The Breakdown
of Democratic Regimes
EUROPE

The Breakdown of Democratic Regimes, edited by Juan J. Linz and Alfred Stepan, is available in separate paperback editions:

The Breakdown of Democratic Regimes:
Crisis, Breakdown, and Reequilibration
by Juan J. Linz

The Breakdown of Democratic Regimes: Europe
edited by Juan J. Linz and Alfred Stepan

The Breakdown of Democratic Regimes: Latin America
edited by Juan J. Linz and Alfred Stepan

The Breakdown of Democratic Regimes: Chile
by Arturo Valenzuela

The Breakdown
of Democratic Regimes

EUROPE

Edited by
Juan J. Linz and Alfred Stepan

The Johns Hopkins University Press
Baltimore and London

Manufactured in the United States of America

The Johns Hopkins University Press, Baltimore, Maryland, 21218
The Johns Hopkins Press Ltd., London

Library of Congress Catalog Number 77-28750
ISBN 0-8018-2022-7

Library of Congress Cataloging in Publication data will be found on the last printed page of this book.

Contents

Editors' Preface
and Acknowledgments

How and why democratic regimes break down are the central questions addressed by the contributors to this volume.[1] Such breakdowns have long preoccupied social scientists. However, much of the existing literature on the subject has focused attention on the emergence of nondemocratic political forces or the underlying structural strains that lead to the collapse of democratic institutions.[2] Implicitly if not explicitly, the impression often given by such works is that of the virtual inevitability of the breakdown of the democratic regimes under discussion. While recognizing the scholarly legitimacy and analytic utility of studying antidemocratic movements and structural strains, we have addressed a somewhat different aspect of the breakdown of democratic regimes.

Given the tragic consequences of the breakdown of democracy in countries such as Germany, Spain, and Chile, we believe it intellectually and politically worthwhile to direct systematic attention to the dynamics of the political process of breakdown. In particular, we felt it important to analyze the behavior of those committed to democracy, especially the behavior of the incumbent democratic leaders, and to ask in what ways the actions or nonactions of the incumbents contributed to the breakdown under analysis. Did the prodemocratic forces have available to them other options that might have alleviated the crisis of democracy? Was the breakdown of democracy indeed inevitable? A closely related concern of the participants was the endeavor to abstract from the historical record recurrent patterns, sequences, and crises involved in the dynamic process of breakdown.

This publication has a long and complex history. Juan J. Linz's involvement with the question of the breakdown of democracy began with his concern with the fate of Spanish democracy, a fate that affected him as a child in Spain and as a citizen. Linz's reading of the monumental work on the breakdown of the Weimar Republic by Karl Dietrich Bracher led him to ask broad theoretical questions, which he explored with Daniel Bell at Columbia University in the mid-1960s. Linz and Alfred Stepan met at Columbia during this period, when Stepan was beginning to write a dissertation on the breakdown of democracy in Brazil, a process he had seen at first hand while writing articles in Latin America for the *Economist*. Other contributors who were at

Columbia University at the same time included Paolo Farneti, Peter Smith, Arturo Valenzuela, and Alexander Wilde.

In order to encourage scholarly exchange on the political aspects of the breakdown of democracy, a panel was organized under the auspices of the Committee on Political Sociology. This panel met at a number of sessions at the Seventh World Congress of Sociology, held at Varna, Bulgaria, in 1970. Before the congress, Linz circulated a short paper titled "The Breakdown of Competitive Democracies: Elements for a Model," which became the focus of discussion by the members of the panel engaged in studies of individual countries and attending the congress. Among the contributors to the complete hardcover edition of this volume presenting initial drafts of the papers at Varna were Erik Allardt on Finland, Paolo Farneti on Italy, Rainer Lepsius on Weimar Germany, Juan Linz on Spain, Walter Simon on Austria, Peter Smith on Argentina, Alfred Stepan on Brazil, and Alexander Wilde on Colombia. Arend Lijphart was a stimulating commentator.[3]

After fruitful exchanges at Varna, we dispersed, with the firm commitment to continue working on the project and to hold a conference in a few years focusing on the comparative and theoretical aspects of our work. In order to introduce other important cases and different perspectives, Stepan encouraged Guillermo O'Donnell to write on the crisis of democracy in Argentina in the decade after the fall of Perón, and Julio Cotler and Daniel Levine to discuss the Peruvian and Venezuelan cases. After the overthrow of Allende in Chile, the editors invited Arturo Valenzuela to analyze the tragic events leading to the end of democracy in Chile.

With the generous support of the Concilium of International and Area Studies of Yale University, and the Joint Committee on Latin America of the Social Science Research Council and the American Council of Learned Societies, the augmented group met at Yale University in December 1973, at a conference chaired by Linz and Stepan, by then both members of the Yale faculty. At this meeting the papers presented benefited from the able suggestions of Douglas Chalmers, Edward Malefakis, and Eric Nordlinger, who acted as discussants. At the end of the conference the participants decided to revise their work in the light of one another's findings and the collective discussion of areas of similarity and dissimilarity. A year at the Institute for Advanced Study in Princeton allowed Linz to revise his introduction and maintain contact with the co-authors.

Despite the group's interest in underlying, recurrent patterns of breakdown, there has been no attempt to force individual contributors into the procrustean bed of the editors' own thinking. The reader will discover important differences in the authors' intellectual orientations, which grew in part out of the diversity of the democracies studied and reflect in part genuine differences of opinion on the relative weight to be attached to political forces, even after these forces had been given due consideration by all contributors.

It should be stressed that this volume is an initial social scientific effort at middle-level generalizations about complex historical reality. Such a work is, of course, never a substitute for fundamental historical studies of individual cases; rather, it builds upon such studies and, we hope, draws the attention of historians to more generalized propositions, propositions they can in turn pursue further in their own work. Although we are concerned with middle-level generalizations, it is the editors' view that the historicity of macro-political processes precludes the highly abstract generalizing of ahistorical social scientific models of the type susceptible to computer simulations and applicable to all past and any future cases. It is our hope, nevertheless, that scholars interested in developing more formal models may build on our work and incorporate into their models the complex realities here discussed. At this stage of the analysis our collective attention to the political dynamics of the breakdown of democracies has brought to light a number of recurring elements which are discussed at length in Linz's introductory essay. The independent contributions made to breakdowns by political incumbents is a theme that emerges in almost all the papers and has justified our attention to this aspect of the problem, an aspect all too often overlooked. Indeed, in reference to the democratic breakdown in many if not most of the cases analyzed, the editors concur with the remark made by the great German historian, Friedrich Meinecke, upon hearing of the appointment of Hitler to the chancellorship: "This was not necessary."

The individual studies shed new light on some of the most historically important cases of breakdown of democracy, such as Germany, Italy, Spain, and Chile. In addition, some of the less well-known cases forcefully illustrate hitherto neglected aspects of the question of the survival of democracy. Daniel Levine's study of Venezuela examines a fascinating case of political learning. Ten years after the breakdown in Venezuela in 1948, many of the institutional participants in the breakdown—the church, the army, the political parties—consciously and successfully devised strategies to avoid such a breakdown when a new attempt to forge democratic institutions began in 1958. Alexander Wilde's discussion of the reequilibration of Colombian democray in the 1950s also shows how political learning was crucial for the construction of a consociational democracy. The chapter by Risto Alapuro and Erik Allardt discusses the little-known case of Finland, in which, despite intense conflict, the process of breakdown described in other chapters was avoided. The analysis of nonoccurrence as well as of occurrence increased our understanding of the breakdown process.

With the publication of this project, many of the contributors are turning their attention to closely related issues that loom large on the scholarly agenda. High priority for further work along these lines should now be given to the analysis of the conditions that lead to the breakdown of authoritarian regimes, to the process of transition from authoritarian to democratic regimes, and especially to the political dynamics of the consolidation of postauthoritarian democracies.

The editors want to thank The Johns Hopkins University Press for its help in publishing a project of such large intellectual scope and sheer physical size as this one. We want to give special thanks to Henry Tom, the social sciences editor of the Press, for his great assistance. The project would not have arrived in the reader's hands without extensive copy editing. Jean Savage and Victoria Suddard helped in the early stages of copy editing.

Yale University   JUAN J. LINZ

ALFRED STEPAN

NOTES

1. An extensive discussion of the definition of democracy and the criteria for the selection of cases is found in Juan Linz's introductory essay, entitled *The Breakdown of Democratic Regimes: Crisis, Breakdown, and Reequilibration.* This essay is also available separately as a Johns Hopkins University Press paperback.
2. Much of this literature is discussed in the work by Linz just cited.
3. The crisis of democracy in Portugal in the 1920s, France in the 1950s, Peru and Greece in the 1960s, and the continuing conflict in Northern Ireland were also discussed in papers presented by Herminio Martins, Steven Cohn, David Chaplin, Charles Moskos, and Richard Rose, respectively. Conflicting obligations did not permit them to continue with the project. Richard Rose developed his paper in a somewhat different direction and published it separately as a book, *Governing without Consensus: An Irish Perspective* (Boston: Beacon Press, 1971).

The Breakdown
of Democratic Regimes
EUROPE

1.

Social Conflict, Parliamentary Fragmentation, Institutional Shift, and the Rise of Fascism: Italy

Paolo Farneti

Introduction

The working of a parliamentary system can be viewed as based on a "division of labor" between civil society, political society, and institutional set. By the first we mean the set of cleavages such as Center-periphery, city-countryside, etc., including class cleavages and their political expressions, that give rise to conditions of interest or solidarity. By the second we mean those groups (from clubs to mass parties and labor unions) that are based on the principles of association or organization. By the third we mean those structures, mostly regulated by legal order, that can be analyzed primarily in terms of consent or force.

To be sure, while these three structures define the complexity of any political system, they are particularly visible as determinants of the complexity of parliamentary systems. As such, they are the results of distinct historical processes. The civil society is the outcome of the industrial revolution; the institutional set is the outcome of the bureaucratic rationalization and centralization performed by the monarchies of the *ancien régime*. The political society is the outcome of the democratic revolution, that is, the democratic development of the principles stated in 1789, through the 1848 revolution and the political and social struggles of the second half of the nineteenth and the first decades of the twentieth centuries.

For many states, especially in Europe, the process of state building has been one through which the tensions and the conflicts arising from the basic cleavages of nineteenth-century societies found a provisional mediation, if not a

3

solution. With the progressive democratization of politics, with the institution of elected parliaments, and with the entrance of new groups into the political arena, this basic function of conflict mediation was taken over by the political society and by an elected political elite composed of professional politicians rather than state functionaries. This process meant the emancipation of the realm of politics and policy-making from both civil and institutional forces. And in effect the "division of labor" stems from the relationships between mutually emancipated structures: civil, political, and institutional.[1] As a relatively emancipated structure, the political society finds its basic resource in redefining the cleavages emerging from the civil society—transforming them into specifically political cleavages and political issues. In fact, an issue becomes political when it is able to aggregate the society into a basic cleavage of *pro* and *contra* the alternative solutions. Of course, it is also part of the art of politics to prevent issues from becoming political. This means that the relationships between civil, political, and institutional structures are in continuous tension. In fact, civil and institutional structures tend to become "politicized," that is, to become part of political society and to transform their own cleavages into political cleavages. The political society tends to monopolize the practice of politics and political issue-making, thereby absorbing into its own structure and logic of performance both civil and institutional forces. In all these cases there is a disruption of the division of labor of the political system in general, and of parliamentary systems in particular.

A crisis of parliamentary system can therefore be analyzed as a failure of the political society to maintain the rules of this division of labor, a balance that demands a restraint on itself and a systematic effort to deter the civil and institutional forces from any attempt at disrupting this balance. When this does not happen, a loss of autonomy of the political society marks the initial stage of a crisis process, together with a polarization of politics and issue-making to civil and institutional forces; this polarization results in the "politics of the streets" and the "politics of the barracks."

Neither the first nor the second kind of politics, however, is a long-term political project, unless it is a "planned" revolution or coup d'état. When neither revolution nor coup d'état is the outcome, the loss of autonomy of the political society is followed by a stalemate situation or a "power vacuum"[2]: the situation is defined by small groups and few persons. The diffusion of the political arena that characterizes the first crisis phase is followed by a shrinking of the political arena during this second phase. Any political project able to aggregate enough forces to resolve the loss of autonomy and overcome the stalemate is likely to take over the political power.

In the case of Italian fascism, this aggregation of forces happened neither through revolutionary outbreak nor purely institutional force (coup d'état), but essentially through the use of private violence.

Political and Socioeconomic Structure

In the framework of a diffusion of the political arena, loss of autonomy of the political society, and a consequent reduction in the number of workable solutions within the rules of the division of labor, we can verify the existence of critical elements that have been suggested in the introductory essay by Juan Linz. In the process of the political society's loss of autonomy we can understand the emergence of issues that cannot be solved within the rules of the division of labor (Linz's "unsolvable problems") but demand a new arrangement of relationships between civil, political, and institutional forces. We can also understand the tendency of the political forces in the existing alignment to lose their identities in favor of civil and institutional forces and therefore to question both their "loyalty" toward the existing arrangement ("semiloyalty" and open "disloyalty") and their own willingness to assume responsibility in it.

In the reduction of the political arena, and above all in the number of possible solutions within the rules of the game, we see the "fragmentation" of the political forces and their "polarization" around one dominant cleavage: for or against the existing institutional arrangement. When one pole of the alignment is supported through private violence, "crisis strata" become decisive for the political balance. It must be emphasized that the use of violence cannot be considered to be at the same level as the other critical elements. It is much more essential to and decisive in fostering the crisis, for at least two reasons. First, if the modern state is defined by the achievement of internal pacification and the reduction of maintenance of public order to a function performed by professional administrators, then the use of private violence and its acceptance is a break with an essential element. Second, if the political alignment is polarized, and one pole of the alignment has the capacity for the use of violence, then the weight of that one pole is such that no contractual relationship is any longer feasible.

This focus on a specific political mechanism should not make us overlook the economic and social determinants of the crisis process, and in particular, their timing. They are significant in a market economy when powerful minority interests succeed in aggregating a larger and larger part of the population—in a word, when the crisis fosters a solidarity otherwise very difficult to achieve. In particular, this happens when the traditional cleavage between "property classes"—based on rent—and "acquisition classes"—based on profit—is blurred by the rise of a common interest on the part of both classes in the dismissal of the existing institutional arrangement, and whenever the "safety of contracts" is threatened.[3] From this point of view, changes in the structure of the property classes and the acquisition classes are of momentous importance, because they can contribute to the formation of this common interest. Therefore, economic crises are of little importance as long as they do not bring about a change within and between the two class systems of a partially industrialized market economy. This change can be a rearticulation of interest in which the role of political forces, as much as political emergency procedures (such as early elections and so forth), can be decisive.

There is, however, in the framework of the model proposed here, a slightly different way to consider the relationship between socioeconomic structure and political structure in a critical situation. We defined the model of relationships between civil, political, and institutional structures as a division of labor because in effect it is based on differentiated role performances. From this point of view, a crisis, i.e., a redefinition of roles, can be seen as paralleled by the introduction of a new technical discovery in the technical division of labor, which also demands a redefinition of roles. A new piece of machinery or a new technical device creates new jobs and eliminates old jobs. Similarly, a profound economic and social crisis can be seen as creating and eliminating jobs in a system of division of labor between civil, political, and institutional tasks. The result is, as in the case of the introduction of a new device, not necessarily a further differentiation of roles: it can very well be a consolidation of roles and therefore a return to a less differentiated condition in the relationship between the three structures, depending on the nature of the socioeconomic crisis and the specific historical situation.

The two perspectives do not contradict each other. The first one is, in effect, a case of the second one, because it depends on at least two conditions: a market economy with a sizable business class, and a partially industrialized economy with the consequent coexistence of acquisition classes and property classes. It is one of the tasks of this discussion to verify the hypothesis in the Italian case of the early twenties.

An Outline of the Italian Crisis of the Early Twenties

In the pages to follow we will try to give evidence of the three phases as they existed in postwar Italy: *loss of autonomy* of the political society ("loss of power," "power deflation," and "fragmentation," are used as synonyms); *exhaustion of legitimate political alternatives* (or "reduction of the political arena," "stalemate situation," etc.); and *takeover of power*. We start from one major assumption: the reshuffling of political cleavages as a result of the issue of participation in the war, and the crisis of relationships between property and acquisition classes consequent to the war mobilization. In the specific Italian case, therefore, the war is accountable for (1) the potential for political and social crisis and (2) for their *convergence* and consequent disruption of an already shaky parliamentary system.

During the first phase the old alignment of Right, Center, and Left is broken up by the dual cleavage of interventionism and neutralism, the international situation being, at least in part, accountable for the persistence of this cleavage after the end of the war. The loss of autonomy of the political society, i.e., of the political parties in the postwar Parliament, is made visible by a diffusion of the political arena in the politics of the streets (the wave of strikes of 1919 and 1920) and in the political mobilization of institutions, namely the army, during the Fiume adventure (also 1919-20). In this phase the aggregation of old interventionist liberalism begins, in a political space soon to be filled by the Fascist movement.

During the second phase, the game seems to be in the hands of the old neutralist alignment: Giolittian Liberals, Socialists, particularly the Reformist wing of the Socialists—led by Filippo Turati—and the Popolari—led by Luigi Sturzo. Internal contradictions prevent an aggregation of these forces, thereby creating a stalemate: a visible exhaustion of political alternatives within the framework of the existing institutional structure. The silence of the streets at this point encourages the exercise of political violence on the side of the Fascist squads. The silence is paralleled by the withdrawal of the army and the police forces, whose loyalty toward the existing arrangement is more and more questionable.

During the third phase, starting with the resignation of Giovanni Giolitti from the cabinet in the twenties, the political alignment is in effect displaced both by the politics of the Fascist parliamentary group and by the restless Fascist violence all over the country. Step by step, the issue becomes the exercise of force and violence on two sides: the institutional side (represented by the army and the crown) and the Fascist side. Late attempts to control the situation, through last-minute agreements on the side of the political forces loyal to the parliamentary system, are ineffective, and end on the night of 27-28 October 1922.

The fragmentation of political forces, as the result of the war and the war-commitment of the country, is in sharp contrast with the aggregation of social forces consequent to the war mobilization. There are at least three key factors that in our view account for a joining of property and acquisition classes in a common struggle and for their political relevance. The wave of strikes in the first postwar years (1919-20) marked, for the first time in the history of the country, a common and relatively homogeneous mobilization of both industrial workers and peasants (agricultural daily workers and small peasants).[4] This meant a mobilization of "negatively privileged classes," according to Weber's definition, both in the system of acquisition classes (industrial workers) and in the system of property classes (peasants).[5]

The energy mobilized by the strikes was finally exhausted, but considerable improvements in labor legislation had been achieved, both for industrial

workers and agricultural workers, including the obligatory hiring of labor in the fields ("imponibile di mano d'opera"). It had not achieved—but the slogan remained as a threat—"the land to the peasants."

In this situation the possibility of an alliance between "positively privileged classes" in the two systems was created: property-owners in the countryside (including small property-owners), and industrialists and financiers in the urban-industrial areas. The alliance was formed on the grounds of a common feeling that the government was "in the hands of the subversives," i.e., the Socialists. This feeling was supported by Turati's policy, which blocked the government without participating in it, and thus gave way to collective reactions.

The result was the aggregation of the interests of a social minority with the interests of a social majority, that of the property classes. It was a social novelty that soon became a political novelty: the Fascist movement became a mass party (section 1).

The second phase—which we have defined as the stalemate of the traditional political alignment (mostly coinciding with the old, Neutralist forces)—was characterized by the Giolittian attempt at coopting fascism at a parliamentary level together with the social and political effects of Fascist violence, by then massive and systematic. Last but not least, the final attempt of the Bonomi government to find a workable solution incorporating both the inclusion of the Popolari in the cabinet and the "pacification pact" between the Fascists and the Socialist labor unions will be considered as the last step in the exhaustion of the legitimate alignment and of the stalemate that preceded the final breakdown of the political system (section 2).

With the first and second Facta governments, the political arena had shifted from the legitimate political alignment, and therefore the representation of the political society, to a different political axis, based on the show of force. The institutional setting, represented by the crown and the army (the latter with its questionable loyalty) was on one side, and the Fascist movement, with its show of force and goal of dividing the last forces of the traditional alignment, on the other. The failure of the "legalitarian strike" and the silence of the streets before and after the March on Rome can be considered as further evidence of the desert, social and political, in which the final destruction of the parliamentary system took place (section 3).

1. The Loss of Autonomy of the Political Society

New Political Cleavages

World War I had the effect of reshuffling political cleavages, especially for the Liberals. Democrats and Socialists were split by the interventionism-

neutralism cleavage, and so were the Popolari, even if opposition to intervention in the war was expressed only by the minority in their group. However, those most affected by this division belonged to the old Liberal ruling group.[6] We can summarize the two cleavages in the following way:

	Left	*Right*
Interventionists	*Democrats* (Francesco Nitti) *Social Reformists* (Leonida Bissolati, Ivanoe Bonomi) *Independent Socialists* (Arturo Labriola)	*Liberals* (Antonio Salandra, Sidney Sonnino, Vittorio Emanuelle Orlando) *Popolari* (Filippo Meda) *Nationalists* (Luigi Federzoni)
Neutralists	*Socialists* (Filippo Turati) *Leftist Popolari* (Guido Miglioli)	*Liberals* (Giovanni Giolitti)

The new cleavage weakened the Giolittian Liberals on both the right and the left: on the right, by the split with men like Salandra and the moderate Catholics such as Meda and his followers; on the left, the gap between Giolitti's group and the Democrats and Social Reformists was deepened. Yet this split did not draw Giolitti's liberalism, Turati's socialism, or Sturzo's Popolari nearer to each other. They had all inherited ancient aversions, and their neutralism had radically different roots, both ideological and pragmatic. On the contrary, interventionism could serve as an aggregating force for the Right: divided, until then, into the major political forces of the Giolittian alignment, it finally found a common ground of action. Its practice, as indicated by the way the Salandra-Sonnino cabinet forced the Chamber of Deputies into the declaration of war, was extraparliamentary.

Interventionism had a political space with potential for expansion and reaggregation, notwithstanding the crisis of the *Fascio Parlamentare di Difesa Nazionale*. The political space of neutralism, on the contrary, was occupied by forces that tended to neutralize each other: Socialists, Popolari, and the Giolitti group. In this situation issues had a divisive rather than an aggregating function. In particular, the issues of the immediate postwar period raised the possibility that the alignment would be immobilized by "unsolvable problems."

The elections at the end of 1919 increased rather than simplified these divisions, because they increased the internal articulation of interventionism and neutralism and, while keeping neutralism and interventionism as a significant cleavage, made any coalition government more and more difficult at a time in which coalition was increasingly indispensable.

The remarkable institutional innovations of the 1919 electoral system (proportional representation, reduction of the voting age from thirty to twenty-one and from twenty-one to eighteen for those who had been drafted during the war) did not bring about any solution to the already complicated alignments that had survived the war. In fact, these innovations fragmented the old alignment (Liberals, Democrats, etc.) without aggregating the new one (Socialists and Popolari).

If we compare the data from 1913–19 to 1919–21 (table 1), a number of things become apparent: the enormous increase in neutralism (the Socialist group is larger than any other political group in the Chamber of Deputies); the even more conspicuous increase of the Popolari group; the weakened condition of the Giolittian group and the reduction of rightist liberalism (Salandra Liberals, the Economic party, the Agrarian party, etc.); and finally, the fragmentation of "leftist interventionism," i.e., Radicals, Republicans, Independent Socialists, and Reform Socialists.

The change from the Orlando cabinet to the Nitti cabinet meant a change from a coalition led by conservative interventionism to one led by Democratic interventionism: both alternatives became more difficult after the 1919 elections as the two groups were weakened. Coalitions with Neutralist groups

Table 1. Political Cleavages, Old and New, in the Chamber of Deputies for 1913–19 and 1919–21

1913–19

	Left		Right	
Interventionists	Radicals	73	Constitutional Democrats	29
	Republicans	17	Democrats	11
	Independent Socialists	8	Liberals (non-Giolitti)	70
	Social Reformists	19	Catholics	20
			Conservative Catholics	9
		N=117		N=139
Neutralists	Socialists	52	Giolitti Liberals	200
		N=52		N=200
		N=508		

1919–21

	Left		Right	
Interventionists	Republicans	9	Salandra Liberals	23
	Radicals	57	"Economic Party" and	
	Independent Syndicalists and Social		"Agrarians"	15
	Reformists	22		
	"Rinnovamento"	33		
		N=121		N=38
Neutralists	Socialists	137	Giolitti Liberals	
	Communists	17	("Democrazia Liberale")	91
		N=154		N=91
	"Right" and "Left" Popolari		99	
			N=99	
		N=503		

SOURCE: Ugo Giusti, *Dai plebisciti alla costituente* (Rome: Faro, 1945), pp. 47 and 75.

became a necessity: the only logical alternative in this situation was a Socialist-Popolari government aided by some leftist Interventionists. But the self-exclusion of the Socialists on one side and of the Popolari on the other brought the choice toward Giolitti's group, the oldest group of Neutralists. Giolitti could not turn to right-wing interventionism because of his old Neutralist attitudes, nor to the Socialists without having them face a split, nor to the Catholic Popolari, because they considered him an old anti-clerical. The result was the early election of 1921. In other words, the war, as long as it lasted, had forged an emergency coalition; once it was finished, new cleavages appeared without erasing the old ones. There accumulation made cabinet formation more and more difficult, i.e., neither the Parliament nor the country could bring about a solution. It is no wonder, therefore, that political society, under the pressure of the mobilization of the streets and the mobilization of the army, at least at the beginning of the Fiume adventure, was losing its relative autonomy and control.

After 1919 we see the exhaustion of three possible alternatives: a coalition led by Democratic interventionism; a coalition led by Democratic neutralism—namely the Socialists—that had not yet been tried, but was already exhausted with the exhaustion of the mass mobilization in the streets; and a coalition led by centrist neutralism, namely Giolitti. Three major governmental chances were exhausted during the one and one-half years between the end of 1919 and the middle of 1921. The fourth possibility, a full-fledged coalition with the Popolari, was actually tried after the fall of Giolitti, led by Bonomi, but it faced: (1) a Fascist movement that was already a massive force and (2) a developing political space precisely in the area of right-wing interventionism. The following analysis of the internal cleavages of the mass parties of the alignment should validate this contention.

The Socialist forces had mobilized since the end of the war, and their success in the 1919 elections seemed to be a validation of this practice. However, the Socialists were divided by a double cleavage: (1) reformism versus revolutionarism, and (2) political versus strictly syndicalist practice in the labor unions. These cleavages resulted in a set of contradictory consequences. The revolutionary wing of the PSU (Partito Socialista Ufficiale)— the *Massimalisti*—had been the majority in the party since the Rome convention of September 1918. (They got 74 percent of the vote, while 13 percent went to the Reformist wing led by Turati, Treves, and Modigliani and 13 percent to an undecided "Center.") The result was that the secretariat of the party was in the hands of the Massimalisti, and the parliamentary group was in the hands of Turati's *Riformisti,* the two groups checking and finally paralyzing each other. It was the other way around inside the leading group of CGI: (Confederazione Generale del Lavoro) at the end of the 1920s the "syndicalist" group led by Buozzi had 54 percent of the votes, while 37 percent went to the Massimalisti and 9 percent were abstentions. This was enough to impose both syndicalist and political mobilization and enough to maintain the mobilized masses' expectations beyond the achievements obtained by the governments (and within an inflationary economy), with the result that the resource of political mobilization was exhausted.[7]

A parallel cleavage appeared to divide the Popolari. Their tremendous increase in membership after the war reinforced their domestic contradiction, thereby making attempts at coalition difficult if not impossible, and in any case always subordinate to the initiatives of other political forces. The leadership of the party, in fact, was centered in Sturzo's line and ideology, both anti-Socialist and anti-Liberal: this excluded most of the major forces of the political alignment. It did not prevent the Popolari from cooperating even with the last Giolitti cabinet, albeit with diffidence and despite profound tensions. But the parliamentary group (Meda and De Gasperi) was certainly more moderate, and for this reason was on several occasions in disagreement with the party leadership. It was in any case more bound to the Vatican, which had followed with unconcealed distrust the development of a Catholic party.

Parliamentary groups in both parties (the PSU and the PPI, or Partito Popolari Italiano) were expressions of the electorate; both parties' leaderships were expressions of their active participants. The gap between and the contradictions within the two major mass parties of the alignment were therefore *both* in the country and in the Parliament. The cleavage that divided the party leadership and the parliamentary leadership in both parties was not subject to bargaining; this is one more reason to believe in the formation, *a contrario,* of a political space in which the old interventionist forces, the discontent of property classes and acquisition classes, the disarray of the young officers' generation, and the demands of some institutional personnel for "order" could find a political expression through a fast, almost emergency-like aggregation.

If we turn to the other side of the alignment, we find equivalent cleavages, namely, liberalism and radicalism. The Liberal side was numerically enfeebled (it declined from 300 representatives in 1913 to about 100 in 1919) and divided between neutralism and interventionism. But even within neutralism there were two opposite tendencies toward the Socialists: cooptation versus thorough rejection. Radicalism, both "leftist" and "interventionist," was also numerically enfeebled and politically fragmented around personalities like Bissolati, Nitti, and Bonomi; this eliminated any possibility of mediation between the two mass parties, the Socialists and the Popolari. Radicalism turned out to be no alternative to Giolitti's liberalism.

New Social Aggregations

There is some evidence to support the hypothesis that a convergence between property classes and acquisition classes (both positively and negatively privileged) led to their consequent mobilization, which initiated the loss of autonomy of the political society. In the first place, workers and peasants were able to mobilize simultaneously in a way unprecedented in the country's social history (table 2). It is true that the political leadership of the Massimalisti, their dream of an Italian October Revolution, was initially responsible for the wave of strikes that allied the middle and upper classes against socialism. However, the readiness of the population to mobilize on purely political issues remains to be explained. There is little question that this postwar mobilization was a consequence of the impact of wartime mobilization, especially on the peasants and agricultural workers who were the rank and file of the army. From this point of view, the war had the effect of dissolving the traditional regional divisions that had prevented the Socialist party from becoming a modern, centralized, mass party with an available *masse de maneuvre*. The political leadership of the Socialist party inherited a condition of unity and a capacity for social and ideological mobilization of the electorate that, had it not been for the war—and *that* war—would have taken many years of painstaking organizational and political activity to achieve.

In the second place, the convergence might have been favored by the postwar industrial demobilization consequent to the conversion of war industries to a normal market economy. For instance, the number of industrial workers in a city like Turin, in which the war industry was particularly important, had returned, during 1919, to 1914 levels. Demobilized workers, provisional industrial workers returned to the fields, are a mobilizable force, and in any case constitute a force that contributes to the simultaneous mobilization of city and countryside. The same observation can be extended to the large industrial cities of the north, Milan and Genoa, both of which suffered from the first steps toward a return to a "normal" market economy. The government's early commitment to a return to a market economy, which was encouraged by Liberal economists, can be seen as a further cause of political instability. In fact, the discontent that this return produced in the working classes could have had an immediate impact on a political structure that had undergone a rapid democratization. The dismissal of the controls over the division of labor—controls appropriate to a wartime economy—was coupled with the sudden increase of mass parties in Parliament consequent to the introduction of proportional representation and the lowering of the voting age. Two things happened simultaneously: the expulsion of part of the population from the labor market (i.e., social citizenship) and input of the whole adult population into the political society (i.e., political citizenship). It overloaded the political society and, to some extent, the labor unions, and posed the dilemma of the whole postwar period, i.e., whether to follow the mobilization of the social classes or perform the control function that had been relinquished by the institutional structure.

A second and most important variable in the aggregation of the property and acquisition classes was the enormous increase, right after the war, in the

Table 2. Number of Strikers in Industry and Agriculture, by Region: 1913 and 1919–21 (in percentages)

Regions	1913		1919		1920		1921	
	Industry	Agriculture	Industry	Agriculture	Industry	Agriculture	Industry	Agriculture
Piedmont, Liguria, and Lombardy	65	9	65	51	56	18	58	38
Veneto	2	3	3	14	4	10	6	8
Total—north	67	12	68	65	60	38	64	46
Emilia	6	50	3	13	4	26	2	25
Tuscany	10	—	5	10	9	25	6	—
Rest of center	9	19	5	11	6	9	9	5
Total—center	25	69	13	34	19	60	17	30
Campania	3	—	13	—	13	—	9	—
Apulia	1	8	1	4	2	8	1	21
Sicily	3	1	3	—	5	3	8	1
Rest of south	1	—	2	—	1	2	1	2
Total—south	8	9	18	—	21	13	18	24
Total industrial strikers	384,725		993,558		858,133		589,259	
Total agricultural strikers	79,842		487,208		1,045,732		79,298	
Total strikers	464,567		1,480,766		1,903,865		668,557	

SOURCE: *Annuario statistico italiano, 1913* (Rome: Bertero, 1914); *Annuario statistico italiano, 1919–1921* (Rome: Librería dello Stato, 1925).

agricultural middle class, small landowners, and tenants (table 3). Favored by the inflation in the payment of debts, many peasants had hurried to purchase the land made available by large landowners who were both frightened by Socialist strikes and attracted by the possibility of speculation. This "new class" was limited and often threatened by the mobilization of salaried workers in the fields (*braccianti*) and their powerful leagues. It is plausible to guess that these millions of new landowners and their families, about five million people altogether, could become a mass of support for agrarian fascism. They were interested not only in defending their new property against the collectivization of the land proposed by the *leghe braccianti* and therefore against the salaried workers' mobilization, but also in regular functioning of the market, in order to pay the debts incurred in buying the land. There is no social force as interested in law and order as an agricultural middle class of small landowners. These landowners were ready to see any government grant of rights to the leagues, including the compulsory hiring of daily workers, as a betrayal and a concession to "red subversivism."

Apparently, the government effectively protected the Socialist leagues. The protection of the workers' wages was pursued thoroughly, and the wages themselves were kept relatively high in relation to the progress of inflation. This was the outcome of the joint effort of leagues and cooperatives. The cooperatives, which were organizations that had not merely a syndical purpose, like the leagues, but shared products, tools, and working personnel, claimed "the land for the peasants," while the leagues insisted upon collectivization of the land. The appeal was double and contradictory and, combined with the agrarian reform promised during the war but not delivered afterward, may have resulted in in a wide disaffection of salaried agricultural workers with their labor organizations and the Socialist party.

While the political cleavages had the cumulative effect of fragmenting the political elite and complicating the possibility of an effective and stable government, these social cleavages underwent a powerful trend toward aggrega-

Table 3. Occupations in Agriculture, 1871–1936 (in percentages)

Census Year	Land-owners	Managers	Share-croppers	Workers	Other	Total
1871	18.0	7.7	17.0	56.9	.4	100 (5,616,482)
1881	18.1	6.6	13.7	61.2	.4	100 (5,450,127)
1901	24.9	8.5	19.8	46.4	.4	100 (6,411,001)
1911	18.3	9.3	18.7	53.3	.4	100 (6,052,623)
1921	32.4	7.2	15.4	44.7	.3	100 (7,085,124)
1931	36.7	12.7	19.7	30.5	.4	100 (6,544,663)
1936	32.9	18.4	20.0	28.4	.3	100 (6,306,742)

SOURCE: Arrigo Serpieri, *La struttura sociale dell-agricoltura italiana* (Rome: Edizione italiana, 1947), p. 123.

tion, thereby increasing their pressure over the political society. Social classes, until 1919, were sharply divided by the traditional cleavage of country and city, industry and agriculture. Property-owning classes were dominant in the countryside and acquisition-oriented classes were dominant in the city. The two sectors now joined and split according to a class cleavage: salaried workers and small peasants and industrial workers were aligned on one side, small and large property and business owners on the other. With the war, class society had taken a leap forward.

This new situation divided a political elite into new cleavages that overlapped with the old ones. Moreover, this elite was bound to a way of looking at politics and society that belonged to the Giolittian era: personalities rather than groups, clienteles rather than organized parties, and patronage rather than mass politics. Therefore, the loss of autonomy of the political society can also be seen as a *lag* between political and civil societies following the war. The political society failed to anticipate the reshuffling of social divisions that followed the war and did not adapt to them once they became manifest. Once again, the political society laid the groundwork for an alternative mobilization: that of the institutions.

New Institutional Cleavages

The Fiume enterprise revealed a potential cleavage in the institutional personnel, mainly in the army: nationalism, victorious war, crown, and expansion of Italy in the Mediterranean were arrayed on one side; internationalism, subversion, redistribution of wealth to labor, and last but not least, republic on the other. The career officers, the veterans, and their associations were politicized on the first side of the cleavage, and this group found its hero in D'Annunzio and his slogan of the "betrayed victory." To be sure, the Fiume adventure remained a partial mobilization of the army against the orders of the legitimate government, and from this point of view it was a break with the century-old tradition of an army loyal to political power. Yet it failed to become a mobilization of the whole army and therefore it failed to make the army the backbone of a Nationalist "block" to overthrow the institutions through a coup d'état. However, it became a rallying point for the radical Right in the country and paved the way for consent to fascism.

Part of this picture is the slowness in the demobilization of the army itself, kept on duty mainly for reasons of public order. Yet this delay in the return of noncareer officers to the labor market did not prevent them from feeling the frustrations of readjusting to civilian bourgeois life in an atmosphere of hostility—from the Socialists and the mobilized masses—toward the war, the soldiers, and the officers.

Against this background we have the first assaults against Socialist headquarters such as that against the offices of the "Avanti!" in Milan, led by

Futurist crackpots and above all by the "Arditi" officers. They, together with the Fiume mobilization, set the style for the exercise of private violence against both the Opposition forces and the legitimate institutional forces.

The weakness shown by the Nitti government against the protagonists of the Fiume adventure had momentous consequences for the creation of a political space for the extreme Right.[8] In fact, if it is true that the Fiume mobilization failed to become a general mobilization of the army, it is also true that it died more from its own exhaustion than from effective governmental reaction, at least until Giolitti's return to power. The government failed to involve the crown with its full responsibility, and this surprising pattern of leniency was probably based on a lack of communication between the two constitutional powers necessary to restore order.

In this way, the yielding of the political society to the "politics of the streets," which we have identified as the first element of its loss of autonomy and of crisis of the political system, finds its counterpart in the government's failure to restore order in the face of a partial essentially minimal mobilization of the army for purposes that were clearly illegal and clearly ran counter to the international commitment of the whole country to its allies.

The Fiume adventure failed in its stated goals, but it set the stage for a series of concessions by legal authorities and abuses by those who saw the possibility of unpunished systematic violence that led to the final overthrow of an incipient democracy.

The Political Space of Fascism

There are two key issues in the development of fascism as a political force, and they are both bound to the process of "loss of autonomy" of the political society. The first is the monopolization of the rightist space of the political-ideological alignment through antisocialism. This allies, at least provisionally, rightist Liberals, Arditi, Nationalists, and Dannunziani. The second is the entrance of facism into the social movement, which resulted from the convergence between property and acquisition classes, "positively privileged," as they were defined. This second phase is called also "agrarian fascism."

The process of monopolization of a political space implies two tasks: the precise identification of a constant enemy and the aggregation and hegemonization of friends or allies.[9] In the case of fascism, the constant enemy was, beyond any doubt, socialism. If the beginnings of fascism, the foggy ideological statements of the meeting of 23 March 1919 and of the October convention in the same year, can give the impression of being "leftist," they must be seen as components of a search for political space. This search, in order to maintain its constant antisocialism, obliged the Fascists to borrow some weapons from the enemy, particularly ideological weapons.

Fascism borrowed its whole ideology from the Nationalists, who combined populism and expansionism ("imperialism"). Nationalists were, to some extent, "respectable," and rejected violence as a political practice; fascism combined the Nationalist motive with the practice of violence, on the grounds of provocation (but the technique of violence came directly from the collaboration with the Arditi, few and fragmented though they were). The lesson of Fiume and the Dannunziani was that a rightist upheaval based on the army was impossible, and therefore it was necessary to coopt the moderate opinion; second, the most important, was that locally limited violence was being tolerated, particularly when it was directed against the Socialists. Finally, if liberalism—and especially Giolitti—was the real and most frightening enemy, its public support showed the necessity and importance of the moderate opinion, the importance, therefore in insisting repeatedly on the motive of the restoration of law and order.

It was of crucial importance for fascism to show that the exhaustion of Socialist mobilization and the failure of the Fiume mobilization, both threats to the order of the state, could not be followed by the restoration of legitimate political order. It was not a "victory" of the legitimate alignment; on the contrary, it could be settled once and for all with the victory of fascism itself.

It is in this framework of a double technique, the result of two years' experience at claiming to support order and attacking it at the same time, that we must see the decision to participate in the 1921 early elections. Mussolini used the entrance into the Parliament for two equally important purposes: to appear as a legitimate force, and to have a position from which to maneuver in the Parliament itself. They are both part of the same fundamental project: to use as a resource the fact that the threats to the parliamentary regime, from both Left and Right, had failed.

Mussolini himself expressed the difficulty of an aggregation of the electorate on this political space in reference to the 1921 elections:[10]

. . . in any case who would vote for us? Not the mass of the workers, because it is indoctrinated by Leninism [leninizzata]. The middle class reads the "Avanti!" as you can see it everywhere. Therefore it will never vote for the lists of the "Electoral Blocks," which include the class of the small merchants [esercenti], the homeowners, or other categories of this kind!

There was only one way to turn the apparent defeat of any system-breaking attempt, Left or Right, into a political resource: continue the threat through the systematic use of violence based precisely on the exhaustion or failure of the other attempts, and on the leniency of the government toward such violence.

That is why, on purely political grounds, 1921 marks the period of the toughest Fascist violence against not only the Socialists and their organizations, both leagues and cooperatives, but against decentralized bureaucratic authorities like the prefects. Fascist violence found a precise political location at the very end of two alternative attacks against the legal order: the mobilization of the streets and the mobilization of the institutional personnel, mainly the army. And in this way "law and order" could become not only a slogan but a bloody banner.

2. The Stalemate of the Political Alignment

We can find a number of reasons to account for Giolitti's failure to reestablish the legitimate game of politics from 1920 to 1921, i.e.: the unquestionable worsening of the economic situation; his inability to turn the failure of the occupation of the factories and the Fiume mobilization into a successful parliamentary alignment; the decision to coopt fascism on an electoral level rather than face a frontal engagement with a party that was increasing in violence and number of adherents; the confusion, rather than clarification, of the political horizon that resulted from the 1921 early elections.

Economic Difficulties

There are those who insist, rightly but perhaps excessively, on the purely political determinants that led fascism to power, but the economic difficulties that marked the whole postwar period were a powerful determinant of the success of fascism. The period 1920–21 was marked by increasing unemployment, but the government continued to make provisions for the employed working class, both in industry and agriculture, under the pressure of social mobilization.

As any Liberal leader would have done, Giolitti in effect oriented his policies toward a rigid balance of the public budget (pareggio del bilancio). This, however, could neither eliminate the commitments of previous governments nor go against organized labor's demands, particularly in view of a possible split and subsequent alliance between Giolitti and the Reform Socialists.

Most important was the decrease in units employed in industry (from 4.36 in 1920 to 4.35 in 1921)[11] and the "rigidity" of the number of units employed in the tertiary sector (from 3.40 in 1920 to 3.45 in 1921).[12] This meant that in a period of conversion from a war to a market economy, there was an increase in nonproductive labor that overloaded the distribution of the GNP.

In this situation, if a social policy of "squeeze" was needed, it demanded a stability that these cabinets lacked. Nor had they the courage to declare an emergency (as the situation in fact was), because the emergency theme had already been monopolized by fascism.

The Giolitti cabinet, even from the economic point of view, concluded the phase of "loss of autonomy" of the political society. In the fall of 1920, two important bills were passed by this cabinet: the conversion of all bonds and securities, both private and public, to the name of the possessor (until then they had been held by the bearer) and a favorable solution of collective contracts for the *Federterra,* the union of the agricultural workers. In a sense this was the farthest point that a "liberal" economy could reach at that point, and Giolitti's insistence on balancing the budget, as we have seen, was the indication of a turning point in the economic and social policies not only of that government but of the governments to come, as long as no Socialist alternative was in view.

Giolitti's project, therefore, was particularly difficult because it passed bills favorable to the Socialists in order to gain Socialist support in the Parliament, but the social and economic resources needed to lead a joint government with the Socialists had been exhausted. The Socialists were being rewarded for entering the cabinet, but not for staying in it, as there were no resources to carry on basic reforms. Yet, this was inevitable, given the resources of the economy and the political isolation of Italy in the international setting, which precluded international financial help.

On one side the period of favorable concessions to the working classes, both industrial and agricultural, was being concluded: it had been a blank check, so to speak, to the leftist members of the alignment, social and political. But at the same time that the Left was once more invited to enter a coalition in order to achieve a stable government, the resources for social policies were exhausted. It was objectively difficult to make a leftist political move and a rightist economic move. Inflation was the last, but dangerous, resort, and in fact between 1920 and 1921 there was an increase of nearly 50 percent in the prices of such necessary goods as bread (from Lit. 0.83 to Lit. 1.41), pasta (from Lit. 1.24 to Lit. 2.14), and meat (from Lit. 9.64 to Lit. 12.96). But inflation arouses the discontent of all the strata of the society: working classes and middle classes together, urban and rural strata, property and acquisition classes (except, of course, speculators, who represent a politically irrelevant minority).

Missed Chances and Missed Collision

The failure of the cabinet to use the end of the strikes and Fiume as a resource was coupled with its avoidance of a frank acknowledgment of the breakup of public order by the Fascist squads. Both failures became a paradoxical legitimation of fascism.

The occupation of the factories marked the final stage of Socialist and working-class mobilization. Giolitti had a crucial role in avoiding a bloody conclusion to the occupation by keeping the police outside the factories, despite the pressures from the newly organized *Confindustria.*[13] He had a role also, when the movement was exhausted, in reaching an agreement favorable to the *maestranze* by providing some commitment, on the side of the management, to workers' control of the factories. In a word, Giolitti helped to save the symbolic value of the movement for the occupation of the factories, while it was evident to the main actors that the movement had failed and that in general working-class politics in Italy had taken a step backward. But this symbolic *sauvetage* was exactly what prevented the government from using the end of the factory-councils as a victory and a symbol of the restoration of order. At least it did not succeed in giving the public the sense that the Socialist upheaval and turmoil were over and that order was being restored under the banner of the traditional forces of the political alignment. In this way, the whole affair turned from a chance at increased credibility into a loss of credibility for the last workable cabinet.

The Fiume enterprise was ended by the signing of the Rapallo treaties, and the consequent demobilization of the Dannunziani from Fiume by the navy. This showed that the army, in general, was loyal to the government, and the whole issue could have been used to demonstrate the success of the government in restoring normal relationships, inside and outside the country, even if, in the whole issue of dismissing Fiume, Giolitti had the silent help of Mussolini.[14] But precisely as in the case of the occupation of the factories, the end of the Fiume enterprise was not used by the government as a resource to increase its credibility if not its legitimacy.

Legitimation, during a period of crisis and public disorder fomented by the Left and the Right, would have required deeper roots, namely, the concentration of public commitment on the issue of public order and the repression of violence. In fact, the issue of order would have had two different destinies according to which political force decided to monopolize and use it. Faced with two alternatives—monopolization of the issue of public order and identification of fascism as "disorder," or cooptation of fascism into the political arena and permitting violence as long as it was directed against the Socialists—Giolitti and his group chose the second, thereby leaving to fascism the possibility of causing civil disorder and using that disorder as an excuse to overthrow the parliamentary system.

According to some historians, this "electoral cooptation" of fascism by Giolitti was due to his disappointment in the results of the Socialist convention at Leghorn in the fall of 1920.[15] There the Socialist party split, not on the right, thereby leaving the moderates free for a coalition with Giolitti (despite all the difficulties that have been just pointed out), but on the left, thereby creating a further element of fragmentation because of the inevitable isolation of the newly formed Communist party. However, this can hardly be an explanation for such a momentous decision on the part of Giolitti and his group. His decision in fact was based on the erroneous idea that Fascist violence could neutralize Socialist violence, without thinking that if one of the two groups had won, it would have demanded all the power in exchange for its "services."

Fascist violence, which was in fact directed mostly against the strongholds of socialism, as Szymanski has shown, increased tremendously during 1921.[16] At the same time, its electoral cooptation in the lists of the Liberals compensated the Fascist movement, which, during the same year, increased its membership by more than 50 percent (see table 4).

It was necessary for fascism to prevent a return to normality in any case by directing violence against the structures created by the Liberal and Socialist traditions. Fascism in fact directed violence against the Parliament (thrashing and killing deputies), the municipalities (breaking up municipal councils), and the labor unions (burning down the *camere del lavoro*).

If the ebb of liberalism and socialism explains both the numerical force of fascism and the speed with which this size was reached, violence explains its internal articulation and geographic distribution. Fascism increased particularly in regions bordering on Yugoslavia, which had been most involved in the Fiume enterprise and in which nationalism meant an expansion into the Dalmatian coast. Fascism increased in central Italy as well, where socialism was strongest and where the Socialist postwar mobilization had been not only deeply felt but also rewarded in terms of governmental measures.

Therefore, fascism monopolized *de facto* anti-Socialist resentment. As an anti-Socialist mass movement using violence (until then identified with So-

Table 4. Increase in Fascist Membership during 1921 and Early 1922, by Region

Regions	March 1921	December 1921	Change (in percentages)	May 1922	Change (in percentages)
Piedmont	2,411	9,618	+75	14,526	+34
Lombardy	13,968	37,939	+63	79,329	+52
Liguria	2,749	7,405	+63	8,841	+16
Veneto	23,549	44,740	+47	46,078	+3
Northern Italy	*42,677*	*99,702*	*+57*	*148,774*	*+33*
Emilia	17,652	35,647	+50	51,637	+31
Tuscany	2,600	17,768	+85	51,372	+65
North Central Italy	*20,252*	*53,415*	*+62*	*103,009*	*+48*
Umbria	485	4,000	+88	5,410	+26
Marches	814	2,072	+61	2,311	+10
Latium	1,480	4,163	+64	9,474	+57
Abruzzi	1,626	6,166	+74	4,763	−22
South Central Italy	*4,405*	*16,401*	*+73*	*22,231*	*+26*
Campania	3,550	13,423	+73	13,944	+4
Apulia and Lucania	4,211	19,619	+78	20,683	−5
Calabria	*712*	*2,406*	*+70*	*2,066*	*−14*
Sicily	3,569	10,110	+65	9,546	−5
Sardinia	1,100	3,372	+67	2,057	−39
Southern Italy	*13,142*	*48,930*	*+73*	*48,296*	*−1*
Italy	80,476	218,448	+63	332,310	+32

SOURCE: Computed from Renzo de Felice, *Mussolini il fascista,* vol. 1, *La conquista del potere, 1921–1925* (Turin: Einaudi, 1966), pp. 8–11.

cialist "street politics"), it gained for its cause the industrial management, a group with little or no penchant for veterans, Nationalists, and middle-class mobilization.[17] With this, fascism constituted a block that could replace the political alignment on one condition: that it operated quickly, precisely because it was a provisional aggregation.

We have seen that the Giolitti government, the last government with a chance to stabilize parliamentary democracy, had missed its chance to acquire credibility. This failure is the origin of Giolitti's failure to face a direct confrontation with the Fascists. Lost chances of restoring the government's credibility brought about an evaded confrontation with a movement that systematically destroyed public order. The appearance of Fascists in the 1921 electoral lists of the Liberals signifies the Liberals' surrender of their responsibility to rule the country.

Further Political Fragmentation in the Parliament

The early elections had three basic effects on the political scene. First, both by presenting their candidates together with those of the Liberals, Nationalists, Democrats, and Social Reformists in the *Blocchi Nazionali,* and by obtaining a parliamentary group. Fascists became "respectable" in the eyes of moderate public opinion. Second, the elections increased the fragmentation of the political alignment, which was further exacerbated by fragmentation of the parliamentary groups. Finally, consequent to this stand of the political forces, Giolitti resigned, thereby leaving the scene at the very moment in which a strong hand was needed. In fact, one can date the takeover of fascism from mid-1921, precisely after these elections.

Giolitti's parliamentary force, in effect, was less than half that of the same group of *Democrazia Liberale* in 1919: the distinction, if not the split, was on the right, the splinter group being headed by De Nava. The *Democrazia Sociale* group, was split on the Right: Nitti, prime minister during the immediate postwar period, was left with forty-two representatives, about half the membership of his group in 1919, and the splinter group was headed by the Sicilian, Duke Colonna di Cesarò, who was not only a Rightist but sympathized with fascism. The fragmentation of the Socialist group is known; its overall decrease was minimal when the loss of power of the Socialists in the country as early as 1921 is taken into consideration. The Salandra group remained the same and represented the destiny of right-wing liberalism, torn between its allegiance to existing institutions and its sympathy toward fascism. The disappearance of Bonomi's group, i.e., the supporters of the man who was to become prime minister after Giolitti's departure, was evidence of the further deterioration of "leftist interventionism" (table 5).

The outcome of Giolitti's early elections highlighted two negative aspects of the overall situation in the country: the fragmentation of the Left and of neutralism, and the consistency and potential solidarity of the Right, of the old interventionism.

In the 1922 Chamber of Deputies, the Liberal group of Democrazia numbered forty-two representatives and was chaired by Giolitti. It was a very heterogeneous group, as the different political destinies of its members later showed. Nitti's *Democrazia Italiana* (thirty-six representatives) had more or

Table 5. Fragmentation of Parliamentary Groups from 1919 to 1922

1919–21

Seats Corresponding to the Electoral Slate		Seats Corresponding to the Later-formed Parliamentary Groups	
Liberals	41	Liberal Democracy (Giolitti)	91
Democrats	60	Radical group (Nitti)	57
Radicals	12	Liberal group (Salandra)	23
Lists of Liberal, Radical,		Social Reformists (Bissolati)	21
Democratic candidates	96	"Gruppo Misto" (including	
Front-fighters	20	Republicans)	24
Economic party	8	Renewal group (Bonomi)	33
Social Reformists	6	Popolari	99
Republicans	4	Official Socialist party	137
Lists of other candidates	5	Communist party	17
Popolari	100		
Official Socialist party	156		
Total	508	*Total*	508

1921–24		*1921*		*1922*	
Liberals	43	Liberal Democracy		Democrats	
Liberal Democrats	68	(Giolitti)	78	(Giolitti)	42
Demo-Socials	29	Demo-Socials		Liberal Democrats	
Social Reformists	25	(Nitti)	64	(De Nava)	23
National blocks	105	Social Reformists	24	Italian Democrats	
Republicans	6	Liberal democratic		(Nitti)	36
Official Socialist		group (Salandra)	17	Demo-Socials	
party	123	"Gruppo Misto"	28	(Di Cesarò)	41
Communist party	13	Agrarians	27	Social Reformists	26
Popolari	106	Fascists	35	Liberal democratic	
Others	17	Nationalists	10	group (Salandra)	21
		Official Socialist		"Gruppo Misto"	32
		party	123	Agrarians	23
		Communist party	14	Fascists	32
		Popolari	107	Nationalists	11
				Official Socialist	
				party (Turati)	83
				Socialist group	
				(Serrati)	40
				Communist party	14
				Popolari	106
Total	535	*Total*	527	*Total*	530

SOURCE: Ugo Giusti, *Dai plebisciti alla costituente* (Rome: Faro, 1945), pp. 75, 85–86.

less the same structure as the Giolitti group but a less lenient attitude toward fascism, as did Bonomi's group of Social Reformists (twenty-six representatives); both were hardly relevant, either politically or intellectually. These three groups, by and large, made up the Center of the political alignment of 1921. Without the Popolari, the Center amounted to 104 representatives, one-fifth of the Chamber. Even combined with the 106 representatives of the Popolari, it could not constitute the majority needed to form a cabinet. The Center needed help that, once again, could not come from the Left (Socialists and Communists), but rather from the Right, with all its equivocal consequences, including the thirty-two Fascists of the National Block.

The Center, composed of the right-wing of neutralism (Giolitti's group) and the left-wing of interventionism (Nitti and Bonomi) was less equipped to run the government than it had been in 1919. Once again, interventionism and neutralism had irrevocably split the old Liberal Center, and the consequences of this split were evident in each electoral test.

The Center, the old Liberal Center, was split more than it had been in 1919. In fact, to the cleavages Left and Right, Neutralism-Interventionism, the more subtle cleavage of the attitude pro and contra Fascism, with numberless nuances, had been added. The Center needed the help of other forces, no matter who those other forces were, since it would not have been able to reach a majority even if it had been more homogeneous. Moving toward the right wing of the alignment, we find the twenty-three representatives of De Nava's Democrazia Liberale and the forty-one representatives of Colonna di Cesarò's Democrazia Sociale, both "liberal" in their origins, both to the right of Giolitti's group, and both willing to cooperate with the Fascists.

The Right is clearly defined as composed of the Salandra group, labeled "Liberal democratic," with twenty-one (a year earlier, seventeen) members; the most conspicuous representation of the *Confindustria* (Benni, Celesia di Vegliasco, De Capitani d'Arzago, etc.); the Agrarians (twenty-three representatives, earlier, twenty-seven); the Fascists (thirty-two, earlier, thirty-five); and eleven Nationalists (earlier, ten). In 1919 the clearly defined Right amounted to thirty-five representatives, in 1922 eighty-seven.

The Left, Socialists and Communists together, decreased, although it remained a numerically powerful group. However, it could not be counted upon in any parliamentary "combination" to form a government (see table 5).

The Socialists were not disposed to enter the cabinet. Had they split they would have sustained a substantial loss: forty *Massimalisti* and fourteen Communists, besides all the consequences to the party, including the relationship with the CGL. But even if they had not split, they would enter the government, any government, not on a cresting wave, so to speak, as would have been the case two years or even one year earlier; they would enter at a time when their influence, both political and moral, was ebbing.

The Popolari—whose numbers slightly increased—became of crucial importance. However, the old clerical-anticlerical cleavage, plus the personal idio-syncrasies of Sturzo and Giolitti, prevented any agreement between the Popolari and the only group that could take the initiative inside the old Liberal Center—that is, the group supporting Giolitti, and in particular Giolitti himself. Without the "old man," this group counted for very little, and in fact the Popolari's sup-port for a member of this group, such as Facta (according to the naive politics of having a "Giolittiane" but not Giolitti), was disruptive. The Popolari then could take the initiative, but the only acceptable man of that group was the mod-erate (and ex-interventionist) Meda, who represented a tiny minority inside the Popolari's parliamentary group. The result was that the Popolari did not take the initiative in forming a cabinet, at least a seriously feasible one, but pre-vented the formation of a large political support for the Giolitti group.

In this situation, the only "disposable" forces were those of the Right; they were small and contradictory, but they were "disposable." One was practi-cally dominating the streets and could therefore bargain on a different table than that of all the other forces, the table of force, i.e., in a location practi-cally above any contractual relationship. In fact, sooner or later, that force would have to deal with the only real "opponent" who could mobilize the army against it: the crown.

From a purely parliamentary point of view, with this situation of the Left, the Center, and the Right of the alignment, there was a visible reduction of the political arena to groups of the old Liberal Center and groups of the Right.

3. The Takeover of Power

The Fascist takeover of power was essentially political, not military, and from this point of view the March on Rome was the conclusion of a strategy based on the exercise of violence and, above all, on the enfeeblement and division of the forces of the political alignment. This division insured that the issue of order as a basic one able to aggregate political and social forces into an anti-Fascist front would be avoided, and resulted in a weak political leader-ship being made the arbitrator among forces that were both weakened and willing to be the "gate-keepers" of power for fascism.

In this perspective, we can consider a sequence of events in the Parlia-ment and in the country, but the starting point of the analysis is no longer the Parliament or the sociopolitical forces in the country, but fascism itself. From the fall of Giolitti to the March on Rome, fascism defined the situation.

The "pacification pact" (August 1921) between Fascists and Socialist unions must be seen as an attempt to detach the Socialist party from its syndicalist basis, thereby disconnecting political socialism from labor so-cialism. The reaction of the squadristi leaders (concluded at the Augusteo Theater in November 1921) was not merely in terms of a "class struggle"; they reacted against the useless salvage of an organization already in critical condition, particularly since such salvage would only have put obstacles in the way of the squadristi's planned violence.

The Bonomi government fell because of the failure of the pacification pact that it had supported: one more indication that fascism defined the political situation, its stability, and its recurrent crises. The story that followed is one that, at the level of analysis, appears as the exhaustion of possible combinations and alternatives, but in none of these failures (when success might have endangered the chance for fascism to take over power), was fascism (or Mussolini) absent.

It is worth reviewing the several possible combinations, all alternatives to a Fascist takeover and sometimes even to Fascist participation in the government, and all containing one basic element: street violence by the Fascists, now prompted by the prospect of certain political combinations in the Parliament. In this sense, Parliament was subjugated to the streets.

Failure of Alternative Arrangements

Parliamentary life comprises all the occasions for political alliances: issues, events, and critical situations. Consideration of a few of them should make clear the contradictions among the political forces of the legitimate alignment and the Fascist technique of dividing the forces from one another and all of them from the country.

The fall of Bonomi's cabinet opened two possibilities. The first was an alliance between Giolitti, De Nicola, and Orlando (the Center-Right), with a program to reintroduce majority rule in the elections. This arrangement failed because of Sturzo's opposition (this was Sturzo's first "veto" to Giolitti). The veto was in the obvious interest of mass parties, including the Fascists, so it therefore blurred the cleavage between fascism and antifascism. The second arrangement was an alliance between Facta (a member of Giolitti's group) and the Popolari party. (This resulted in the first Facta government, which lasted until the end of July 1922). Facta and the Popolari party agreed on the promise of a favorable consideration of the statewide exam in public schools, which was granted by a Popolari member (Anile) in the Ministry of Public Education. The issue of church versus state blurred the basic cleavage that was breaking up the country.

During the first Facta cabinet, a Socialist attempt at isolating the Fascists in Parliament (as a consequence of a series of eruptions of violence), supported by the Popolari (the *mozione* Longinotti of 19 July 1922), met the opposition of rightist Liberals, particularly Salandra. This group permitted the Fascists to join the *mozione* as a vote of no confidence against the cabinet. A political victory for Mussolini resulted, though it was based on the presence of allies.

The fall of Facta's cabinet opened another series of alternative arrangements that are worth being compared with the first ones after Bonomi's fall. Orlando's design of assembling a grand coalition of Liberals, Fascists, and

Popolari met the opposition of the Popolari (Sturzo in particular) to having either Fascists or Giolitti in the government. The king tried to appoint Ivanoe Bonomi a second time (the first Bonomi cabinet had fallen on 2 February 1922). But Bonomi, who had the support of the Popolari, faced the opposition of Salandra Liberals, Demosocials (Nitti), Giolittians, and of course, Fascists.

At this stalemate there was an attempt by the Socialists and Popolari to respond, "patronized" by Bonomi. The task of canceling this alternative, the only feasible and anti-Fascist course of action, was performed by Giolitti: the newspaper *La Tribuna* published a letter by Giolitti in which the old leader cast many doubts over "a union of Sturzo, Treves, and Turati." Giolitti was the only figure who still had enough power—by himself—to veto such an important initiative, and he did it solely to return the veto to Sturzo.

When Bonomi gave up his attempts to form a cabinet, a series of impossible appointments followed, which showed the impotence of the traditional alignment of forces: Meda (Popolari), De Nava (rightist Liberal), and a projected appointment to Orlando, which was again interrupted by the news about the "legalitarian strike." Turati was consulted by the king on 29 July 1922, and a legalitarian strike was declared. This had disastrous consequences, including the second, definite appointment of Facta ("from factà to facta" while the storm was gathering), which passed in the emergency situation.

It was this atmosphere of division and fragmentation that prevented the Socialist-Popolari coalition, the only alliance with any hope of stability, from forming. The gains made by fascism during this period are manifested by an episode that took place when Orlando was first appointed. Shortly after he announced his design for a grand coalition (21–23 July 1922), Orlando had a talk with Mussolini, who, in order not to be isolated, asked for a cheap exchange: three undersecretaries (one to the presidency) for three inconspicuous Fascists. At the time of his second, prospective appointment, Orlando had another talk with Mussolini (28 July 1922). During that one-week interval Mussolini's price had risen to two ministries, including one for himself, the Ministry of the Interior. It was only a short step from this demand to the demand for total power, as Mussolini declared in the newspaper *Il Mattino* (11 August 1922) after the week of Fascist violence in retaliation for the "legalitarian strike" (1–3 August 1923).

The great victory for fascism resulted from the failure of the coalition between the Socialists and the Popolari. If it was a logical coalition, it was also immature in 1919, and during the three crucial years it had apparently deteriorated, rather than matured. In fact, it is difficult to believe that an agreement as important as that between the Socialists and Popolari turned out to be so vulnerable that it could be broken up by a simple column inspired by an old man.

The second Facta government, the one that fell with the March on Rome, witnessed a further reduction of the political arena and the entrance of new actors into the politically decisive arena, such as the king or even the Masons. Socialists and Popolari did not enter the last game, and the streets were silent, after the noise and violence. Violence was, however, being performed by the squads. Even the Vatican (as opposed to the leftist leadership of Sturzo) took a position in the game. The political parties were on the way out.

Reduction of the Political Arena

The failure of workable alternative arrangements further reduced the political arena and created a power vacuum that made the possibility of a government "imposed by the streets" more and more feasible. The streets, after the failure of the legalitarian strike, were monopolized by the Fascists; they could, however, be controlled by the army. As the "army" meant the "crown," in the middle of September 1922 Mussolini approached the monarchy in the well-known talk at Udine.

The power vacuum was not solely the result of the reduction of the political arena to four actors: the cabinet, the crown, Giolitti, and Mussolini. It was created in part by their internal relations, which gave the last-minute alternative of Giolitti versus Mussolini a complex aspect that resulted in the "lack of drama" with which the takeover was carried through.

The self-exclusion of the political forces from the arena reduced the situation to the alternative of Giolitti or Mussolini. The cabinet was quasi-paralyzed; the crown, according to the formal procedures, could come into the picture only on the initiative of the cabinet. There is sufficient evidence that Facta was negligent in contacting the king, for largely conjectural reasons that are of no interest here.[18] However, from the analysis of the government's decisions and nondecisions it appears that it was divided by two contrasting lines that neutralized each other: the Taddei line, which favored strong intervention against mounting Fascist violence, and the Facta line, which favored letting things go, based on the provisional task of paving the way for the return of Giolitti.

The lack of any reaction to the constant civil disorder gives, of course, a different weight to the two last-minute competitors and to their projects, but it is not the only reason for the difference in bargaining power.

Mussolini made no secret of his project of a dictatorship. As early as August of the same year in the interview to *Il Mattino* he had posed the dilemma of "either Parliament or seizure of power" and had stated that "it is out of the question that fascism wants to become the state." This kind of statement made the attempts by Salandra, Nitti, and of course by Giolitti himself to coopt fascism seem grotesque.

We have no evidence that Giolitti had a definite project in mind, unless we consider the scuttling of the tentative Socialist-Popolari agreement that we have mentioned and later the demand for a "strong government" led by a "prestigious man" that appeared as an editorial in *La Stampa* on 13 September 1922 but is considered a self-proposal by Giolitti.

The difference in "weight" in fact resulted from several elements, most of them in favor of fascism. First, Giolitti planned to include the Fascists in the government, while Mussolini carefully avoided any mention of Giolitti for a parallel project. Second, Giolitti had uncertain allies, if not enemies, in Salandra and other representatives of the old Liberal alignment. In other words, the old cleavages and the old hostilities did not melt away in this emergency situation, partially because there was no dramatization on the side of Giolitti or of the Giolittiani of the situation in terms of "*sauvetage* of democracy" versus "the end of democracy." This happened, however, precisely because a basic element of Giolitti's program was the inclusion of Fascists in the government.

The frontal collision, already repeatedly avoided in order to maintain public order, was avoided even at the last minute, thereby giving Mussolini a monopoly to define the political situation. There is also the question of "style," which becomes important during crises, because groups are replaced by personalities and therefore the whole existing arrangement is more vulnerable. Given his uncertain allies, Giolitti should have remained in Rome, physically present, in order to aggregate his existing forces. However, his absence from the arena of the match, the aloofness with which he responded to the pressures to come and start talks concerning the formation of a new cabinet, all make the observer think that his strategy was opposite to the one demanded by the situation. Giolitti employed the traditional parliamentary tactic of playing the role of the indispensable man—a tactic used by those who

Table 6. Progressive Absenteeism in Parliament for the "Vote of Confidence" in the Government, 1919–22

Cabinets	Date	Confidence	No Confidence	Abstentions	Present	Absent
Orlando	23 June 1919	78	262	—	340	168
Nitti	11 May 1920	112	191	4	307	201
Nitti	21 May 1920	146	264	—	410	98
Giolitti[a]	26 June 1921	234	200	6	440	95
Bonomi	2 February 1922	368	11	3	382	153
Bonomi[b]	2 February 1922	127	295	1	423	112
Facta	19 June 1922	103	288	—	391	144
Facta	1 July 1922	122	247	—	369	166
Mussolini	30 October 1922	215	80	—	295	240

SOURCE: Computed from data in Francesco Bartolotta, *Parlamenti e governi d'Italia dal 1848 al 1970* (Rome: Vito Bianco, 1971), vol. 2.

[a]From 1921 on, the total number of deputies rose from 508 to 535 due to inclusion of the provinces previously under Austrian-Hungarian rule.

[b]The *ordine del giorno* that caused the resignation of the Bonomi cabinet had two different parts that were voted on separately. Here we have the results of the two votes.

resign the minute they think of themselves as being irreplaceable. It is, however, a tactic that often has proved to be wrong.

The self-exclusion of Giolitti left the field open to the leader of fascism. The technique of waiting was paralleled by the Fascist decision to anticipate the showdown of the march, which they were sure would have failed had the army seriously intervened. The rest is known, as the dilemma of Victor Emmanuel reproduced the dilemma that the political forces had refused, with different degrees of intensity, to face thoroughly.

The quasi-progressive absenteeism from the sessions of the Parliament (table 6) is also an indication of the final reduction of the political arena, to the point that Mussolini presented his first cabinet, with the well-known "Bivouac speech," to a semideserted House.

Fascism and Crisis

What was the relationship between the crisis of the Liberal state and the takeover of fascism? In these pages we have tried to illustrate the thesis that fascism was more the outcome of the crisis of the parliamentary state than an irresistible force. We have tried to identify those elements of the crisis of the Liberal-parliamentary state in Italy that are common to other parliamentary systems undergoing rapid transformation and mobilization. (The war caused this transformation in Italy; today it could result from serious economic crisis.) In such cases the rules of the "division of labor" between civil, political, and institutional elements of society—the rules on which the European parliamentary system is based—are turned upside down. Since the political society is the "protagonist" of the parliamentary system, because it maintains the rules of the game of this division of labor, our attention was inevitably directed to the contradictions within the political elite in general and the Liberal political elite in particular.

Fascism was finally able to exploit the confused reaction to the process of democratization of Italian society, when the Liberal, Socialist, and Catholic political forces renounced their role of redefining the tensions arising from the contradictions of the society and the state. In particular, Italian fascism was an answer to two political elites: the Liberals, who were not willing to accept the passage from liberalism to democracy, and the Socialists, who were equally unwilling to forgo the passage from democracy to socialism. Fascism grew out of the crisis of both the governing and the opposition forces of Giolittian Italy. As the crisis of the governing force was decisive, a few points are worth considering. A part of the Liberal elite was unwilling to accept passage from a political system managed by a social minority that, because of the electoral system it had given to itself, was overrepresented as a political majority, to a political system in which social and political majorities tended to coincide, both in numbers and in power. There is a statement by Antonio Salandra, one of the stauncher supporters of fascism within the group of the Liberals, in a letter written to the Liberal philosopher Benedetto Croce, that clearly reveals the mood of Liberals (and also of the so-called Democrats), i.e., of the basic political forces of Italy before World War I: "The victory of Giolitti and his associates over Pelloux and his government marked a turning point not from Reaction to Liberalism, but from Liberalism to Democracy. Italy was profoundly immature and badly adjusted to Democracy. From this came all the events that later followed."[19]

This was precisely the mood of the Liberals, of the force that, whether interventionist or neutralist (it did not really matter), was the continuous loser during and after the World War I. In this sense we can say that fascism was the outcome of the incapacity (or unwillingness) of liberalism to turn into liberal democracy based on universal suffrage and proportional representation. In the same sense we can say that fascism was also the outcome of the incapacity (or unwillingness) of socialism to become social democracy, rather than turning into a rather wishful revolutionarism. Fundamentally, fascism exploited the incapacity of political forces of the Liberal state to aggregate and organize themselves as a mass party capable of coopting the middle classes. Italian liberalism, and above all, its most able representative, Giolitti, failed to aggregate the interests and the solidarities of the Italian middle class, both industrial and rural. It failed to coopt the increasing Italian middle class in a liberal democratic project of government, as Franklin D. Roosevelt succeeded in doing with his "New Deal," once in power.

Giolitti would probably have succeeded in this project of social and political cooptation had Italy not entered the great European conflict that brought out the most irrational feelings of the Italian middle class, especially that petty "humanism"—made of rhetoric, resentment, and low income—that a careful observer of his own contemporary politics had rightly identified as a fundamental matrix of that climate of opinion that contributed to the Fascist takeover of power.[20]

However, there is little doubt that the Fascist regime marks the beginning of that upward trend of the middle classes, their political and economic expansion, that was interrupted by neither World War II nor its aftermath. This phenomenon constitutes one of the most interesting problems of our modern political systems.

NOTES

1. Paolo Farneti, "Introduzione," in *Il sistèma politico italiano*, ed. Paolo Farneti (Bologna: Il Mulino, 1973), pp. 12–26.
2. Karl Dietrich Bracher, *Die Auflösung der Weimarer Republik* (Stuttgart: Ring Verlag, 1955).
3. Max Weber, *Wirtschaft und Gesellschaft: Grundriss der Verstehenden Soziologie*, vol. 1 (Cologne and Berlin: Kiepenheuer and Witsch, 1964), pp. 223–26.
4. A. F. K. Organski, "Fascism and Modernization," in *The Nature of Fascism*, ed. J. S. Woolf (London: Weidenfeld and Nicolson, 1968), pp. 9–14.
5. Weber, *Wirtschaft und Gesellschaft*, pp. 224–25.
6. Roberto Vivarelli, *Il dopoguèrra in Italia e l'avvènto del fascismo, 1918–1922*, vol. 1, *Della fine della guèrra all'impresa di Fiume* (Naples: Istituto Italiano per gli Studi Storici, 1967); Giampiero Carocci, *Stòria del fascismo* (Milan: Garzanti, 1972); Axel Kuhn, *Das Faschistische Herrschafts-system und die Moderne Gesellschaft* (Hamburg: Hoffman and Conze, 1973); Adrian Lyttelton, *The Seizure of Power: Fascism in Italy, 1919–1929* (London: Weidenfeld and Nicolson, 1973); Nicola Tranfaglia, *Dallo stato liberale al regime fascista* (Milan: Feltrinelli, 1974); Giovanni Sabbatucci, ed., *La crisi italiana del primo dopoguèrra: La stòria e la crìtica* (Bari: Laterza, 1976).
7. R. Frank, "Les classes moyennes en Italie," in *Inventaires III: Classes moyennes*, ed. Charles Bougle (Paris: Alcan, 1939), pp. 82 ff.; N. Tranfaglia ed., *Fascismo e capitalismo* (Milan: Feltrinelli, 1976) (see in particular the essay by Valerio Castronovo); Paolo Farneti, "La classe polìtica italiana dal suffragio allargato al suffragio universale," in *Sistèma Polìtico e società civile* (Turin: Giappichelli, 1971); Giampiero Carocci, *Stòria d'Italia dall'unità ad òggi* (Milan: Feltrinelli, 1975); Giorgio Rochat, *L'esèrcito italiano da Vittorio Veneto a Mussolini* (Bari: Laterza, 1967), pp. 26–66.
8. Nino Valeri, *Da Giolitti a Mussolini: Momenti della crisi del liberalismo* (Florence: Parenti, 1956).
9. Carl Schmitt, *Der Begriff des Politischen* (Berlin: Duncker and Humblot, 1932).
10. Renzo De Felice, *Mussolini il rivoluzionàrio* (Turin: Einaudi, 1966), p. 636.
11. *Annuario statistico italiano, 1919–1921* (Rome: Librerìa dello Stato, 1925), p. 400.
12. Paolo Ercolani, "Documentazione statìstica di base," in *Lo sviluppo econòmico in Italia*, vol. 3, *Studi di settore e documentazione di base*, ed. Giorgio Fua (Milan: Angeli, 1969), p. 413.
13. Alfredo Frassati, *Giolitti* (Florence: Parenti, 1959), pp. 29–30.
14. Renzo De Felice, *Mussolini, il fascista*, vol. 1, *La conquista del potere: 1921–1925* (Turin: Einaudi, 1966), pp. 276 ff.
15. Gabriele De Rosa, *Stòria del Partito Popolare italiano* (Bari: Laterza, 1966), pp. 27–37.
16. Alfred Szymanski, "Fascism, Industrialism, and Socialism: The Case of Italy," *Comparative Studies in Society and History* 15 (1973): 400.
17. Piero Melograni, *Gli industriali e Mussolini: Rappòrti tra confindustria e fascismo dal 1919 an 1929* (Milan: Longanesi, 1972); Roland Sarti, *Fascism and the Industrial Leadership in Italy, 1919–1940* (Berkeley and Los Angeles: University of California Press, 1971).
18. Efrem Ferraris, *La marcia su Roma vista dal Viminale* (Rome: Leonardo, 1946); Antonino Repaci, *La Marcia su Roma* (Milan: Rizzoli, 1972).
19. Quoted in Paoll Alatri, *Le orìgini del fascismo*, 2nd ed. (Rome: Editori Riuniti, 1971), p. 36, n. 3.
20. Luigi Salvatorelli, *Nazionalfascismo* (Turin: Piero Gobetti, 1923).

2.

From Fragmented Party Democracy to Government by Emergency Decree and National Socialist Takeover: Germany

M. Rainer Lepsius

The breakdown of the Weimar Republic was more than the collapse of a government or the dissolution of a political system. The seizure of power by the National Socialist party and the dictatorial regime of Adolf Hitler demonstrated the possibilities for self-destruction of a modern society. This change, revolutionary in its consequences, happened in a nonviolent way, observing the legal provisions of a democratic constitution in an economically developed, socially tightly organized, and culturally highly diversified country.

Since its occurrence, more than forty years ago, a great many attempts have been made to analyze the breakdown of the Weimar Republic. However, as a historian of that period recently said: "Despite the plethora of studies dealing with Nazism and the Third Reich, those phenomena in no sense belong to a closed chapter of history. Instead, they remain the focus of a vigorous and ongoing body of international scholarship. Historians and social scientists have as yet far from plumbed the full depths of the sea of documentation they generated."[1] One could add that the social sciences are still struggling to develop adequate systematic categories to analyze this event in theoretical terms.

This essay will not attempt to give a systematic analysis or a general interpretation, nor will it give an account of the sequence of events that led to the breakdown. The former would not be possible because of the lack of theoretical analysis that has still to be done, the latter is unfeasible because of space and is unnecessary in view of the available literature.[2] The following paragraphs will attempt to discuss some dimensions of the complex process and propose a number of analytical accounts that will be neither exhaustive nor evaluated in regard to their relative weight for the explanation of the total historical phenomenon.

1. The Democratic Potential

The strength of a democratic regime rests with the popular support of a democratic conception of government. The Weimar Republic, it has often been stated, was a republic without republicans and a democracy without democrats. While both statements are too rigid, they certainly point toward one of the basic hazards of the Weimar Republic: a very narrow democratic potential.

With the term "democratic potential" we do not refer to theories of a peculiar authoritarian German modal personality nor to conceptualizations of a specific German value system. In this context the democratic potential is defined by democratic conceptions of the political order institutionalized in the party system. The institutionalization of democratic and nondemocratic concepts of political order in the political system does not need to correspond with the distribution of personality types. Democratic personalities may have an identification with authoritarian parties, just as authoritarian personalities may have acquired a political affiliation with parties committed to democratic institutions. The institutionalization of social behavior cannot be reduced to underlying motivations or attitudes; it makes social action to a certain degree independent of them and defines legitimated alternatives of behavior for people with all kinds of personality structures.[3] The strength of the democratic potential of a political system, hence, can be measured by the votes for parties committed to democratic institutions. The more components of the political process are committed to democratic institutions, the greater is the institutionalized democratic potential. The more homogeneously the part system is oriented toward a democratic political order, the less the democratic regime becomes endangered by shifts in party identification and by sudden disaffections with a particular government. If, however, competing conceptions of the basic political order are firmly institutionalized in the party system, changes in the respective strength of the parties may have repercussions on the nature of the political regime. The more the strength of the institutionalized democratic potential is based on some parties only, the more risks a democratic regime runs by changes in voter alignments or protest movements in times of crisis.

In the Weimar Republic one can distinguish three major conceptions of political order firmly institutionalized in the party system: the democratic, the authoritarian, and the Communist. To these we will add a fourth residual category comprising splinter parties organized along particularistic regional and economic interests with ambivalent or undefined conceptions of the national political order. Table 1 shows the general distribution of votes along those groupings for the period of 1907 to 1933 according to the results of the national elections.

The democratic camp was formed by a coalition of the Social Democrats, the Catholics, and the Left liberals, who were striving for a democratization of the *Kaiserreich* and proposed peace negotiations in 1917 (the Interfraktionelle Ausschuss). This "Weimar coalition" took responsibility for the armistice in 1918, established the democratic constitution of the new Republic in 1919, and defended a democratic political order in the years of turmoil from 1918 to 1920. It founded the Republic, but it was a coalition of parties with very divergent political interests and lacked a homogeneous political platform. It had a unique strength in the National Assembly of 1919 that it never regained. This was partly due to the fact that at the time of the election, 19 January 1919, only two months after the armistice, the demission of the Kaiser, and the collapse of traditional order and imperial illusions, the authoritarian camp found itself in a state of organizational and political weakness. However, it soon recovered and by July 1920, at the first *Reichstag* elections, it had regained its prewar strength. The second factor, leading to the majority for the democratic camp in 1919, was the organizational unity of the Socialist party. The radical wing of the Socialists had not yet established an organization throughout the country, and only by the end of 1920 did the Communist party become a party with mass support. The permanent institutionalization of the Communist conception of a political order became an uncompromising opposition to the democratic order and drew its support from strata that formerly had voted for the democratic camp; this, then, weakened it below its prewar strength.

The authoritarian conception of political order was not only a carry-over from imperial times, a nostalgic resentment against the present state of affairs, believed to be caused by Allied reparations and political mismanagement, and anxieties of the middle classes toward Socialist reforms. It was deeply rooted in a widespread intellectual conviction that there was a distinctly German road to modernity, which was not to follow the lines of the West. This conception had a number of long-standing leitmotifs: power should be wielded by an elite of virtue and competence, not by functionaries of the impersonal parliamentary mechanisms; social conflicts should be solved by reason of the public good rather than settled by compromises of conflicting interests; integration should be achieved by national commitment and a quest for community, not by particularistic interest mediation and institutionalized procedures; and the state should have ultimate authority and moral dignity in regard to the autonomous forces of society and the individual pursuit of goals. These ideas coalesced in a distrust of democracy and the free organization of social interests and in the belief in state intervention and constitutionally secured elite author-

Table 1. **National Elections in Germany, 1907–33 (Reichstagswahlen)**

Percentage of Votes in National Elections

Conceptions of Political Order	1907	1912	1919	1920	1924_1	1924_2	1928	1930	1932_1	1932_2	1933
Authoritarian[a]	33	27	15	30	36	35	26	30	45	42	55
Democratic[b]	59	63	76	47	46	50	49	43	38	36	33
Communist[c]	—	—	7	20	13	9	11	13	14	17	12
Particularistic[d]	8	10	2	3	5	6	14	14	3	5	2

[a]For the elections in 1907 and 1912 these are the Deutsche Konservative Partei, Reichspartei, National-Liberale Partei, Bund der Landwirte, and the Deutsche Reformpartei. For the elections in 1919 and after they are the Deutschnationale Volkspartei, Deutsche Volkspartei, Nationalsozialistische Deutsche Arbeiterpartei, and the Landbund.

[b]For the elections in 1907 and 1912 these are the Fortschrittliche Volkspartei, Zentrum, Sozialdemokratische Partei. For the elections in 1919 and after they are the Deutsche Demokratische Partei (Staatspartei), Zentrum and Bayerische Volkspartei, and Sozialdemokratische Partei.

[c]Unabhängige Sozialdemokratische Partei and Kommunistische Partei.

[d]Regional protest parties of ethnic minorities and splinter parties of peasant and middle-class economic organizations.

ity. It should be made clear that such a concept of political order was neither totalitarian nor Fascist: it did not call for a unitarian mass movement but for a cooperation of social units in their own right (*berufständische Ordnung*); it did not believe in a military policing of society but in the authority of welfare-oriented paternalism; it did not advocate an uncontrollable charismatic leader bound only by his fortune and his idiosyncratic judgments but an open elite committed to the public good and responsible to publicly shared values of honor and individual virtues subject to law. These ideas were formed in the course of the nineteenth century under the impact of industrialization and the French Revolution. They were directed toward a double goal: to overcome the backwardness of Germany rapidly and at the same time to avoid the negative consequences of modernization clearly evident in the Western countries. The German way to modernity was believed to be superior in terms of efficiency as well as in terms of humanitarian values.[4]

The democratic concept of political order was in a precarious situation. However, its potential support was not so weak that democracy had no chance to survive. In 1919 it had a unique strength, and in 1932 it still had not lost a chance for a majority. The democratic potential could increase under favorable conditions.

To substantiate this argument, it is useful to analyze two presidential elections: 1925 and 1932. The presidential elections forced a polarization and concentration, as an absolute majority (in the second ballot, a relative majority) was necessary. They also led to a symbolic dramatization by the personalization of the election. While in the parliamentary elections numerous parties provided many and often indistinct alternatives, the presidential elections restricted the choices and mobilized the democratic and authoritarian potential more clearly. Table 2 condenses the voting results according to the different conceptions of political order in the two ballots for *Reichspräsident* and adds the results of the preceding national parliamentary election.

There is a two-step process of concentration and polarization. The first occurs between the parliamentary elections and the first ballot for the presidential elections, where the alternatives are reduced from about fifteen parties to five or seven candidates for the presidency. Thereby, the voters of the particularistic parties have to make a choice between the major orientations of the national party system.

In the second ballot a further reduction of alternatives takes place, with three candidates representing the three basic conceptions of political order. While the Communists can retain their hard-core support, despite having no chance to win, the ambivalent situation between the democratic and the authoritarian orientations becomes clearly apparent. The victorious candidate in both elections was Field Marshal von Hindenburg, who was the candidate for the authoritarian camp in 1925 and the candidate of the democratic camp in 1932. In 1925 his candidacy pulled 12.8 percent of the electorate toward an

Table 2. Relative Strength of Basic Orientations in the Elections for
Reichspräsident in 1925 and 1932 Compared to the Parliamentary
Elections of 1924 and 1930

	Percentage of Votes		
Conceptions of Political Order	*Reichstag 7 December 1924*	*Reichspräsident 1925*	
		1st ballot	*2d ballot*
Authoritarian	35.5	39.9	48.3
Democratic	49.5	53.0	45.3
Communist	9.2	7.0	6.4
Particularistic	5.8	0.1	—
Turnout	77.7	68.9	77.6
Conceptions of Political Order	*Reichstag 14 September 1930*	*Reichspräsident 1932*	
		1st ballot	*2d ballot*
Authoritarian	30.3	36.9	36.8
Democratic	42.9	49.6	53.0
Communist	13.1	12.2	10.2
Particularistic	13.7	0.3	—
Turnout	81.4	86.2	83.5

authoritarian orientation; in 1932, however, it pulled 10.1 percent toward the democratic orientation. In contrast to these effects, there was a comparatively good economic situation in 1925, which should have favored the democratic forces, while in 1932 the economic crisis was at its peak, which should have favored a radical protest vote. It seems that the polarizing effect of the candidacy of Hindenburg, in both elections, could not break up the basic strength of the authoritarian and the democratic potential; it could, however, swing the ambivalent electorate to either one or the other. In rough calculations on the aggregate election results—with all its known fallacies—it seems to be safe to conclude that the three major institutionalized conceptions of political order had a respective potential throughout the Weimar Republic of about 45 percent for a democratic political order, 35 percent for an authoritarian political order, and 10 percent for a Communist political order. It was for the remaining 10 percent of the electorate, which was undecided between the democratic and the authoritarian camp, to decide the fate of the democratic order.

The democratic potential of the Weimar Republic rested on the coherence and integrative capabilities of its intermediary organizations, parties, and interest groups to safeguard its basic core and to win support from segments of the population that were ambivalent or attached to the other conceptions of order. The coherence between the organizations was by and large maintained throughout the period. There were important breakups, particularly when the

Bavarian branch of the Catholic party decided to desert the democratic camp in the second ballot in the election of the Reichspräsident in 1925, which made Hindenburg the winner rather than the Catholic candidate, Wilhelm Marx, and caused the first major symbolic shift to the right in the political structure. But despite great internal differences and struggles, the organizations of the democratic camp maintained close connections and formed the government of Prussia continuously until its enforced dissolution of Chancellor von Papen on 20 July 1932.[5] The integrative abilities of the parties and intermediary organizations of the Catholic and Socialist segments of the democratic camp lasted until the Nazi seizure of power in 1933. In the end, the democratic camp lost because the liberal and Protestant segments had already disintegrated in the late twenties.

The democratic potential could have grown through the disintegration of either the authoritarian or the Communist camps. The Communists, however, became more and more uncompromising during the Weimar period.[6] In the course of its internal Stalinization during the years 1924 to 1928, the Communist party moved further away from the Socialists and made them their main target after 1929. Ideologically as well as organizationally, the Communist camp was tightly integrated and ready to absorb the protest vote of the unemployed working class.

The authoritarian camp compromised on occasion between 1925 and 1927. Altogether it lost popular support, but many of its followers moved toward the ambivalent group of regional or economic particularism rather than toward the democratic camp. The authoritarian camp returned to a course of system opposition in 1928–29; but it was not the traditional forces that regained popular support. It became completely reorganized and energetically strengthened by the Nazi party, which not only unified different groupings but was able to attract most of the ambivalent segments, and by the end of the period it had also made some inroads into the solid basis of the democratic camp, thereby creating a relative majority for the authoritarian camp.

The democratic potential remained stagnant. It might have been enlarged by integrating the ambivalent sector or by destroying the two other camps. This could have been achieved by the successful performance of democratic governments or by expanding the integrative capability of the respective intermediary organizations. The first was hard to achieve, given the basic differences of the political forces inside the democratic camp on major issues of internal policy and the general obstacles created by the war and the economic development. The second possibility was not pursued because of the subcultural fixation of the organizations, parties as well as interest groups. The Catholic Zentrumspartei was enclosed by religious boundaries, the Sozialdemokratische Partei by class boundaries. The disintegration of the authoritarian potential in 1919 and 1928 could not be utilized for a permanent growth of the democratic camp. It rather enlarged the ambivalent segments from 1928 to 1930 and provided an unstructured reservoir for recruitment by the Nazis. It was their vigorous campaigning and unscrupulous tactical agitation that restructured the authoritarian camp, moving it beyond the boundaries of Protestant middle-class conservatism into a highly politicized mass movement. This process, of course, was enormously aided by the disruptive effects of the economic crisis. The democratic regime was not doomed by the weakness of the democratic potential, but by its internal fragmentation and overall stagnation. The authoritarian potential did not win because of its traditionally institutionalized concepts of political order and organization but through its renewed internal cohesion and the vitality provided by the Nazi movement. The basic weakness of the democratic potential, however, limited the elasticity of the democratic regime in times of severe crisis because it did not allow for a change of government and coalition of political forces within a common democratic conception of political order. Change of government always implied the danger of a change of regime. A stable democratic regime should allow for a change of government without a threat to the regime. In this sense the Weimar Republic was not a stable democracy.

Parliamentary democracy, established during the turmoil of the German defeat in 1918–19, remained an "improvised democracy."[7] Legitimacy rested less on value commitments than on instrumental considerations. As perceived efficiency declined during the economic crisis after 1929, so did the legitimacy of the parliamentary regime. A substantial part of the population shared what Thomas Mann expressed in 1918: "I don't want politics. I want objectivity, order, and decency."[8] Mounting difficulties led to new improvisations during the period of presidential cabinets (1930–33) and to an erosion of parliamentary procedures. The political system did not satisfy the quest for leadership and symbolic integration so prominent in Nazi agitation.

2. The Party System

The German party system was formed in the Kaiserreich from 1870 to 1890 and carried over into the Weimar Republic without basic changes. This had two major consequences for the political process in the Weimar Republic. Firstly, the party system was based on the social and cultural cleavages of the seventies and eighties, and preserved them over a period of fifty years, while fundamental changes in the social structure took place. Second, in the Bismarckian political culture and within the imperial constitution with its pseudo-parliamentary government, the parties became used to acting as representatives of their respective sociocultural milieus rather than as responsible units of government. This traditional attitude led, within the parliamentary regime of the Weimar Republic, to an unconstructive inclination to regard uncompromising representation of traditional goals more highly than participation in government.

The basic fragmentation of the German party system consisted of four major groupings: a conservative political formation resting on the Protestant, agrarian segments of the population, located primarily in north and east Germany and oriented toward premodern authoritarian values; a liberal political grouping resting on Protestant urban and agrarian populations and organized along the influence patterns of local *Honoratioren*, divided into a nationalist right wing and a democratic left wing; the Center party, binding together the Catholic population in agrarian, middle class, and industrial areas primarily in west and south Germany; and the Socialist labor movement, integrating the secularized working class in the industrialized urban centers, dedicated to democratic and Socialist emancipation. The party system was structured along religious, class, regional, and ideological lines in a complex way that did not lead to a clear grouping of opposing coalitions; it evoked within any coalition high sensitivity on issues of firmly instutionalized interests.[9] In the course of the Weimar Republic the fragmentation grew further, thereby weakening the traditional party system. The Socialists split into the Social Democratic and the Communist parties. In the Catholic camp, the Bavarian branch became independent. The conservative and liberal milieus, however, experienced the greatest disintegration in numerous splinter parties of particularistic orientation.[10] Figure 1 tries to represent the party system of 1928 in a two-dimensional space. One dimension is a democratic-authoritarian continuum, the other dimension is a capitalist-socialistic continuum. The placement of the parties within this property space is, of course, always somewhat difficult to decide. The sketch should be used as an indication of the relative standing of the parties to one another and not as an indication of their absolute standing on questions of the political or the socioeconomic order. The percentages in the sketch refer to votes obtained in the elections of 20 May 1928 and are used to define the relative size of the parties.

The party system of the Weimar Republic offered two main alternatives for broad coalitions. Each, however, had to overcome a major internal cleavage. The democratic dimension united the parties of the Weimar coalition, the Social Democrats, the Catholic parties, and the liberal Democratic party. They could compromise on constitutional issues, as they endorsed the democratic regime, and on foreign policy, as they agreed on a revisionist strategy toward the Versailles treaty. They could not compromise on social issues, particularly when the Deutsche Volkspartei was included in a coalition, as they were too heterogeneous along the capitalist-socialistic dimension. The other coalition of forces was structured along homogeneity on the capitalist dimension and could include the Deutschnationale Volkspartei, the Deutsche Volkspartei, the Catholic parties, and the Democratic party. These parties

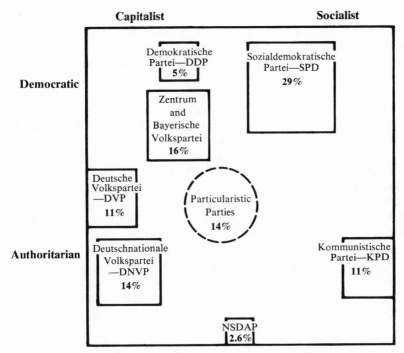

Figure 1. Germany Party Structure in 1928

could compromise on social and economic issues but not on constitutional and foreign policy issues. This led to a situation in which a coherent policy became impossible for any government. Both types of coalition had been tried: the democratic coalition was chosen during five years, the bourgeois coalition during two years. For seven years neither was attainable and minority or presidential cabinets were in office.

The development of the German party system before the advent of the Nazi movement had led to a disaggregation of interests within the parties. The mediation of political, economic, and social interests could not be achieved within parties and had to be secured on the level of the formation of a government coalition. This caused extreme instability in the governments of the Republic, as continuous tension management had to be maintained by means of government alterations. In the period from 13 February 1919, the date of the formation of the first parliamentary government, to 30 January 1933, when Hitler became chancellor, there were twenty cabinets. In only about half of these fourteen years did the governments have a parliamentary majority. This liability of the political process led to a complicated process of government by issue. For any major political issue a separate coalition and cabinet had to be formed. The governments did not rest on firm coalitions of parties on a common platform for a certain period of time but on short-term negotiations on policy actions for specific issues. The coherence of a government was achieved by the interaction of a few personalities who could exert influence within their parties to make them tolerate the government from issue to issue. This caused an alienation between government and Parliament quite in contrast to the principles of parliamentary democracy. The government became more dependent on the prerogatives of the Reichspräsident and saw itself as an independent agency that had to continue governing by continuous crisis management despite the fragmented Parliament. The parties, however, felt that reluctant toleration of government provided them with veto power on symbolic issues without the necessity of becoming entangled in the ongoing crisis management, which could be used to secure the *Gesinnungsgemein-schaft* within the party and its symbolic mediation into their respective electorates. As a contemporary observer wrote: "What we have today is a coalition of ministers, not a coalition of parties. There are no parties committed to the government any more, only opposition parties. That we have arrived at such a situation is a more severe hazard to the democratic system than ministers and parties foresee."[11] This is the clear perception of the crisis of the parliamentary regime under the conditions of the existing party system in 1929, at a time where neither the economic crisis nor the impact of the Nazi movement were dominating the political scene.

An awareness of the malfunctioning of the parliamentary system grew rapidly. It led to widespread resignation within the democratic camp and to a widely encouraged search for new forms of government, thereby revitalizing the authoritarian critique of democracy. A simultaneous development of disaffection with parliamentarianism and a quest for government authority came into being independent of the Nazi agitation against the political system. Even defenders of democracy lost their belief in its effectiveness. "In the entire period there was no government with real authority. It was a philosophy of 'somehow one must govern' which guided, and given the circumstances, had to guide political action but simultaneously led to a complete resignation, deadly to the vitality of a parliamentary democracy."[12]

Ferdinand Hermens, whose judgment we just quoted, pointed out as early as 1932 that one of the causes of the disintegration of the party system was of an institutional kind. He held that the electoral system of unrestricted proportional representation was crucial for the political crisis of the *Parteienstaat*. It facilitated the formation of small parties and the foundation of ever more by giving them the chance of winning a few seats in the Parliament. With about 60,000 votes out of an electorate of thirty-five million voters a splinter group could count on one seat. In 1930 there were nineteen parties that polled less than 100,000 votes each, some of them having the character of politicized sects, like the party against alcohol, which received 1,170 votes. It is obvious that such parties were without any influence, but they reduced the strength of the parliamentary system. After the election in 1928 there were eighty-eight members of Parliament elected by parties polling less than 5 percent of the national vote each. If one assumes only a modified proportional representation system by which no party polling less than 5 percent of the total vote gets seats, 18 percent of the members of Parliament in 1928 would have been excluded. Hermens suggested a majority system which would not only have inhibited the creation of new parties but would also have forced the traditional party system to reorient itself and try to aggregate diverse particularistic interests. While it is quite true that the electoral system of the Weimar Republic facilitated the disintegration of the party system, it did not, of course, originate it. However, it was a condition for the parliamentary crisis that had been widely discussed since 1924, but no alteration of the election system could be achieved by a Parliament that was paralyzed on so many issues.[13]

By 1930, the situation had worsened, and the party system changed. The disintegration of the party system, already clearly visible in 1928, had developed into a regime crisis under the impact of the severe economic crisis. None of the traditional parties, entrenched in old boundaries, was able to reintegrate the substantial segments of the population that were drifting out of the established political order either by voting for particularistic groups or by increased abstention.

Three major components of the traditional party system moved to the right; the conservative Deutschnationale Volkspartei under its new leader, Hugenberg; the Deutsche Volkspartei, after the death of its leader, Stresemann, in 1929, and the Catholic Zentrumspartei, under the more conservative chairmanship of the prelate Kaas.

The DNVP and DVP, which until 1928–29 could be regarded as the semiloyal opposition to the democratic system, now became disloyal. In the Socialist camp the strength of the disloyal opposition of the Communists was likewise growing. The Social Democrats, loyal to the democratic process to the very end, were unable to absorb the drifting voters of 1928. They had nothing to offer these voters, primarily peasants and those of middle-class origin, as they reinforced the traditional labor movement goals in order to defend their basic constituency against the competition of the Communists.

The main event, however, was the breakthrough of the Nazi movement. It became by far the strongest party and reversed the process of slow disintegration into a rapid reintegration of the party structure. The Nazis succeeded in absorbing the unattached and ambivalent voters of the splinter parties and former supporters of the Protestant middle-class and conservative parties. They pulled a substantial number of voters, who were still bound by semiloyal and even loyal parties prior to 1930, into a movement of uncompromising disloyalty to the democratic system. Together with the Communists, the Nazis made the disloyal opposition in 1932 a majority—a majority, however, which was internally antagonistic and unable to form a government (see table 3).

The crisis of the democratic regime was closely connected with the nature of the German party system—its fragmentation and its reluctance to accept the functions of parties in a parliamentary government.[14] To be sure, the tasks with which a German government was confronted in the postwar period and the subsequent economic crisis were extraordinary. The weakness of the democratic potential, furthermore, put severe limits on the formation of governments and loyal oppositions. But while continuous crisis in the years 1919–23 (adjustment to the lost war, assassinations, rightist putsches and leftist upheavals, occupation of the Ruhr, and inflation) could be overcome, the less threatening problems of 1928 to 1930 overburdened the party system. To reiterate, even without the threat of Hitlerism and the consequences of the mass unemployment of 1931 and 1932, the democratic parties were prepared to suspend the democratic procedures and resort to a presidential rule. By early 1930 they had accepted the government of Chancellor Heinrich Brüning, which rested on presidential power rather than on parliamentary majority. This signals the degree of frustration and timidity which became so dominant by the end of the Republic in 1932.

It is likely that the combination of presidential rule, politics of issue coalition, and short-term crisis management could have been carried on for a longer time and that the total collapse of democracy could have been avoided, despite the economic crisis that was further weakening the traditional structure of the German society and polity. There might also have been a chance for a revitalization of the party structure in 1934 or 1935 when the international economy recovered. However, the fragmentation of the party system and the strategy of temporary retreat from government participation and crisis management by emergency decrees were certainly preconditions for the breakdown of democracy.

Table 3. Strength and Composition of the Disloyal Opposition to the Democratic Regime, 1928–33

| | Votes in Reichstag Elections (in percentages) | | | | |
	1928	1930	1932₁	1932₂	1933
DNVP	14.2	7.0	5.9	7.2	8.0
NSDAP	2.6	18.3	37.2	33.0	43.9
KPD	10.6	13.1	14.2	16.8	12.3
Disloyal opposition	27.4	38.4	57.3	57.0	64.2

3. The Constitutional Framework

Any political process is influenced by the constitutional framework in which it takes place. In the case of the breakdown of the Weimar Republic the constitutional framework deserves special attention, as the breakdown and the seizure of power by Hitler has a curious double character. It is a regime change observing legal provisions while using revolutionary means.

In this context a systematic analysis of the Weimar constitution is not to be given, but a few remarks concerning the prerogatives of the Reichspräsident and the famous Article 48 must be made.[15] The constitution basically endorsed parliamentary rule but granted special rights to the president of the Republic. This duality of a parliamentary and a presidential rule was deliberately introduced into the constitution, partly influenced by the former imperial constitution and partly as a means of strengthening the authority of the state and counterbalancing the power of the parties and the Parliament. The president could claim greater personal legitimacy than the chancellor, as the former had a plebiscitarian basis and the latter only an indirect legitimation by Parliament. The president could bring a government into office without active participation of the Parliament as long as the Parliament was not casting a vote of no confidence. The president could dissolve the Parliament without its consent. The president could issue decrees in states of emergency to restore public order with the endorsement of the chancellor, which the Parliament later could revoke or merely tolerate by not casting a vote against the decree. Taken together, the presidential prerogatives allowed for government without active participation of the Parliament. The Parliament could fall back on a passive role of toleration and resort to its veto powers without being forced to formulate a political course of action of its own. There is a certain correspondence between the party structure and the constitution. This could be seen as functional, given the fragmented party structure; it could, however, also prolong a party structure dysfunctional for a parliamentary democracy.

In the first years (1919–24) of the presidency of Friedrich Ebert the emergency powers of the president became widely used to cope with upheavals and revolts within the narrow sense of the constitutional definitions. However, by 1923 and 1924 the presidential prerogatives were also used to cope with economic matters that had no relation to any state of emergency or public disorder. They were, however, only used for a short period of time, since the Parliament always retained its ultimate authority. President Ebert, a Social Democrat who was deeply committed to a democratic form of government, never intended to abuse the emergency powers in order to change the power distribution between the legislative and executive branches of government.

With the appointment of Chancellor Brüning on 30 March 1930, a new situation was created. His government was put into office by the Reichspräsident without consultation with the parties and was declared deliberately to be a nonparliamentary government resting on the authority and the constitutional power of the president. The right to issue emergency decrees was now used as a permanent substitute for formal legislation. Its precondition was the internal paralysis of the Parliament, which would only agree not to pass a vote of no confidence. When in July 1930 an emergency decree on the budget was not tolerated by the Parliament, the president resorted to his right to dissolve the Parliament. The emergency decree was issued again, now not faced with any acting Parliament to resist its legality. Sixty days later, however, new elections had to take place. By combining the three constitutional rights of the president, a government could be kept in power without the explicit endorsement of Parliament, distorting the nature of the constitution. The countervailing powers of the president became the dominant focus of political authority. A shift of power from the legislative to the executive branch took place, which changed parliamentary rule into presidential rule. To hold a national election in September 1930, at the start of the economic crisis and with a Nazi movement already on the way to mobilize and radicalize the electorate, was a politically fatal decision. Its only result was to increase the incapacity of the Parliament. The Nazis, who had had 12 deputies in the Reichstag of 1928, returned now with 107; the Communists enlarged their faction from 54 to 77. However, the decision to dissolve the Parliament was not taken with the aim of restoring parliamentary rule but of prolonging presidential rule. The party crisis had led to an extension of the constitution. The government was no longer conceived as an agent of the Parliament but of the presidential authority. The awareness of the parliamentary crisis became now an awareness of a constitutional crisis. Conservative forces, opposed to parliamentary democracy, saw their opportunity gradually to transform the political system into a semiparliamentary rule with a government "above the parties" and responsible only to the president legitimated by the plebiscite. The more reactionary circles thought the time for exclusion of the labor movement from the political process and a reduction of social legislation had come, restoring not only the prewar political order but its social order as well. Presidential rule became a new form of legal government, opening up a chance for permanent dictatorial rule. As long as Brüning was chancellor, the latter possibility was not contemplated by the government. He aimed at an eventual return to a parliamentary regime.[16] It was only after his dismissal by Reichspräsident von Hindenburg on 30 May 1932 that the essence of the constitution was violated.

The new chancellor, von Papen, appointed by Hindenburg on 1 June 1932, did not even have a chance to be tolerated by the Parliament. Before even a vote of no confidence could be cast, the Parliament was dissolved by presidential decree. New elections were to take place within the constitutional limits of sixty days. This caused an election at the peak of the economic crisis, which could only lead to an enormous increase of Nazi strength in the Reichstag. There had already been three nationwide elections in 1932 that Hitler had used for a continuous campaign. The new Reichstag saw the NSDAP, with 37.2 percent of the votes, as by far the largest faction. However, the Reichstag elected on 31 July 1932 was immediately dissolved on 12 September and a fifth election was called for 11 November, again observing the constitutional provision of the sixty days. The rationale for the two dissolutions and elections of Parliament, however, was an abuse of the constitution, namely, to install a presidential government without parliamentary support. Neither von Papen nor General von Schleicher, who became chancellor on 3 December 1932, were committed to a democratic regime. They were, however, unable to establish an authoritarian rule by either an enforced permanent dismissal of Parliament or a military coup d'état. They succeeded in further discrediting parliamentarism, in providing new occasions for agitation and mobilization of the population by useless elections and in unintentionally justifying Hitler's claims that the present system was rotten and that Germany could only be saved by a truly authoritarian leadership based on his own mass support.[17] Table 4 indicates the breakdown of parliamentarism well before the Nazi seizure of power.

With the gradual shift of power from the Parliament to the president, the arena of decision-making became confined, and legal procedures were replaced by personal relations. The leadership of the parties and factions lost influence. The mediation of interests in the political arena shifted from organized procedures between agencies to obscure informal conferences and confidential agreements. The personal likes and dislikes of Hindenburg, his understanding of the political situation, and his physical health became of utmost importance to the political fate of the country. Rooted in the tradition of the imperial army, living in a world of conservative national commitments, he had no clear understanding of a democratic parliamentary system. Overburdened by the decisions he had to make or at least to justify by his signature, eighty-five years of age and in poor health, he was placed in the center of the remaining arena of legal decision-making,[18] Personal access to Hindenburg rather than constitutional procedures defined political events. The appointments and dismissals of Brüning, Papen, and Schleicher, and finally also the appointment of Hitler, were effected in the influence on Hindenburg of a very small and publicly irresponsible group of people. A process of gradual denaturation took place, covering up even the most obvious violations of constitutional rights. The depossession of the Prussian government by the

Table 4. Erosion of Parliamentary Power

	1930	1931	1932
Laws passed by Parliament	98	34	5
Emergency decrees by the president	5	44	66
Days in parliamentary session	94	41	13

Papen government on 20 July 1932 could still pretend to be legally justified by a presidential decree.[19] This blurring of the categories of legality and legitimacy also served to make the seizure of power by Hitler look legal.[20] He was appointed by the president but could not win a vote of confidence in Parliament. Therefore, the Reichstag was dissolved once more two days after his appointment, and new elections were scheduled for 5 March 1933. Hitler had five weeks without a constitutional basis to establish his rule and in particular to take over the police in Prussia, suppressing leftist forces and intimidating all opposition. On 28 February 1933 an emergency decree was issued, which pretended to be constitutionally legal while it suspended the very basis of the constitution with no Parliament to cast a vote on the decree. The election on 5 March 1933, conducted under the unrestricted impact of Nazi propaganda, using all the suppressive powers of the government, brought the Nazis 43.9 percent of the vote and, only by the coalition with the Deutschnationale Volkspartei and their 8 percent of the vote, a narrow majority. Pseudo-legality was transformed into a nominal legitimacy, which in turn was used to destroy constitutional legality and to establish an undemocratic rule.[21]

Attitudes are formed and actions are taken within an institutional framework. This framework is not neutral but gives rise to a dynamic of its own. It not only defines the normal procedures but makes certain alternatives more accessible than others. The constitution and the election system, both hailed as most democratic, did not cause the breakdown of the Weimar Republic. However, they did not serve to strengthen the democratic political process. The imperial regime, with its authoritarian political order, remained an alternative preferred by many parts of the elite—the civil servants, the military, the professors, the industrialists, and of course, the landed aristocracy. Democratic procedures and institutions did not gain consensual legitimacy with the population, either. Open interest mediation was mistaken for efficiency. At best, the Germans became *Vernunftrepublikaner,* at worst they were longing for a restoration of the monarchy or a charismatic *Führergestalt.*

4. Economic Situation and Social Structure

The impact of the economic depression on the rise of Nazism and the breakdown of democracy in Germany cannot be overestimated. It has often been stated, and the assumption is very plausible, that without the disruption of the economic situation, the political system would not have entered a prolonged crisis, nor would a large segment of the population have been mobilized by the Nazi movement. The rise of the Nazi movement and the unemployment curve show a close similarity. Germany was hit particularly hard by the world depression. Next to the United States, she suffered most, much more than France, Great Britain, the Scandinavian countries, Holland,

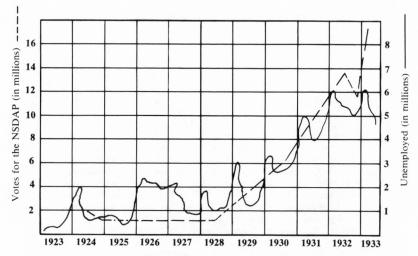

Figure 2.   Unemployment Rate and Vote for the National Socialist Party. Reprinted from Werner Kaltefleiter, *Wirtschaft und Politik in Deutschland* (Cologne and Opladen: Westdeutscher Verlag, 1968), p. 37

and Belgium. This severe economic crisis, which led to a decrease of the gross domestic product in 1932 to 63 percent of its 1928 level, and to the unemployment of six million people in the first months of 1932 and 1933, was caused by the international depression, structural domestic problems, and political factors.[22] The main cause, however, rested in international economic developments and was external to the German political and social system. However, the question of whether the economic crisis was aggravated by German actions and why the economic crisis led to a breakdown of the total political system must be raised.

After a disastrous inflation in 1923, the German economy recovered quickly. Foreign, particularly American, loans provided short-term investment funds; these were used to modernize the industrial production system,

Table 5. National Income, 1929–32 (1929 = 100)

	1929	1930	1931	1932
Germany	100	92	75	61
United States	100	94	78	60
United Kingdom	100	98	87	85
France	100	99	93	84
Sweden	100	107	108	100

SOURCE: League of Nations, *Economic World Survey 1933–34* (Geneva, 1934), p. 158.

Table 6. Unemployment, 1928–33 (Annual average as percentage of labor force)

	1928	1929	1930	1931	1932	1933
Germany	8.6	13.3	22.7	34.3	43.8	36.2
United States	4.4	3.2	8.9	15.9	23.6	24.9
United Kingdom	10.8	10.4	16.1	21.3	22.1	19.9
France	4.0	1.0	2.0	6.5	15.4	14.1
Sweden	10.8	10.2	11.9	16.8	22.4	23.3

SOURCES: The figures for Germany, the United Kingdom, and Sweden are from Walter Galenson and Arnold Zellner, "International Comparisons of Unemployment Rates," in *The Measurement and Behavior of Unemployment*, National Bureau of Economic Research (Princeton, N.J.: Princeton University Press, 1957), p. 455. The figures for France are estimated rates among wage and salary earners in manufacturing, mining, and construction. This represents the total unemployment picture adequately. See Galenson and Zellner "International Comparisons of Unemployment Rates," p. 523. The figures for the United States are from Stanley Lebergott, "Annual Estimates of Unemployment in the United States, 1900–1954," in *The Measurement and Behavior of Unemployment*, p. 215.

which, due to the war, had a ten-year backlog of demands for new equipment. The internal war debts were liquidated by the currency reform of 1923/24, diminishing large sums of private savings, thereby impoverishing the middle classes and causing a lasting, psychological trauma.

The reparations demanded by the Allies became the great political issue; they were thought of as the cause of the German economic difficulties. At first undefined in their amount, they were the subject of continuous negotiations leading to the Dawes Plan of 1924, which regulated the procedures and amount of the annual payments, and later to the Young Plan of 1930, which set up a definitive schedule of payments to end in 1988. The capitalized present value of all payments was computed at just below 37 billion marks, which was a remarkable reduction from the sum of 132 billion marks set up by the Reparations Commission in 1921. In addition to the financial and economic burden, the reparations played an enormous symbolic role in the German political scene. The sum was regarded as totally unjust, much more than what was needed to compensate for the war damage caused by the German army in occupied territories. It was seen as being a means for the permanent enslavement of Germany by France and as a basis for direct intervention in German affairs. A severe limitation of national sovereignty was clearly perceived in the occupation of the Ruhr area as a sanction for alleged German noncompliance in 1923, in the setup of an Allied control commission in Berlin, and in the imposition of foreign experts on the board of the *Reichsbank,* the German central bank, and the national railways. Their controlling power was to secure a guarantee for the reparations payments. By the provisions of the reparations agreements, the German authorities saw themselves as hampered in embarking on any policy of credit expansion to counteract the depression.[23]

The German reparations were linked with the regulation of French and British war debts to the United States, and this interdependence caused a fatal immobility in the international fiscal system and contributed to the enormous decline in international trade during the world depression. In the German political scene the reparations became the overriding issue, as the depression was seen as an ideal opportunity to achieve an international agreement to abolish the reparations altogether. The Brüning government concentrated all its efforts on this goal regardless of the repercussions on the domestic economic and political situation. The strategy was first to prove to the Allies the German incapacity to pay reparations and only then to embark on a policy of public works and credit expansion. And indeed as the Reparations Conference in Lausanne from 16 June to 8 July 1932 brought about the final settlement, Brüning had already been dismissed.

The nationalistic opposition had denounced the policy of compliance and gradual negotiations on the reparation question from the very beginning in the early twenties. The NSDAP embarked on a violent campaign against the reparations and the Versailles treaty, both symbols of national degradation, both alleged tools of an international conspiracy of world capitalism and in particular Jewish manipulations against the German people. The experience of misery served as proof for these allegations, which converted economic problems into ideological commitments of a mythical character.

The domestic economic difficulties started with an agrarian crisis in 1927–28. Violent demonstrations, particularly in Schleswig-Holstein, gave rise to a peasant movement directed against the Parteienstaat and demanding special legislation that would keep agriculture outside the market economy (*berufsständische Ordnung*). Its basis was a delayed adaptation of agriculture to the new market conditions. The war and the postwar period had been boom years for the peasantry because of the shortage of food. The annulment of debts by the inflation that took place until 1923 and the currency reform had secured a period of ten years during which agriculture in Germany had not had to face the conditions of the market. A high renewed indebtedness (partly for new machinery, partly for consumption, as the harvest of 1923 was sold for the old, inflated currency) and falling agricultural prices had put certain agricultural areas, particularly those in the north and east, in a severe slump. Public sales of farms (because of failure to pay interest or taxes) aroused the peasant population against the perceived immorality of the economic and political system.

The *Landvolkbewegung* became a violent populist movement with strong anti-Semitic overtones. The outburst of violent protest in 1928 led first to the formation of regional agrarian protest movements and to the erosion of the voter basis of the Protestant middle-class and conservative parties. By 1930 the agrarian protest movement had turned to the NSDAP. Agrarian voters in Protestant areas provided the Nazis with their first success, in the national elections of 1930. In Schleswig-Holstein the NSDAP won 27 percent of the vote, and in 1932 this was the only district in which the Nazis polled more than 50 percent of the vote. This development took place on a local level and within the regional agrarian subculture. The new leaders of the spontaneous Landvolkbewegung converted to the NSDAP rather than the NSDAP going out to win them.[24]

The party did not react to the agrarian protest until late in 1930. Walther Darré, the agrarian expert, was put in charge of a special organization on 1 August 1930; the first party meeting with representatives of the peasantry convened on 9 February 1931. It must be noted that the alliance of the Landvolkbewegung with the NSDAP was not the result of a special propagandistic effort on the side of the Nazis nor of the personal experience of mass rallies conducted by Hitler. Rather, the Nazi party, being in a state of rapid, disorganized growth, was open for the most diverse activists' particularistic interests and protest moods. The vague reference to a *berufständische Ordnung,* the radical attack on the political system and its open hierarchy made it attractive as a nationally unifying body for regional and social protest, opening up political careers for young activists. The mediation between the agrarian structural crisis and the Nazi movement was provided by the breakdown of traditional intermediary organizations and the unavailability of alternative political organizations in Protestant areas. The Socialists never really managed to care for the peasants; they concentrated on the working class and, via some unions, on the agricultural day laborers. The independent farmer was supposed to die out and become transformed into a new agricultural worker in a Socialist society. As late as 1927 the first agrarian program was proclaimed by the SPD.[25] Only the Catholic milieu, always concerned with the peasants as faithful Catholics, was able to absorb the unrest of the peasants, but, of course, the Catholic Center party was no alternative for the Protestant sectors of the peasantry.

The large landowners in East Elbia, also caught in an economic crisis of long standing, were accustomed to political and economic protection from the aristocratic elite of prewar Prussia. They felt threatened by the new political order and particularly by the Social Democrats, who proposed to nationalize their estates. With the election of Hindenburg as the president of the Republic, a new avenue to state subsidies became available. Hindenburg, belonging to the old Prussian elite and a landholder himself (an estate was presented to him as a gift in 1927), became an advocate of the demands of the landowners. When Hindenburg appointed Brüning as chancellor of the presidential government in 1930, he made it quite clear that a special relief program for the East German estates had to be enacted by the government, the Osthilfe. The dismissal of Brüning in 1932 again was influenced by distrust in Brüning's willingness to continue the Osthilfe. It is remarkable that throughout the severe economic crisis from 1930 to 1932, the government paid 170 million marks to the approximately 13,000 large landowners, much more than was given to industry in direct or indirect subsidies.[26] This curious one-sidedness can only be explained by the specific mediation of the interests of the Junkers, which was easier to achieve in the presidential than in the parliamentary regime.

The structural crisis in agriculture had different political results. The landowners found an avenue to meet their interests and stayed conservative. The peasants did not see an avenue for relief and special treatment via the affiliation with the traditional parties, so they deserted them and formed regional protest movements of their own. As these proved ineffective, they shifted to the Nazis, who in turn, after 1931, skillfully infiltrated the agrarian interest organizations and converted them to supporters of the NSDAP.[27]

The international financial crisis following the crash of the New York stock market in October 1929 caused the stop and recall of the foreign loans in Germany. The German banking system was, due to the inflation, very limited in capital and relied heavily on foreign loans. The investment boom in German industry, as well as in German cities, was financed by short-term loans from the banking system, but these loans were placed on long-term projects. Only 58.6 percent of the total credit volume was financed with long-term credits, as compared with 91.5 percent in 1913. The German banking system, therefore, was more endangered by the international financial crisis than other banking systems. The breakdown occurred in July 1931, when the international financial system did not succeed in saving the Austrian *Kreditanstalt,* and its insolvency reached the German banks. The failure of the international banking and credit system was related to rivalries between France and Great Britain, triggered by a plan to create a tariff union between Austria and Germany, which was preceived by the French as a violation of the peace treaties.

Chancellor Brüning and the president of the Reichsbank, Hans Luther, in close cooperation with the leaders of the major German banks, solved the crisis by more or less nationalizing the banks. Though the handling of the banking crisis can be considered a great success for the government, the crisis itself was most unfortunate for the economic and political situation. The dysfunctions of the credit system led to a further weakening of trust in the economic development. The central bank rate was raised from 5 percent to 8 percent, tightening the credit market further, discouraging the investments vital for a recovery of the economy. The political consequences were equally negative. The bank crisis heightened the distrust in the existing system. The bank managers saw themselves in close dependency on the government and feared direct state control, particularly in case of a Socialist regime. Some of them began to establish relations with Hitler to secure future autonomy.[28]

By 1930 industrial production had declined sharply (see table 7). German industry relied heavily on exports. International trade, however, was falling even more than domestic consumption. From an index of one hundred in 1929, the total imports of seventy-five countries, measured in millions of gold dollars, declined to an index of forty in 1932.[29]

Big industry in Germany had two major interests. The export industry advocated a policy by which it could retain its position on the world market. It favored lower production costs to meet the devaluation of the pound sterling. Since the relative position of the German export industry could not be bettered by an alteration of the exchange rate, as Germany had to observe the gold standard due to reparation treaties, a lowering of wages was thought to be the only remedy. The export industry, particularly the big corporations in the chemical and electrical industry, therefore supported the deflationary policy of the Brüning cabinet, hoping that eventually the international economy would recover. The minister of economics during the period of October 1931 to January 1933, Warmbold, was a former board member of the I. G. Farbenindustrie, a huge chemical corporation created in 1925.

The steel industry, on the other hand, was more oriented toward the domestic market and in general less liberal in economic persuasion. Its leaders were inclined to see a long-term solution only in government spending, particularly in the rearmament of the German army. Nationalistic stands were taken by some leading managers and particularly by Hugenberg, the leader of the Deutschnationale Volkspartei, a former member of the board of Krupp. Their interests were also directed toward a definitive cutback in social legislation and union influence; they were fiercely antisocialistic and opposed the Brüning government for its conciliatory policy toward labor. Representatives of the coal and steel industries, notably Fritz Thyssen and Emil Kirdorf, were among the first industrialists to establish close relations with Hitler. The majority, however, remained ambivalent and preferred to support the truly conservative and authoritarian politics of men like Papen.[30]

Small business, retail trade, and small artisans were under great pressure. They found themselves in a structural crisis, faced with the need to change from the productive trades to the repair and service trades, as well as to cope with the rising trend toward department stores and chain stores. The cause of

Table 7. German Industrial Production (1928 = 100)

	1929	1930	1931	1932	1933
Total industrial production	100.1	87.0	70.1	58.0	65.7
Production goods	102.4	84.3	62.3	47.3	56.1
Consumption goods	96.6	91.0	81.7	74.1	80.0

SOURCE: Ernst Wagemann, ed., *Konjunktur-Statistisches Handbuch 1936* (Berlin: Hanseatische Verlagsanstalt, 1935), p. 49.

their difficulties was seen to be the double attack from capitalist big business and Socialist labor. These segments developed the classic attitude of the struggle against the class struggle, activating all the moral sentiments of the prewar world. Moral indignation and the feeling of political powerlessness had already radicalized them before the advent of the economic crisis. The coincidence of a structural adjustment crisis with the general depression made them particularly vulnerable and ready to believe in Nazi propaganda.[31]

As the effects of the depression on the self-employed do not clearly show up in the unemployment figures, it must be kept in mind that the situation of the population was even worse than the unemployment figures make evident. Germany suffered the worst unemployment of any country during those years (see table 8).

There was already an average of 1.3 million people unemployed in 1927 and 1928, before the depression occurred, which was an unemployment rate of about 9 percent. According to present standards, this would be considered severe structural unemployment. As the unemployment rate went up to 22.7 percent in 1930 and 43.8 percent in 1932, the situation became disastrous. A total disruption of everyday life occurred for about half of the industrial working class. But the white-collar workers were also hit severely, and although they retained a better relative degree of employment, they were less accustomed to unemployment than the working class and felt emotionally more degraded by being out of work.[32]

On 31 January 1933, the day Hitler became Reichskanzler, there were 6,014,000 unemployed: 578,000 white-collar workers and 5,436,000 blue-collar workers, one-quarter of whom were below twenty-five years of age.[33] Many young people never made the transition into a stable working life. They were particularly easy to mobilize into militia-like organizations and were always available for street demonstrations and fights at party rallies. These militia-like organizations threatened public security and on occasion created an atmosphere of civil war, especially the storm troops (SA) of the Nazis and the *Rote Frontkämpferbund* of the Communists. For the young and unemployed men they provided clothing, food, and most of all, a feeling of belonging and comradeship that meant a meaningful structuring of their daily life.[34]

Table 8. Employment In Percentage of the Employment Capacity of Industry

	Annual Averages				
	1929	*1930*	*1931*	*1932*	*1933*
Hourly wage earners	70.4	61.2	50.7	41.9	46.3
Salary earners	87.8	83.2	73.5	61.2	60.5

SOURCE: Wagemann, *Konjunktur-Statistisches Handbuch 1936*, pp. 17 and 38.

The more unemployment rose, the greater became the number of people who had to live on less than a minimum income. In 1932, of the 5.6 million unemployed, 19.4 percent received unemployment insurance, 25.8 percent got support from a special relief fund, 36.6 percent were on welfare, and 18.2 percent did not get any aid.[35] The unemployment insurance program, created in 1927 to handle about 900,000 unemployed, had already become insolvent by 1929. The municipalities, responsible for the welfare payments, were bankrupt or in a severe financial crisis by 1931. Therefore, all relief payments were lowered substantially. But the population still at work also experienced a mood of deprivation and fear of becoming unemployed. By 1932, the situation of the majority of the population was desperate, disrupting life expectations and conceptions of social and political order. This is also reflected in the birth rate, which fell to the level of the war years 1916–18.

As the supply of labor exceeded the demand for labor, the strategic position of the labor unions became weaker. In April 1930 20 percent of union members were unemployed; in April 1932 the figure was about 44 percent, with an additional 20 percent working reduced hours.[36] The capacity of the unions to exert political pressure and, as a last resort, to conduct a general strike, decreased. Unemployment and depression presented the unions with problems for which they had neither an economic program nor a political strategy. Not until 1932 did they adopt a plan for modest credit expansion and public works; they were politically on the defensive, trying to maintain the status quo and preserve their organizations against the attacks of the Communists and the Nazis.[37] On the other hand, the influence of the employers rose steadily because of the labor market situation and their growing impact on the government. They used their strategic advantages to reduce social legislation and to cut back on union influence in general. The changed power relation became clearly visible and politically important as early as 1930, when an attempt to reconstruct the unemployment insurance program failed because labor and industry would not compromise on the proposed increase of the contributions employees and employers should pay. On this issue the last parliamentary government of the Weimar Republic collapsed; the Social Democrats retreated from active participation and left the field to the conservative forces.[38] The economic crisis had changed the distribution of power and the influence structure within the political system.

The white-collar strata were particularly vulnerable in this crisis. This group had expanded very rapidly in the preceding twenty years and was less integrated than the workers. Their interest groups, primarily the Deutschnationaler Handlungsgehilfen-Verband, were traditionally conservative in orientation, representing the aspirations of the white-collar employee to gain in status and to secure a social position like that of the civil servants. Only after the war did the Socialist and democratic orientations gain in influence via the new white-collar unions. The majority, however, became radicalized in favor of nationalistic and authoritarian political ideas, supporting antidemocratic tendencies and, in the end, the Nazi movement.[39]

General economic developments are reflected in the figures in table 9. They show a decline in the gross domestic product, a decline in private consumption, which corresponds to the decline in the wholesale prices, a much greater decline in gross investment, and a decline in state expenditures. The incomes from wages and salaries and from property and proprietorship declined at the same rate. With the reduction in the state income, expenditures for relief payments rose, which led to an increase in the excise tax from 0.8 percent to 2 percent in 1931. This, together with the high level of the central bank rate, was counterproductive for a revival of the economy.[40] The deflationary policy aggravated the economic situation. The hesitation of the Brüning government to put a public works program into action added to the feeling of helplessness and despair.[41]

To return to the question raised at the beginning of this section, it seems that the economic crisis in Germany was aggravated by peculiarities in the German situation. The coincidence of diverse structural strains in the economy produced by an arrested adaptation of some traditional segments of the economy, particularly agriculture, retail trade, and the trades, an enforced modernization of the industrial production apparatus in the years 1924–29, and a crisis of the structurally weak banking system were immensely heightened by the world depression. Excessive concern with the reparations problem led the government to an economic policy that aggravated the depression in search for a solution.

The second question raised was why the economic crisis led to a breakdown of the political regime. A crisis of everyday life of this sort mobilizes the population to a higher degree than any propaganda can possibly achieve. The mobilization activates parts of the population that under normal conditions do not participate in the political process and therefore are not integrated into the

Table 9. Indicators of Economic Development, 1928–33 (1928 = 100)

	1928	1929	1930	1931	1932	1933
Gross national income (includes net export, at market prices)	100	101	93	78	63	65
Private consumption	100	103	99	84	67	68
Gross domestic investment	100	77	60	28	33	41
Government purchases	100	103	90	81	72	74
Income of households:						
Wage and salary incomes	100	101	94	80	62	63
Property and proprietorship income	100	99	89	74	60	62
Public transfer payments	100	113	124	131	122	111

SOURCE: Data from Dietmar Keese, "Die volkswirtschaftlichen Gesamtgrössen für das Deutsche Reich in den Jahren 1925–1936," in *Die Staats-und Wirtschaftskrise des Deutschen Reiches 1929/33*, ed. Werner Conze and Hans Raupach (Stuttgart: Klett, 1967), pp. 43, 49.

structure of intermediary interest groups and parties. It is likely that this nonintegrated population will turn to the most radical parties available. The outcome of the protest mood of the population depends, then, on the nature of the party system. The radical parties available in a given situation may be less radical than the mood of their voters or more radical; they may be loyal to the system or disloyal. The willingness to support a radical party is determined by the power of the moderate parties to absorb the protest mood and the success with which they can produce a plausible interpretation of the situation. The strength of the moderate party structure depends on the capacity of the radical parties to produce a more plausible interpretation of the situation as well as an organizational network that links divergent protest movements into unified political forces.

In the German case, the economic crisis was most influential for the political mobilization. However, there were several filters that channeled the effects of this mobilization. Prior to the economic crisis, there was a firmly institutionalized disloyal opposition to the democratic regime, consisting of Communists as well as conservative nationalists. Any radicalization of the voters would lead to reenforcement of the disloyal opposition. This, however, could take place only when the moderate parties could neither retain their voters and interest organizations nor absorb the respective protest vote reciprocally. While the Catholics and the Social Democrats were fairly successful in the first respect, they were not in the latter. The Protestant middle-class parties, both liberal and conservative, however, were unable to secure their bases—neither the individual voters nor the interest organizations that had been affiliated with them. The farmers' organizations, the trade associations, and a substantial part of the intellectual and white-collar groupings were searching for new alignments. They could not join the Catholics, because of cultural tradition, nor the Social Democrats, because of class interest and status resentment. Nor did either party try to win them. The Communists were unlikely to attract the middle class, and only a few intellectuals switched to them. So the conservative nationalists would have been the most likely choice for the protest orientation. They, however, did not succeed even in retaining their voter basis.[42]

The availability of the vital Nazi movement, uncompromised by former involvement with the governments and rapidly expanding a wide network of devoted young functionaries and organizations, provided the most plausible protest opportunity. It also presented a definition of the situation that corresponded with the irrationality of contemporary life. Action and the power of will would be the means by which the impact of international conspiracy and the impotence of decadence would be crushed, and the German virtues restored.

To assess the overall impact of the Nazi movement on the breakdown of the political system at the peak of the economic crisis, one could try a rough and,

Table 10. Changes in the Protest Vote, 1924, 1930, and 1932

	1924	1930	1932
Percentage unemployed	13.1	22.7	43.8
Percentage of voter turnout	76.3	81.4	79.9
Protest vote of the Right (DNVP and NSDAP)	24.9	25.3	40.2
Protest vote of the Left (KPD and USPD)	13.2	13.1	16.8

of course, very questionable method, and compare the elections in May 1924, September 1930, and November 1932 (see table 10). The election in May 1924 followed the inflation crisis and a period of great internal disruption, including the occupation of the Ruhr by France and upheavals in middle Germany and Bavaria; they showed the highest percentage of leftist and rightist protest votes prior to the depression. By 1930, at the beginning of the depression, the rightist and leftist protest vote had regained its 1924 strength. With the worsening of the situation until 1932, the leftist protest vote grew by about 27 percent, comprising 16.8 percent of the total vote. Assuming that the rate of growth of the rightist protest vote would be comparable, one could project a total growth in the rightist protest vote to about 31 percent. Instead, it gained 40 percent. It can then be argued that the impact of the Nazi movement prompted about 10 percent of the population, which otherwise would have stayed within the realm of the moderate traditional or splinter-party system, to turn to a rightist protest vote. It was due to the particular aggressiveness of Hitler's movement and the weakness of the moderate liberal parties and Protestant middle-class organizations that the regime collapse entered the realm of possibility in 1932.

5. Adolf Hitler and the Nazi Party

The previous sections have dealt with the framework within which the breakdown took place. But none of the factors discussed so far has been of decisive importance for the final outcome. The active and, in the end, fatal role was played by Hitler and the Nationalsozialistische Deutsche Arbeiterpar-tei. In underlining Hitler's importance for the breakdown of the Weimar Republic we are not resorting to a demonology of Hitler or the conceptions of *"Männer machen Geschichte,"* it is men who make history. Rather, we will emphasize the structural aspects of Hitler's role.[43]

The conceptual tools for this attempt are derived from Max Weber's theory of charisma.[44] Weber proposes four dimensions to define charismatic author-ity. First, there is a belief in the exceptional qualities of an individual. This belief calls for absolute trust in the leader and makes recognition of his legitimacy a duty. Second, the influence of the leader rests on the recognition of his charismatic qualities as proved by his success. The attributed charisma is subject to proof. The chances of a leader to achieve recognition of his assumed charismatic qualities are increased psychologically by complete personal devotion on the side of his followers, arising out of enthusiasm, despair, or hope. Sociologically, they are determined by the definition of the situation in which the charismatic leader is forced to prove his qualities. Third, the realm of authority is a charismatic community, not a firmly institutionalized organization. The administrative staff consists of trusted agents who have either been provided with charismatic authority by the chief or possess charisma of their own. There is no bureaucratic organization, no principle of formal rules, no supervisory or appellate body, and hence no process of rational judicial decision-making. Fourth, the economic basis is not derived from systematic economic activities but rests on voluntary contributions and booty.

In line with these propositions we will first describe the simultaneous development of Hitler's claim on ultimate authority and the belief in his charismatic qualities. We will then discuss the breakthrough of Hitler's ''charismatic community'' into a mass movement and a dominating force in the German political scene.

Hitler's ascent comprised a series of successful claims on ultimate authority conducted despite high risks to his personal career. The capacity for unscrupulous tactical decisions and hazardous risk-taking is undoubtedly a personal precondition of his success. On 21 July 1921 he forced the then sectarian party to acknowledge him as the leader, unbound by any formal regulations, by declaring his resignation when leading party members suggested a coalition with other racist-nationalistic organizations, or *völkische Verbände*. This first seizure of power put him in the central position of the Nazi party and established for the first time his claim of ultimate and personal authority. After his defeat at the putsch on 9 November 1923, during his trial and imprisonment, he deliberately kept the party organization in a state of disorganization to avoid the establishment of a new leadership. Upon his release from prison he founded the party anew on 27 February 1925, denouncing all organizations that had formed in the meantime. The new party lost many followers and members because of Hitler's rigid actions. But his was the second successful seizure of power, by now already founded on his artificially built-up reputation as the hero of the Munich putsch. The third successful defense of his ultimate authority took place on 14 February 1926, when party leaders in northern and western Germany began close cooperation and proposed a revision of the party program with leftist inclinations and new organizational procedures. Hitler summoned the district chiefs on short notice to a meeting in Bamberg, where, after a speech five hours long, no dissent was aired, and Gregor Strasser as well as Goebbels, both spokesmen of the dissenters, expressed their personal loyalty. With this third seizure of power within the party organization, Hitler's ultimate authority was firmly established; no further serious attempts at ideological specification and formalization of the decision-making process were undertaken. Later conflicts, in 1930 with Otto Strasser and SA leader Stennes, in 1932 with Gregor Strasser, and in 1934 with Röhm, were settled by Hitler's unquestioned authority, the dissenters losing any personal charismatic authority they might have had the moment Hitler turned against them.[45] Every successful claim on ultimate authority was in itself a verification of Hitler's charisma, proof of his extraordinary gifts. The challenge to his authority was converted into renewed personal loyalty.

This process of gradual increase in Hitler's charismatic authority rested on some preconditions which are independent of his personality, his extraordinary ability to persuade and convince people in face-to-face contact. The first of these preconditions lies in the peculiar organizational structure of the party. The *Führerprinzip* as basic rule meant the total abolition of any formal regulations for decision-making and legitimation of authority. There were no collective bodies, no representative mechanisms, no procedural limitations for actions.[46] Ultimate authority rested with the leader of the party, who became legitimized by undefined acts of plebiscitary consent. He in turn appointed the subleaders, who held in their own areas ultimate authority as bestowed upon them by Hitler, independent of the formal consent of their subordinates. Furthermore, Hitler designed an intricate net of competing realms of jurisdiction, thereby placing himself in the all-important position of supreme conflict manager. Personalized rivalries without an institutionalized claim on competence kept the organization of the party in a state of artificially created disorganization, which only Hitler could control by arbitrary decisions without any limitations by procedure or precedent. There is a correspondence between organizational anarchy and need for ultimate authority, which, in a process of circular stimulation, enhanced Hitler's position, and the dependence of the subleaders on personal loyalty. Hitler's extreme autonomy from the demands of the party gave him the chance to take any action, and also to leave conflicts and competing ideologies unresolved, thereby integrating very divergent interpretations of the aims and the ideological basis of Nazism.

This leads to the second precondition of Hitler's charismatic authority: the lack of an officially defined ideology. The party program as expressed in the twenty-five points of 1920 was a rather arbitrary collection of sentiments and particularist demands, lacking intellectual consistency and pragmatic implementation. Hitler declared this program unalterable in 1926, thereby avoiding any intellectual discussion of ideological matters. It was he and only he who could interpret the Nazi ideology. His personal beliefs, therefore, played an extremely important role in the policy of Nazism. *Mein Kampf,* written between 1924 and 1926, expressed in much greater detail his personal beliefs than did the party program.[47]

There is in particular the violent anti-Semitism, a tendency not equally shared by other Fascist movements.[48] It rested on Hitler's racist Darwinism, the core of his belief system. Other guiding ideas were also shaped by Hitler's convictions: the extreme antimodernism and the preindustrial conception of social order as a militarized peasant society whose development rests on soil and space and whose blood is to be sacrificed to gain eternal life.[49] Hitler had no genuine interest in economic problems. He denounced capitalism and socialism alike. His intention was not to create a new economic order but to have an effective production apparatus at his command. He did not care for capitalism but he could compromise with capitalists, as long as they were compliant and efficient. Hitler's affinity with the capitalistic system rested on his conviction that only individual leadership unrestricted by bureaucratic regulations would produce efficiency, not on any general conception of economic and social order in an industrial society. In effect, "Nazi *Weltanschauung* was a meaningless abstraction until personified in Hitler."[50] This left Hitler uncontrolled by ideological interpretations of his actions by the party members, since "no legitimate questions can be raised about the leader's conception or interpretation of an idea" where there is no clearly defined and implemented obligatory program.[51] The followers could incorporate their own anxieties and hopes into the vague values of the movement, whose programmatic emptiness allowed for an identification with an ultimate authority regardless of specific and mutually exclusive interests and particularistic aims. On the other hand, Hitler could adjust the ideology to the short-term tactics he felt suitable and obscure his personal implementation of the ultimate cause. His ultimate authority was enhanced by his position as sole ideological interpreter of Nazism.

Third, it should be noted that Hitler most decidedly avoided any coalition with organizations outside his direct realm of ultimate authority. From the very beginning he fought against any cooperation with other rightist and völkische groupings, even when such coalitions would have promised greater influence in the political arena. Internal autonomy and external independence were the guiding principles he observed, rigidly putting aside considerations of growth, influences, and stability of the organization. It was his influence that was important to him, not the development of the party or its impact on a given political situation. He observed this principle throughout the negotiations in 1931 and 1932, which were intended to integrate the Nazis into the traditional authoritarian camp and thereby to tame Hitler.

The charismatic nature of the Nazi movement was not only the result of specific properties of Hitler's personality, magical capabilities, rhetorical fascination, and ruthless tactics, but also of deliberately advanced properties of organization, ideology, and external independence of the movement. Hitler was quite aware of the requirements of the role he had chosen for himself and spent much time on the elaboration of the image he wanted to create. Perhaps the greatest personal burden he willingly carried was the discipline to conform to his self-created role and public image.[52]

The party was formed as a "charismatic community" pledged to Hitler and managed by his agents in the districts, the *Gauleiter*. The only nationwide organizational bond was provided by the Munich head office, which was in charge of the finances and the central membership file. Otherwise great regional independence and diversity existed.[53] Only the storm troopers, the SA, developed an identity of their own. They were militarily organized outside the jurisdiction of the Gauleiter and directly committed to their leaders. Many SA leaders, mostly former army officers and veterans of the war, were torn between loyalty to Hitler and a commitment to form a militia as an auxiliary to the regular army. With all of Hitler's personal ability to persuade, to subjugate opponents, to destroy definite spheres of competence, he did not succeed in fully integrating the SA until he ordered the execution of its core leadership during the Röhm affair in 1934. The independent organization and clearly defined identity of the SA set institutional limits on Hitler's charisma. The Nazi militia, which Hitler used to produce an atmosphere of civil war in 1932, was at the same time the greatest threat to the unity of the party. However, the SA leaders had no political strategy of their own and had to fall back on Hitler for subsidies and ideological justification. Thus Hitler kept the SA leadership in line until he no longer needed them.[54]

Hitler was reluctant to establish any other specific organization outside the party, which, by the contextual properties of its field of operation, would not be able to function as a charismatic community. There was never a serious attempt to create National Socialist unions or interest groups.[55] There were, however, a multitude of auxiliary organizations for nearly every occupational group within the party. But they served only to attract sympathizers and absorb divergent interests, never developing into service organizations for a clientele outside the party membership.

A charismatic community will very likely remain small and insulated, consuming its energies in continuous internal conflict management and purification of the charismatic qualities. Hitlerism was, therefore, not regarded as a formation with political importance, but as a disturbing nuisance. Until 1928 this judgment seemed justified. The NSDAP polled 2.6 percent of the national vote in the Reichstag election of 28 May 1928. The membership comprised 100,000 people. Its financial means consisted of membership fees, revenues from publications, and occasional gifts from idiosyncratic wealthy people.[56]

The prospects for the Nazis looked dim. Even vigorous campaigning by Hitler in 1927 (he was prohibited from making public speeches in most states until early 1927) did not have an effect. The general political and social situation did not give his apocalyptic visions the necessary resonance. There were not enough anxieties to be directed toward the promises of the new order of the Third Reich. Nazism was an internally highly integrated but externally isolated political sect. It had succeeded in absorbing the radical völkische fringe in the political scene but it seemed to be entrenched in the boundaries of those circles, which had received 6.5 percent of the national vote in the crisis election of May 1924. There was but little hope for a breakthrough into the established party system. The strategy of a putsch had been discredited since the debacle of November 1923 and was disregarded by Hitler. Mussolini's example of a March on Rome was no more realistic an option.

The breakthrough came with changing political circumstances rather than through the activities of the Nazi party. In the summer of 1929 the nationalist opposition in the established party system propagated a referendum against the Young Plan, which they considered a national degradation and an attempt to prolong the dependency of Germany with reparations. Led by the Deutschnationale Volkspartei under their new rightist leader, Hugenberg, nationalistic and conservative groups like the organization of veterans of the war (Stahlhelm) and the agricultural associations (Landbund) formed a national committee for the referendum against the Young Plan and coopted the Nazis. This was the first step by the conservative establishment toward the acknowledgment of Hitler and his party, giving him a chance to gain national reputation by association with respectable organizations and personalities. It also provided access to financial means and the popular press, which to a large degree was owned or directed by Hugenberg, who had established the greatest press concern in Germany. Nazi propaganda became nationally recognized, Hitler personally respectable.

The referendum on 22 December 1929 was a failure. However, the alliance with the conservatives opened the authoritarian camp to the Nazis. The state elections on 8 December 1929 in Thüringen saw the first major Nazi victory. They obtained 11.3 percent of the vote and were invited to participate for the first time in a state government in coalition with other rightist forces.

The circle of the völkische fringe was broken up, and the Nazi party gained a national reputation. While the conservatives thought they could utilize Hitler and his movement as drummer and supporters for their aims, Hitler kept clear of any commitment and played his part with complete independence. It was not he who became absorbed in the national opposition of the establishment but rather they who lost their voters to Hitler. The DNVP suffered through the defection of its conciliatory leaders and was outdone by the much more radical and populist propaganda of Hitler's NSDAP. By the Reichstag election of September 1930 the DNVP had lost half its 1928 vote, while the NSDAP won 18.3 percent of the vote, becoming more than twice as strong as the DNVP.

The strategy of the established conservatives that had proved so disastrous for them in 1929/30, the futile attempt to tame Hitler and incorporate his party into a national front under their leadership, was repeated in the Harzburger Front in October 1931 and finally in the negotiations to form a rightist cabinet in August 1932 and in January 1933. Three times Hitler played the same game: he agreed to join forces yet upheld his claim for ultimate authority and his independence of action. Hitler could increase his demands from time to time as his relative weight in the rightist-nationalist coalition rose. In 1929 he was the underdog, in 1933 the top dog, due to the accelerating economic crisis and gains in voter suppport. Aided by the depression and growing unemployment, the defection of functionaries in middle-class interest groups to the Nazis, and their rapid infiltration by young and active men converted to the Nazi party and mobilized by the skillful propaganda activities of the party nationwide, by the end of 1931 the NSDAP had won 26.2 percent of the vote in the state elections of Hamburg and 37.1 percent of the vote in the state elections of Hessen. Nazism had become a major component of the political system. Its voters were primarily of Protestant and middle-class background. The agrarian protest vote went to the NSDAP in areas where it was not retained by the Catholic organizations. The industrial and urban protest vote shifted to the Nazis in areas where the labor unions were weak. In areas with large-scale industrial plants, the unions were strong and contained the protest within the Socialist and Communist parties. Therefore, the Catholic and working-class segments of the population were strongly underrepresented in the NSDAP vote.[57]

In the spring of 1932 an election for Reichspräsident was due to be held. Brüning tried to avoid an election at the peak of the economic crisis. However, the parliamentary majority needed to enact a special law to prolong the period of office of Reichspräsident von Hindenburg could not be obtained. Hitler played an important role, categorically refusing any attempt to keep Hindenburg in office without an election. Despite the fact that Hindenburg represented the national values for which Hitler was agitating, he turned against the field marshal and became a candidate for Reichspräsident in 1932. Only seventeen days before the election, he obtained the requisite German citizenship by a nominal appointment to the civil service of the state of Braunschweig, where the Nazis held the Ministry of the Interior. Hitler's candidacy against Hindenburg was an attempt to gain the undisputed leadership in the nationalistic, authoritarian camp, uniting all rightist opposition to the democratic system. Hitler gained 36.8 percent of the vote on the second ballot in April 1932. His claim to supreme leadership was clearly documented and caused a radical reorientation within the conservative elites.

The military, through its political spokesman, General von Schleicher, started to negotiate with Hitler in April 1932; leading industrialists established contacts with Hitler; some Protestant clergymen openly endorsed the Nazis; and a member of the royal Hohenzollern family joined the party. The conservative establishment symbolically, financially, and politically opened the door to power. In early 1932 they still thought they could tame Hitler and persuade him to tolerate a regime of their own. By the end of January 1933 they were willing to grant him the chancellorship.

Hitler skillfully played a double strategy: the promise of legality and the threat of civil war. He had the necessary means at his disposal for both. For the legal creation of an authoritarian regime, it was his mass support and parliamentary strength that provided the basis. For the threat of civil war and a violent revolutionary takeover, it was his private army, the SA, that could arouse public disorder any time and at any place. The violence in political fights on the streets and at the party rallies, particularly those of the Nazis and the Communists, increased considerably in 1932. From January to September 1932 155 were people killed.[58] The entire year of 1932 saw the deaths of 82 Nazis.[59] The election campaign in June and July of 1932 saw the greatest number of casualties, with 100 persons dead. Attempts to outlaw political violence, the use of weapons, the wearing of party uniforms, and party armies, the SA in particular, remained ineffective. Numerous lawsuits were conducted but only a few resulted in prison sentences, more often against Communists than Nazis.[60] As the national government became more accessible to conservative politicians, the willingness to embark on a forceful policy to prohibit Nazi violence became weaker. Growing sympathy from the younger officer corps and the strength of the SA, nearly 500,000 members strong, made it unlikely that the army would be willing forcefully to subjugate the SA. The double character of the SA as Nazi party organization and an auxiliary militia for the regular army in case of war inhibited the prohibition of the SA from its very beginning.

Hitler's tactics were aimed at a legal takeover of government, but as he declined any offer short of the appointment as chancellor, he ran high risks. His followers were disappointed that despite all their efforts and their victories in the elections, the seizure of power had not yet been achieved in the summer of 1932. There were two tendencies within the party. One was articulated by Gregor Strasser, the most important leader next to Hitler. He advocated participation in the government even without Hitler in the chancellorship. The other was espoused by the storm troopers, who were in favor of a violent takeover of the government, a "real" revolution, as they saw it. Here again Hitler's unique position in the Nazi party becomes crucial. He was faced with the loss of control of his forces, but Hitler's institutionalized charisma was not damaged. Strasser resigned and could not muster party support for his course of action. Hitler's charisma also kept the SA in a precarious state of obedience. Hitler retained his freedom of action, his capability for waiting until the conservative establishment would invite him to the chancellorship and give him the unrestricted power of government. No decision-making body of the party or the Reichstag faction existed to influence his decisions. But had it not been for the intrigues of Schleicher and Papen, the deadlock they had created, and the final submission of Hindenburg to the advices of Papen and his son, the seizure of power by Hitler on 30 January 1933 might not have been the necessary result of Hitler's strategy. It was his nature to risk an all or nothing game.

There were at least two chances for the decline of the Nazi movement in late 1932 and early 1933. The first would have aimed at a destruction of the belief in Hitler's charisma; the second would have been connected with a change in the political and economic situation by which the perceived need for charismatic leadership as the only solution to a chaotic crisis would have become less plausible.

Charismatic authority and a charismatic community rest on the belief in the extraordinary gifts of the leader. This belief must be verified by signs of his extraordinary abilities. The destruction of such a movement will be unavoidable if the charisma of the leader can no longer be proved in the perception of his followers. Until the summer of 1932 proof of Hitler's extraordinary capabilities was provided by continuous election victories, which kept the party in a state of high enthusiasm and mobilization. The experience of the futility of the election campaigns and the losses in the November election were potentially a severe blow to Hitler's charisma, the more so as the financial means of the party were completely exhausted. Had it not been for his seizure of power at the last moment, in January 1933, elections in 1933 and 1934 would most likely have seen a severe defection of NSDAP voters.

Charismatic authority needs a situation in which extraordinary capacities are expected: ordinary situations do not call for extraordinary means or personal gifts. It was the combination of a political and economic crisis in Germany in the years 1929–33 that created an atmosphere conductive to belief in extraordinary gifts. Hitler's chances consisted in his capacity to define the situations as doomed and his leadership as the last chance for salvation. These chances would have been limited by improvement in the economic situation, which was expected in 1933, and by governmental stability as provided by the Brüning cabinet on the basis of emergency decrees. However, developments in 1932 reduced politics to a single issue: chaos or regeneration of Germany. This allowed Hitler to gain support from very divergent segments of the population with heterogeneous interests and aspirations on the level of ultimate values. The eschatological character of Nazism had a peculiar pseudo-religious fascination, extremely favorable for the belief in charismatic authority.

The unprecedented growth of the NSDAP in membership (see table 11) and votes (see table 12) within three years must be seen in the context of a highly emotionalized and anomic situation. Forces of destiny seemed at work; economic interests and social distinctions were superseded by a hope in the "power of will" and the "vitality of youth." Trust in the institutions of the existing system was exchanged for the commitment to ultimate values of an unknown but new order.

It was Hitler and the NSDAP who were best prepared to capitalize on this mood and the underlying disruption of the social fabric after 1930. There was no political leader in the democratic camp who could match Hitler's demagogy and provide an alternative general definition of the situation, less irra-

Table 11. Membership of the NSDAP, 1925–33

1925 December	27,117
1926 December	49,523
1927 December	72,590
1928 December	108,717
1929 December	176,426
1930 September	293,000
1930 December	389,000
1931 December	806,294
1932 April	1,000,000+
1932 December	1,378,000
1933 August	3,900,000

SOURCE: Hans-Gerd Schumann, *Nationalsozialismus und Gewerkschaftsbewegung* (Hannover and Frankfort: Norddeutsche Verlagsanstalt, 1958), pp. 167 ff.

tional but convincing. Stresemann had died, Otto Braun, the popular prime minister of Prussia, was ill, Brüning was an introverted personality without popular appeal, Hindenburg had become senile. The democratic elites were paralyzed.[61] The men who influenced the final decisions to hand over the government to Hitler were without popular resonance and opportunistic in outlook: Papen and Schleicher, the last chancellors, Otto Meissner and Hindenburg's son Oskar, the closest advisers to the Reichspräsident, Hugenberg and Schacht, the spokesmen of industry and finance. The Communists, uncompromisingly attacking the democratic system, provided another general definition of the situation, the collapse of capitalism, but their new order was less empty than that of Hitler. Communist Russia attracted neither the peasants, the white-collar class, nor even the majority of the working class. Their

Table 12. Popular Support of the NSDAP, 1928–33

1928	28 May Reichstag elections	2.6%
1929	27 October Landtag elections in Baden	7.0
1929	8 December Landtag elections in Thüringen	11.3
1930	22 July Landtag elections in Saxony	14.4
1930	14 September Reichstag elections	18.3
1931	17 May Landtag elections in Oldenburg	37.2
1931	15 November Landtag elections in Hessen	37.1
1932	13 March Reichspräsident elections, first ballot	30.1
1932	4 April Reichspräsident elections, second ballot	36.8
1932	24 April Landtag elections in Prussia	37.1
	Landtag elections in Bavaria	32.9
	Landtag elections in Württemberg	30.5
1932	29 May Landtag elections in Oldenburg	46.3
1932	19 June Landtag elections in Hessen	43.1
1932	31 July Reichstag elections	37.3
1932	4 November Reichstag elections	33.0
1933	5 March Reichstag elections	43.9

very existence, however, seemed proof that there was only one alternative: chaos or Hitler. Hitler's impact was that he persuaded not only his voters but also many of his enemies into accepting his definition of the situation.

Not only Hitler but the NSDAP as an organization was able to capitalize on the anomic situation. Led by young functionaries, it mobilized town and country by continuous rallies, parades, and demonstrations. It spread the rhetoric and liturgy invented by Hitler during the numerous election campaigns throughout the country. It was able to absorb the rapidly increasing and changing membership and to infiltrate local associations and interest groups.[62] Hitler was a new type of political leader, and the NSDAP was a new type of political party. It was flexible enough for rapid expansion, and its internal immobilization allowed Hitler a unique freedom of decision. There was no other party that combined these elements. The Communist party was inflexible for ideological reasons, the Social Democrats limited their leadership by high internal bureaucratization, the Zentrum party was entrenched in the Catholic milieu, and the bourgeois and conservative parties had no vital local organizations. The NSDAP was the appropriate instrument for Hitler's strategy, which was to create a threat of civil war that he would trade in for the handing over of power. Hitler's bargaining power rested in the NSDAP. But as the NSDAP had no organized will of its own, Hitler could bargain at no cost to himself as long as he commanded the party as a charismatic community.

6. The Process of Transfer of Power

The dismissal of Brüning by Hindenburg at the end of May 1932 meant the destruction of the tiny chance for a consensual emergency policy of the democratic forces. With the appointment of Papen a government was put in office that had no popular support. It had to rely either on the support of the Nazis or on the intervention of the military. The options were radically narrowed. As the military would not embark on a policy of a military rule, there was only Hitler left. The Papen government tried to buy Hitler's toleration and increasingly became the executive of Hitler's demands. First it lifted the prohibition on the SA, decreed by the Brüning government in April 1934. Second, the Papen government announced new elections, giving Hitler a chance for renewed mass mobilization and reenforced strength in the Reichstag. Third, it dissolved the government of Prussia, still in the hands of the Weimar coalition, which thereby could command the police forces in two-thirds of Germany. Despite all this, Hitler did not support the Papen government at all. Only a military government seemed capable of preventing the final seizure of power by Hitler. In December 1933 General von Schleicher tried to form a coalition between the military and the conservative elites that would be tolerated by the unions, but these were desperate machinations, without a chance. Schleicher's inclinations toward an authoritarian political regime had played an important role in the dissolution of the moderate Brüning regime, in the appointment of Papen, whom he personally suggested to Hindenburg, and finally in his turn against Papen. But by now he had become discredited. The alternatives were further reduced, since not even the possibility of a military rule remained realistic. The conservative establishment had conducted a policy by which they sold themselves to Hitler and at the same time destroyed their own basis of power. The more their own power became deflated, the more the power of Hitler became inflated. Even Reichspräsident von Hindenburg, who disliked Hitler personally and profoundly, saw the final solution only in the appointment of just this man.

The democratic forces saw no chance for a counterattack. Instrumentally they had lost the majority. In the game of personal intrigues around the now all-important Reichspräsident, they were excluded. They had no access to the military, and had lost control over the police forces in Prussia. The labor unions had a diminished capacity for a political general strike because of the great number of unemployed. The forces of the old Weimar coalition were unable to form a firm and united front for the defense of democracy on ideological grounds. A process of intimidation and an atmosphere of fatalistic hopelessness prevailed. Strategies to secure individual survival under an anticipated period of Nazi rule fragmented the democratic forces even further. In desperation, but inactive, they observed and submitted to the transfer of power to Hitler.[63]

The process of transfer of power started with the dissolution of the Weimar coalition in 1930, gained momentum with the cooptation of Nazism by the conservative camp in 1931, and came to a conclusion with the conviction that no alternative but Hitler remained in 1932. The Weimar coalition was established in 1918/19 and rested on the coalition of the middle-class parties with the Social Democrats in the *Interfraktioneller Ausschuss* to end the war, the Stinnes-Legien agreement between industry and labor to secure the economy in the demobilization period, and the contract between the military and the republican government to guarantee internal security. Its effect was the exclusion of the conservative and authoritarian forces after the armistice. The dissolution of the Weimar coalition started with the end of the industry-labor agreement in 1923 and the attempt of the employers to reduce social legislation and limit the influence of the unions during the depression. It was aggravated by the alienation of the military from the republican state and finally by the weakening of the party coalition between the middle-class parties and the Social Democrats. This led to an exclusion of the labor movement and the reentry of the conservative and authoritarian forces into the government. However, in 1931, and more so in 1932, the distribution of power had changed. The conservative and authoritarian forces thought first to use Hitler, then to tame him, and in the end they had to submit to him.[64]

The turn from parliamentary democracy to government by emergency decree had hollowed the constitution. The installation of the Papen and Schleicher governments had created a deadlock in which Hindenburg was put into the decisive position. His sentiments were with the authoritarian camp but he was not prepared to suspend the constitution altogether. In appointing Hitler he thought to retain the constitution, as only Hitler had promised a government with parliamentary majority. The idea of return to constitutional normalcy by including Hitler in the political process clearly shows a profound misjudgment of Hitler and the Nazis.

Hitler had followed a strategy that advanced such misunderstanding. He had cut down on the Socialist trends within the NSDAP since 1930, he guaranteed industry that the status quo would be maintained, he promised the military its autonomy, he observed a neutrality in regard to the churches. He activated the common resentments in the authoritarian camp against socialism and liberalism, and made its latent anti-Semitism overt. On the other hand, he could threaten industry with state socialism, the military with his SA militia, and the churches with a new Germanic religion. His was a precarious strategy of offering legality and threatening civil war.

The situation was commonly defined as unsolvable. In anticipation of the surrender of power to Hitler, industry, the military, churches, and the labor unions embarked, as early as the summer of 1932, on a course of action directed not at combating Hitler but at negotiating with him to ensure their respective survivals after his takeover.[65]

Hitler changed his strategy the moment he was appointed chancellor, discrediting all who believed his regime would only be transitory because (1) the collapse of capitalism would carry away fascism as well; (2) the incompetence of the Nazis to govern would lead to a return of the rule of traditional elites; or (3) disappointment with Hitler's regime would lead to a dissolution of the Nazi movement. Hitler acted quickly after his appointment on 30 January 1933. On 28 February he issued with Hindenburg's *placet* an emergency decree that suspended constitutional civil rights, using the burning of the Reichstags building as a pretext. In an atmosphere of public insecurity and terror for the Communists and Socialists, the last free elections took place. These gave Hitler a vote of 43.9 percent, and together with the 8 percent polled by the conservatives, he gained a tiny majority. Two days after the opening of the new Reichstag, on 23 March 1933, Hitler succeeded in mustering a two-thirds majority to pass the *Ermächtigungsgesetz,* which was to suspend the constitution for a period of four years and to entitle the government to act unbound by the constitution. The Communist deputies were already being persecuted and most of them had been imprisoned. Only the Socialists opposed him. It took Hitler seven weeks to turn the pseudo-legality of his seizure of power into a revolution of the political system. The last remnant of the old system, the institution of the Reichspräsident, was incapacitated by the senility of Hindenburg. When he died on 2 August 1934,

Hitler had firmly established his rule and could combine the offices of the president and the chancellor. Parties were prohibited, unions dissolved, the army sworn to obey Hitler personally, public opinion intimidated, and the media controlled. The political system was changed entirely.[66]

NOTES

1. Henry A. Turner, Jr., Introduction to *Nazism and the Third Reich*, ed. Henry A. Turner, Jr. (New York: Quadrangle Books, 1972), p. 4.
2. Only a few general references that provide basic information and further bibliographical references will be listed. The work of Karl Dietrich Bracher, *Die Auflösung der Weimarer Republik*, 5th rev. ed. (Villingen: Ring Verlag, 1971) remains the most important attempt at systematic analysis, despite the twenty years since its conception. It should be consulted together with a more recent but less comprehensive study by Karl Dietrich Bracher entitled *The German Dictatorship* (New York and Washington: Praeger Publishers, 1970). Also of basic importance are the following publications: Erich Matthias and Rudolf Morsey, eds., *Das Ende der Parteien, 1933* (Düsseldorf: Droste Verlag, 1960); Thilo Vogelsang, *Reichswehr, Staat und NSDAP* (Stuttgart: Deutsche Verlagsanstalt, 1962); Werner Conze and Hans Raupach, eds, *Die Staats—und Wirtschaftskrise des Deutschen Reiches, 1929/33* (Stuttgart: Ernst Klett Verlag, 1967); Gotthard Jasper, ed., *Von Weimar zu Hitler, 1930–1933* (Cologne and Berlin: Kiepenheuer and Witsch, 1968); Anthony Nicholls and Erich Matthias, eds., *German Democracy and the Triumph of Hitler* (London: George Allen and Unwin, 1971); Hans Mommsen, Dietmar Petzina, and Bernd Weisbrod, eds., *Industrielles System und politische Entwicklung in der Weimarer Republik* (Düsseldorf: Droste, 1974); Gerhard Schulz, *Aufstieg des Nationalsozialismus; Krise und Revolution in Deutschland* (Frankfort, Berlin, and Vienna: Propyläen, 1975); and Ernst Nolte, *Three Faces of Fascism* (New York: Holt, Rinehart and Winston, 1966).
3. In the present context no further discussion will be directed toward problems of the German modal personality, authoritarian elements in the German socialization process, particularly of the middle classes, and the political consequences of dogmatism and belief systems. References to these problems will be found in Max Horkheimer et al., *Studien über Autorität und Familie* (Paris, 1936), a study conducted in Germany in the early thirties trying to analyze the social and psychological basis for Nazism; and Erich Fromm, *Escape from Freedom* (New York: Farrar and Rinehart, 1941).
4. For an interesting study of the formation of the ideas of a German way to modernity, see Eckart Pankoke, *Soziale Bewegung-Soziale Frage-Soziale Politik* (Stuttgart: Ernst Klett, 1970). For ideas of leadership in the political thought of liberal and conservative intellectuals, see Walter Struve, *Elites against Democracy* (Princeton, N.J.: Princeton University Press, 1973). For a general analysis of German conceptions of society and democracy, see Ralf Dahrendorf, *Society and Democracy in Germany* (Garden City, N.Y.: Doubleday, 1967). There is an extensive literature on the German cultural development, but we refer in this context only to Hans Kohn, *The Mind of Germany: The Education of a Nation* (New York: Scribner's, 1960); Leonard Krieger, *The German Idea of Freedom* (Boston: Beacon Press, 1957); George L. Mosse, *The Crisis of German Ideology: Intellectual Origins of the Third Reich* (New York: Grosset and Dunlap, 1964); Helmuth Plessner, *Die verspätete Nation* (Stuttgart: Kohlhammer, 1959); Fritz Stern, *The Politics of Cultural Despair* (New York: Doubleday, 1961); and Peter Gay, *Weimar Culture: The Outsider as Insider* (London: Seeker and Warburg, 1969).
5. On Prussia, see most recently Hagen Schulze, *Otto Braun oder Preussens demokratische Sendung* (Frankfort, Berlin, and Vienna: Propyläen, 1977).
6. For the development of the KPD and the influence of the Komintern, see Hermann Weber, *Die Wandlung des deutschen Kommunismus* 2 vols. (Frankfort: Europäische Verlagsanstalt,

1969); Hermann Weber, ed., *Der deutsche Kommunismus: Dokumente* (Cologne and Berlin: Kiepenheuer and Witsch, 1963); Ossip K. Flechtheim, *Die KPD in der Weimarer Republik* (Frankfort: Europäische Verlagsanstalt, 1969); Theo Pirker, *Komintern und Faschismus, 1920–1940* (Stuttgart: Deutsche Verlagsanstalt, 1965).

7. Theodor Eschenburg, *Die improvisierte Demokratie* (Munich: Piper, 1963), pp. 11–60.

8. Thomas Mann, *Betrachtungen eines Unpolitischen*, 10th ed. (Berlin: Fischer, 1919), p. 246.

9. For an analysis of the German party system in the *Kaiserreich*, see M. Rainer Lepsius, "Parteisystem und Sozialstruktur," in *Deutsche Parteien vor 1918*, ed. Gerhard A. Ritter (Cologne: Kiepenheuer and Witsch, 1973) and other articles in that volume. See also Sigmund Neumann, *Die Parteien der Weimarer Republik*, 2d ed. (Stuttgart: Kohlhammer, 1965).

10. Johannes Sass, *Die 27 deutschen Parteien 1930 und ihre Ziele* (Hamburg, 1930) gives a detailed description of the particularistic and partly sectarian small parties.

11. This is the judgment of Gustav Stolper, expressed in the journal *Der deutsche Volkswirt* 13 December 1929, p. 333 (translation by the author).

12. Ferdinand A. Hermens, *Demokratie und Wahlrecht* (Paderborn: F. Schöning, 1933), p. 145 (translation by the author).

13. See ibid., pp. 115–70 or the revised American edition, *Democracy or Anarchy?* (South Bend, Ind.: University of Notre Dame, 1941), pp. 161–240. See also Friedrich Schäfer, "Zur Frage des Wahlrechts in der Weimarer Republik," in *Staat, Wirtschaft, und Politik in der Weimarer Republik*, ed. Ferdinand A. Hermens and Theodor Schieder (Berlin: Duncker and Humblot, 1967).

14. For the basic changes in 1929–30 and their importance for the breakdown, see Bracher, *Die Auflösung der Weimarer Republik* pt. 2, chaps. 1–3; also Werner Conze, "Die Krise des Parteienstaates in Deutschland 1929/30," *Historische Zeitschrift*, 178 (1954); and Conze, "Die politischen Entscheidungen in Deutschland, 1929–1933," in Conze and Raupach, *Staats-und Wirtschaftskrise*.

15. There is an extensive literature on the Weimar constitution and Article 48. See especially Bracher, *Die Auflösung der Weimarer Republik*, pt. 1, chap. 2; idem, "Parteistaat, Präsidialsystem, Notstand," *Politische Vierteljahresschrift* 3 (1960); Karl Löwenstein, *Verfassungslehre* (Tübingen: J. C. B. Mohr, 1959); Martin Needler, "The Theory of the Weimar Presidency," *Review of Politics* 21 (1959); Klaus Revermann, *Die stufenweise Durchbrechung des Verfassungsystems der Weimarer Republik 1930–1933* (Münster: T. Aschendorff, 1959); Ulrich Scheuner, "Die Anwendung des Art. 48 der Weimarer Reichsverfassung unter den Präsidentenschaften von Ebert und Hindenburg," in Hermens and Schieder, *Staat, Wirtschaft und Politik in der Weimarer Republik*.

16. On Brüning, see Heinrich Brüning, *Memoiren, 1918–1934* (Stuttgart: Deutsche Verlags-Anstalt, 1970); idem, *Reden und Aufsätze eines deutschen Staatsmannes*, ed. Wilhelm Vernekohl and Rudolf Morsey (Münster: Regensberg, 1968); and Gottfried Reinhold Treviranus, *Das Ende von Weimar, Heinrich Brüning und seine Zeit* (Düsseldorf and Vienna: Econ, 1968).

17. On Papen and Schleicher, see, in addition to the work of Bracher, Thilo Vogelsang, *Reichswehr, Staat, und NSDAP;* idem, *Kurt von Schleicher* (Göttingen: Musterschmidt, 1965); and Eschenburg, *Die improvisierte Demokratie*, pp. 235–86.

18. On Hindenburg, see Andreas Dorpalen, *Hindenburg and the Weimar Republic* (Princeton, N.J.: Princeton University Press, 1964), and John W. Wheeler-Bennett, *Hindenburg, the Wooden Titan* (London: Macmillan, 1967).

19. On the legal aspects of the so-called *Preussische Staatsstreich*, see, in particular, Arnold Brecht, *Mit der Kraft des Geistes* (Stuttgart: Deutsche Verlags-Anstalt, 1967).

20. One of the most influential legal advisers in constitutional law was Carl Schmitt. His publications served to justify the gradual reinterpretation of the Weimar constitution from a parliamentary *Rechtsstaat* toward a plebiscitarian *Massnahmestaat*. See his *Der Begriff des Politischen: Text von 1931 mit einem Vorwort und drei Corollarien* (Berlin: Duncker and Humblot, 1963), and *Verfassungsrechtliche Aufsätze aus den Jahren 1924–1954* (Berlin: Duncker and Humblot, 1958), in particular, "Legalität und Legitimität (1932)" and "Die staatsrechtliche Bedeutung der Notverordnung (1931)."

21. On the destruction of the constitution by the *Verordnung des Reichspräsidenten zum Schutze von Volk und Staat* on 28 February 1933, see Karl Dietrich Bracher, Wolfgang Sauer, and

Gerhard Schulz, *Die nationalsozialistische Machtergreifung: Studien zur Errichtung des totalitären Herrschaftssystems in Deutschland 1933/34* (Cologne and Opladen: Westdeutscher Verlag, 1960), pp. 82–88.

22. There is an extensive literature on the world depression and the German economic development. See especially Charles P. Kindleberger, *The World Depression, 1929–1939* (Berkeley and Los Angeles: University of California Press, 1973); Robert Aaron Gordon, *Economic Instability and Growth: The American Record* (New York: Harper and Row, 1974). An account of the German development is given in Gustav Stolper, Karl Haüser, and Knut Borchardt, *The German Economy, 1870 to the Present* (New York: Harcourt, Brace, 1967), esp. chap. 4, "The Weimar Republic," by Gustav Stolper; Wilhelm Grotkopp, *Die grosse Krise* (Tübingen: J. C. B. Mohr, 1952); Rudolf Stucken, *Deutsche Geld und Kreditpolitik, 1914–1963* (Tübingen: J. C. B. Mohr, 1964); and Rolf E. Lücke, *Von der Stabilisierung zur Krise* (Zurich: Basle Center for Economic and Financial Research, Series B., no. 3, 1958).

23. The problems of the reparations are dealt with in particular in Wolfgang J. Helbick, *Reparationen in der Ära Brüning* (Berlin: Walter de Gruyter, 1962).

24. For the agricultural crisis, see Werner T. Angress, "The Political Role of the Peasantry in the Weimar Republic," *Review of Politics* 21: 530–49; Max Sering, *Die deutsche Landwirtschaft: Berichte über Landwirtschaft 50* (Berlin, 1932). The Landvolkbewegung is described in Günther Franz, *Politische Geschichte des Bauerntums* (Celle: Niedersächsische Landeszentrale für Heimatdienst, 1959); Hans Beyer, *Die Landvolkbewegung Schleswig-Holsteins und Niedersachsens 1928–1932* (Eckernförde: Heimatgemeinschaft des Kreises Eckernförde, 1957); Rudolf Heberle, *Landbevölkerung und National-sozialismus* (Stuttgart: Deutsche Verlags-Anstalt, 1963); Gerhard Stoltenberg, *Politische Strömungen im schleswig-holsteinschen Landvolk, 1918–1933* (Düsseldorf: Droste, 1962); and Heinz Sahner, *Politische Tradition, Sozialstruktur, und Parteiensystem in Schleswig-Holstein* (Meisenheim am Glan: Anton Hain, 1972).

25. Sten S. Nilson, "Wahlsoziologische Probleme des Nationalsozialismus," *Zeitschrift für die gesamte Staatswissenschaft* 110 (1954), shows how in contrast in Norway the farmers' protest was absorbed by the Social Democratic party.

26. The special situation of East Elbian estate agriculture is discussed in Hans Raupach, "Der interregionale Wohlfahrtsausgleich als Problem der Politik des deutschen Reiches," in Conze and Raupach, *Staats-und Wirtschaftskrise.* ed. See also Gerhard Schulz, "Staatliche Stützungsmassnahmen in den deutschen Ostgebieten: Zur Vorgeschichte der 'Osthilfe' der Regierung Brüning," in Hermens and Schieder, *Staat, Wirtschaft, und Politik;* and Henning Graf von Borcke Stargordt, *Der ostdeutsche Landbau zwischen Fortschritt, Krise und Politik* (Würzburg: Holzner, 1957).

27. The conversion and infiltration of the agrarian organizations to and by Nazism is discussed in Horst Gies, "NSDAP und landwirtschaftliche Organisationen in der Endphase der Weimarer Republik," *Vierteljahreshefte für Zeitgeschichte* 15 (1967).

28. The best account of the banking crisis is given in Karl Erich Born, *Die deutsche Bankenkrise, 1931* (Munich: Piper, 1967).

29. Kindleberger, *The World Depression, 1929–1939*, p. 172.

30. See Wilhelm Treue, "Der deutsche Unternehmer in der Weltwirtschaftskrise," in Conze and Raupach, in *Staats-und Wirtschaftskrise;* Henry A. Turner, Jr., "Big Business and the Rise of Hitler," in Turner, *Nazism and the Third Reich;* Alfred Sohn-Rethel, *Ökonomie und Klassenstruktur des deutschen Faschismus* (Frankfort: Suhrkamp, 1973); George W. F. Hallgarten, *Hitler, Reichswehr, und Industrie* (Frankfort: Europäische Verlangsanstalt, 1955); Henry A. Turner, "Das Verhältnis des Grossunternehmertums zur NSDAP," and Bernd Weisbrod, "Zur Form schwerindustrieller Interessenvertretung in der zweiten Hälfte der Weimarer Republik," both in Mommsen et al., *Industrielles System und politische Entwicklung in der Weimarer Republik;* Eberhard Czichon, *Wer verhalf Hitler zur Macht?* (Cologne: Pahl-Rugenstein, 1967).

31. See Seymour Martin Lipset, *Political Man* (Garden City, N.Y.: Doubleday, 1960), chap. 5; Herman Lebovics, *Social Conservatism and the Middle Classes in Germany, 1914–1933* (Princeton, N.J.: Princeton University Press, 1969); Theodor Geiger, *Die soziale Schichtung des deutschen Volkes* (Stuttgart: Enke, 1932); idem, "Panik im Mittelstand," *Die Arbeit* 7

(1930); Svend Riemer, "Zur Soziologie des Nationalsozialismus," *Die Arbeit* 9 (1932); Peter Wulf, *Die politische Haltung des schleswig-holsteinischen Handwerks* (Cologne and Opladen: Westdeutscher Verlag, 1969); Ernst-August Roloff, *Bürgertum und Nationalsozialismus* (Hannover, Verlag für Literatur und Zeitgeschehen, 1961); idem, "Wer wählte Hitler?" *Politische Studien* 15 (1964); and Heinrich August Winkler, *Mittelstand, Demokratie, und Nationalsozialismus: Die politische Entwicklung von Handwerk und Kleinhandel in der Weimarer Republik* (Cologne: Kiepenheuer and Witsch, 1972).

32. The disruptive effects of unemployment are analyzed in Marie Jahoda, Paul F. Lazarsfeld, and Hans Zeisel, *Die Arbeitslosen von Marienthal* (Allensbach: Verlag für Demoskopie, 1961). See also Heinrich Bennecke, *Wirtschaftliche Depression und politischer Radikalismus* (Munich: Günter Olzog, 1968).

33. See *Statistisches Jahrbuch für das Deutsche Reich 1935* (Berlin: Statistisches Reichsamt, 1935), pp. 322, 323.

34. On the *Wehrverbände* and *Parteiarmeen*, see Bracher, *Die Auflösung der Weimarer Republik*, chap. 5; for the SA, See Andreas Werner, "SA und NSDAP," (Ph.D. diss., Erlangen-Nürnberg, 1964); and Heinrich Bennecke, *Hitler und die SA* (München: Olzog, 1962).

35. See *Statistisches Jahrbuch für das Deutsche Reich 1933* (Berlin: Statistisches Reichsamt, 1933), p. 297. For a general account of social legislation, see Ludwig Preller, *Sozialpolitik in der Weimarer Republik* (Stüttgart: Franz Mittelbach, 1949), and Hans-Hermann Hartwich, *Arbeitsmarkt, Verbände, und Staat, 1918-1933* (Berlin: Walter de Gruyter, 1967).

36. See *Statistisches Jahrbuch für das Deutsche Reich 1933* (Berlin: Statistisches Reichsamt, 1933), p. 307.

37. On the labor unions, see Michael Schneider, *Unternehmer und Demokratie: Die freien Gewerkschaften in der unternehmerischen Ideologie* (Bonn-Bad Godesberg: Neue Gesellschaft, 1975); idem, *Das Arbeitsbeschaffungsprogramm des ADGB in der Endphase der Weimarer Republik* (Bonn-Bad Godesberg: Neue Gesellschaft, 1975); and Hannes Heer, *Burgfrieden oder Klassenkampf: Zur Politik der sozialdemokratischen Gewerkschaften 1930-1933* (Neuwied and Berlin: Luchterhand, 1971).

38. See Helga Timm, *Die deutsche Sozialpolitik und der Bruch der grossen Koalition 1930* (Düsseldorf: Droste, 1952); Werner Conze, "Die politischen Entscheidungen in Deutschland 1919-1933," in Conze and Raupach, *Staats- und Wirtschaftskrise.*

39. See Hans Speier, *Die Angestellten vor dem Nationalsozialismus: Ein Beitrag zum Verständnis der deutschen Sozialstruktur, 1918-1933* (Göttingen: Vandenhoek and Ruprecht, 1977); Jürgen Kocka, "Zur Problematik der deutschen Angestellten 1914-1933," and Larry E. Jones, "The Crisis of White-Collar Interest Politics: Deutschnationaler Handlungsgehilfen-Verband and Deutsche Volkspartei in the World Economic Crisis," both in Mommsen et al., *Industrielles System und politische Entwicklung in der Weimarer Republik.*

40. For more detailed information, see Dietmar Keese, "Die volkswirtschaftlichen Gesamtgrössen für das Deutsche Reich in den Jahren 1925-1936," in Conze and Raupach, *Staats- und Wirtschaftskrise.* The Reichs Kredit-Gesellschaft Aktiengesellschaft in Berlin published semiannual reports on the economic conditions in Germany; they present the contemporary evaluations of the economic situation and a great deal of data. A concise account of the development of unemployment by a contemporary author is Robert Wilbrandt, "Arbeitslosigkeit in Deutschland," in *International Unemployment* (The Hague: International Industrial Relations Institute, 1931). See also Gerhard Bry, *Wages in Germany, 1871-1945,* National Bureau of Economic Research, no. 68. General Series (Princeton, N.J.: Princeton University Press, 1960); Dietmar Petzina, "Hauptprobleme der deutschen Wirtschaftspolitik 1932/33," *Vierteljahreshefte für Zeitgeschichte* 15 (1967).

41. The logic of the economic policy of the Brüning government is discussed by the two leading figures in the policy: Brüning, *Memoiren,* and Hans Luther, *Vor dem Abgrund* (Berlin: Propyläen, 1964). A critical view is presented in Keese, "Die volkswirtschaftlichen Gesamtgrössen für das Deutsche Reich in den Jahren 1925-1936," in Conze and Raupach; *Staats-und Wirtschaftskrise.* A positive view is presented in Ferdinand A. Hermens, "Das Kabinett Brüning und die Depression," in Hermens and Schieder, *Staat, Wirtschaft, und*

Politik, and in Gottfried Reinhold Treviranus, *Das Ende von Weimar* (Düsseldorf: Econ-Verlag, 1968), pp. 170–219. Treviranus was a personal friend of Brüning and a member of his cabinet.

42. Werner Kaltefleiter, *Wirtschaft und Politik in Deutschland*, rev. ed. (Cologne: West-deutscher Verlag, 1969), discusses the effects of the economic crisis on the voting behavior and the differential chances to turn to the NSDAP or the Communists. For an analysis of the appeal of extreme nationalism as advocated by the national opposition, particularly the NSDAP, see also M. Rainer Lepsius, *Extremer Nationalismus* (Stuttgart: Kohlhammer, 1966).

43. There is an ever-growing literature on Hitler. The most recent book with a claim to com-prehensiveness is Joachim C. Fest, *Hitler* (New York: Harcourt, Brace, Jovanovich, 1974). For a new account of the personal life of Hitler, see Werner Maser, *Hitler: Legend, Myth, and Reality* (New York: Harper and Row, 1973). The postwar classic is Alan Bullock, *Hitler: A Study in Tyranny*, 2d ed. (London: Odhams Press, 1965). The most influential prewar study is Konrad Heiden, *Der Führer: Hitler's Rise to Power* (London: Gollanz, 1944).

44. For the ideal type of charismatic authority, see Max Weber, *Economy and Society*, ed. Guenther Roth and Claus Wittich, 3 vols. (New York: Bedminster, 1968), pp. 241–45 and 1111–57.

45. An excellent study on factional conflicts and their resolution by the charismatic authority of Hitler within the authoritarian party organization is Joseph Nyomarkay, *Charisma and Factionalism in the Nazi Party* (Minneapolis: University of Minnesota Press, 1967).

46. A detailed study of the *Führerprinzip* is given in Wolfgang Horn, *Führerideologie und Parteiorganisation in der NSDAP (1919–1933)* (Düsseldorf: Droste, 1972).

47. Adolf Hitler, *Mein Kampf*, 2 vols. (Munich: Franz Eher, 1925, 1927). His second book was published posthumously: *Hitlers Zweites Buch: Ein Dokument aus dem Jahre 1928* (Stuttgart: Deutsche Verlagsanstalt, 1961). See also Werner Maser, *Hitlers Mein Kampf* (Munich: Bechtle, 1966), and Karl Lange, *Hitlers unbeachtete Maximen* (Stuttgart: Kohl-hammer, 1968).

48. See Peter G. P. Pulzer, *The Rise of Political Anti-Semitism in Germany and Austria* (New York: Wiley, 1964), and Werner E. Mosse, ed., *Entscheidungsjahr 1932: Zur Judenfrage in der Endphase der Weimarer Republik*, 2d ed. (Tübingen: J. C. B. Mohr, 1966).

49. See Eberhard Jäckel, *Hitlers Weltanschauung* (Tübingen: Wunderlich, 1969), and Friedrich Heer, *Der Glaube des Adolf Hitler* (Munich and Esslingen: Bechtle, 1968).

50. Nyomarkay, *Charisma and Factionalism*, p. 21.

51. Ibid., p. 22.

52. This is reflected in the total seclusion of his private life from the public, the careful prepara-tion of his public speeches, the elaborate ritual of the mass rallies, the mythological sym-bolism of flags, and the exaltation of his speeches. See Fest, *Hitler*, bk. 6, chap. 2. See also J. P. Stern, *Hitler: The Führer and the People* (Berkeley and Los Angeles: University of California Press, 1975).

53. On the NSDAP and its regional diversity, see Dietrich Orlow, *The History of the Nazi Party: 1919–1933* (Pittsburgh: University of Pittsburgh Press, 1969); Jeremy Noakes, *The Nazi Party in Lower Saxony, 1921–1933* (London: Oxford University Press, 1971); Eberhart Schön, *Die Entstehung des Nationalsozialismus in Hessen* (Meisenheim am Glan: Anton Hain, 1972); Franz Josef Heyen, *Nationalsozialismus im Alltag: Quellen zur Geschichte des Nationalsozialismus im Raum Mainz-Koblenz-Trier* (Boppard am Rhein: Harald Bolt, 1967); William Sheridan Allen, *The Nazi Seizure of Power: The Experience of a Single German Town, 1930–1935* (Chicago: Quadrangle Books, 1965).

54. See Bennecke, *Hitler und die SA;* Werner, *SA und NSDAP;* and Charles Bloch, *Die SA und die Krise des NS-Regimes 1934* (Frankfurt: Suhrkamp, 1970).

55. See Hans-Gerd Schumann, *Nationalsozialismus und Gewerkschaftsbewegung* (Hannover and Frankfort: Norddeutsche Verlagsanstalt, 1958).

56. See Henry A. Turner, Jr., "Emil Kirdorf and the Nazi Party," *Central European History* 1 (December 1968): 324–44, and idem, "Fritz Thyssen und das Buch 'I paid Hitler,'" *Vierteljahreshefte für Zeitgeschichte* 19 (1971): 225–44.

57. On the election results and the propensity to vote for the NSDAP, see Alfred Milatz, *Wähler und Wahlen in der Weimarer Republik* (Bonn: Bundeszentrale für politische Bildung, 1965);

idem, "Das Ende der Parteien im Spiegel der Wahlen 1930–1933," in Matthias and Morsey, *Das Ende der Parteien 1933;* Alexander Weber, "Soziale Merkmale der NSDAP-Wähler" (Ph.D. diss., Freiburg, 1969); Kaltefleiter, *Wirtschaft und Politik in Deutschland;* Karl O'Lessker, "Who Voted for Hitler?" *American Journal of Sociology* 74 (1968–69); Allan Schnaiberg, "A Critique of Karl O'Lessker's 'Who Voted for Hitler?'" *American Journal of Sociology* 74 (1968/69); W. Phillips Shively, "Party Identification, Party Choice, and Voting Stability: The Weimar Case," *American Political Science Review* 64 (1972).

58. Franz Osterroth and Dieter Schuster, *Chronik der Sozialdemokratie* (Hannover: Verlag für Literatur und Zeitgeschehen, 1963), p. 367.

59. Walter M. Espe, *Das Buch der NSDAP* (Berlin: Schönfeld, 1933), pp. 327–34.

60. For the legislation and its results on political terrorism and antidemocratic activities during the Weimar Republic, see Gotthard Jasper, *Der Schutz der Republik* (Tübingen: Mohr, 1963).

61. On the growing paralysis of leadership in the two major parties of the Weimar coalition see Erich Matthias, "Die Sozialdemokratische Partei Deutschlands," and Rudolf Morsey, "Die Deutsche Zentrumspartei" in Matthias and Morsey, *Das Ende der Parteien 1933.*

62. On the membership and the functionaries of the NSDAP, see Wolfgang Schäfer, *NSDAP, Entwicklung und Struktur der Staatspartei des Dritten Reiches* (Hannover and Frankfort: Norddeutsche Verlagsanstalt, 1956); Peter Merkl, *Political Violence under the Swastika* (Princeton, N.J.: Princeton University Press, 1975); Michael Kater, "Sozialer Wandel in der NSDAP im Zuge der nationalsozialistischen Machtergreifung," and Hans Mommsen, "Zur Verschränkung traditioneller und faschistischer Führungsgruppen in Deutschland beim Übergang von der Bewegungs- zur Systemphase," both in *Faschismus als soziale Bewegung,* ed. Wolfgang Schieder (Hamburg: Hoffmann and Campe, 1976).

63. For the final stage of the breakdown, see Bracher, *Die Auflösung der Weimarer Republik;* Matthias and Morsey, *Das Ende der Parteien 1933;* Vogelsang, *Reichswehr, Staat und NSDAP;* Hermann Pünder, *Politik in der Reichskanzlei* (Stuttgart: Deutsche Verlags-Anstalt, 1961); and Hans Otto Meissner and Harry Wilde, *Die Machtergreifung* (Stuttgart: Cotta, 1958).

64. See Franz Neumann, *Behemoth: The Structure and Practice of National Socialism, 1933–1944* (New York and Evanston: Harper Torchbooks, 1966), Introduction.

65. On the diverse strategies of survival, see Matthias and Morsey, *Das Ende der Parteien,* and Fritz Stern, ed., *The Path to Dictatorship, 1918–1933* (Garden City, N.Y.: Doubleday, 1966). For industry, see Arthur Schweitzer, *Big Business in the Third Reich* (Bloomington: Indiana University Press, 1964), and Ingeborg Esenwein-Rothe, *Die Wirtschaftsverbände von 1933–45* (Berlin: Duncker and Humblot, 1965). For the military, see Robert J. O'Neill, *The German Army and the Nazi Party, 1933–1939* (London: Cassell, 1966); Francis L. Carsten, *Reichswehr und Politik 1918–1933* (Cologne and Berlin: Kiepenheuer and Witsch, 1964); and John W. Wheeler-Bennett, *The Nemesis of Power* (New York: Viking Press, 1967). For the Protestant church, see Günther van Norden, *Kirche in der Krise* (Düsseldorf: Presseverband der evangelischen Kirche, 1963). For the Catholic church, see Hans Müller, *Katholische Kirche und Nationalsozialismus* (Munich: Nymphenburger Verlagshandlung, 1963); Guenter Lewy, *The Catholic Church and Nazi Germany* (New York: McGraw-Hill, 1965); and Ernst-Wolfgang Böckenförde, "Der deutsche Katholizismus im Jahre 1933," *Hochland* 53 (1960/61). For the labor unions, see Gerhard Beier, "Zur Entstehung des Führerkreises der vereinigten Gewerkschaften Ende April 1933," *Archiv für Sozialgeschichte 15* (1975); Hans Mommsen, "Die deutschen Gewerkschaften zwischen Anpassung und Widerstand 1930–1944," in *Vom Sozialistengesetz zur Mitbestimmung,* ed. Heinz Oskar Vetter (Cologne: Bund Verlag, 1975); and Schumann, *Nationalsozialismus und Gewerkschaftsbewegung.*

66. For the change from legality to revolution in the process of the Nazi seizure of power, see Karl Dietrich Bracher, Wolfgang Sauer, and Gerhard Schulz, *Die nationalsozialistische Machtergreifung: Studien zur Errichtung des totalitären Herrschaftssystems in Deutschland 1933/34* (Cologne and Opladen: Westdeutscher Verlag, 1960); and Martin Broszat, *Der Staat Hitlers: Grundlegung und Entwicklung seiner inneren Verfassung* (Munich: Deutscher Taschenbuch Verlag, 1969).

3.

Democracy in the Shadow of Imposed Sovereignty: The First Republic of Austria

Walter B. Simon

Ideologies are formulated through the constant interplay between current contingencies and historical legacies.—Reinhard Bendix, "Industrialization, Ideologies, and Social Structures."

Citizens of a state that has been created against their expressed will may be expected to be at best semiloyal. Yet democratic politics prevailed in the First Republic of Austria for over a decade under the most trying circumstances and might well have withstood even the most severe tests if the moderate factions of the three political camps had only been a little more consistent in their willingness to cooperate with one another in defiance of the antidemocratic extremist factions in their own ranks. Even as matters went, the cooperation of moderates in all three camps did endow democratic institutions with a viability and vitality that suggests that their breakdown was not at all preordained.

The three mutually antagonistic political camps whose interrelation determined the course of politics in the First Republic of Austria and again in the Second have been identified, under a variety of party designations, with the ideologies of international socialism, proclerical conservatism, and German-nationalism.[1] These ideologies have a common origin in that all three arose in the 1880s as a protest against various aspects of Austrian liberalism, which had become dominant in Imperial Austria after enactment of the Constitution of 1867.[2] The proclerical camp stood against the liberal position regarding the separation of church and state, the German-nationalists opposed liberal cosmopolitanism, and all three camps rejected laissez-faire capitalism. Their joint opposition to capitalism had initially even brought the founding fathers of the three camps together, but their ways soon parted because their ideologies were essentially incompatible.[3] The anticapitalism of the proclerical camp and of the German-nationalists involved a denial of class antagonism and a romantic longing for a harmonious past that never was.[4] Proclerical and German-nationalist anticapitalism expressed itself primarily in anti-Semitism. The schism between the three camps was deepened by the militant anticlericalism of the Socialists and the German-nationalists. The German-nationalists, in turn, opposed both the proclerical camp and the Socialists who were conciliatory in their approach to the language conflicts that set the different national or ethnic groups of Imperial Austria against one another.

In an important sense it was issues of language conflict that tore the polyglot empire apart. The German-speaking Alpine provinces of the Danube monarchy that were to form the Republic of Austria were involved only marginally in these language conflicts, because here the Socialists and the proclerical conservatives took conciliatory positions in order to keep the multilingual Danube empire together. The uncompromising extremists prevailed, however, in the mixed-language areas (and, one should insert here, at the institutions of higher learning), where their militant obstructions impeded compromise solutions. Even though outnumbered by the moderates, the extremists succeeded in disrupting democratic politics to the point that the government had to suspend the *Reichsrat* and govern by decree.

The Republic of Austria that emerged as one of the successor states of the defunct empire was 99 percent German-speaking, the only linguistic minority of consequence being in southern Carinthia on the Yugoslav border. The effectiveness of democratic politics depended entirely upon the relationships between the three ideological camps. In spite of the anarchic state of affairs left in the wake of military catastrophe and political disintegration, prospects for the success of democratic policies appeared hopeful because initially the leaders of the three camps worked together, jointly assuming the responsibility of coping with the catastrophic situation in the remnant of empire that had now become their country. On 12 November 1918 Socialist, proclerical conservative, and moderate German-nationalist leaders proclaimed the "Republic of German-Austria" and formed its first coalition government.

In the First Republic of Austria the effectiveness of democratic politics depended upon the balance between the commitments to partisan ideologies and the commitments to parliamentary democracy and constitutional government of all three political camps. This balance had in each case been uneasy and delicate from the very beginning. Yet the effectiveness and the achievements of democratic institutions and constitutional government in a decade and a half of precarious existence indicate that the ultimate extreme polarization in all three camps and the resulting disruption of democratic politics were not inevitable.[5]

The close cooperation between their leaders at the establishment of the Republic indicates that such cooperation was certainly not out of the question.

Later instances will likewise support the thesis that cooperation between the camps might well have forestalled the ultimate breakdown of democratic politics brought about by the subsequent polarization.

A statement of democratic politics and political ethics is here indicated. Democratic politics serve primarily to define and legitimize the means to be employed in the resolution of conflicts; pursuit of specific goals is left to contesting political forces. The essence of the democratic political process is perhaps most succinctly stated in a phrase from the American constitution, "To build a more perfect union." In this sense democratic politics are not directed toward the achievement of an objectively ideal state of affairs but toward the provision of an arena in which the codified pursuit of conflicting aims itself effects the amendment of imperfections. It goes without saying that limitations upon the means to be employed rest upon the consent of the contesting parties with the understanding that these limitations apply equally to all of them—whether in the opposition or in the government. It is obvious that democratic politics also limit in the short run the scope of ends that may be realized. Democratic politics should, instead, facilitate constant and gradual social change and concomitant far-reaching reforms over protracted periods. Democratic politics break down when the contesting parties strive to achieve their objectives by means not countenanced by the rules of democratic political contest and when they endeavor to impose their will upon the others by any and all means.

An understanding of the nature of democratic politics will be advanced by making a distinction between the political ethics of partisanship and the political ethics of constitutional means. The former commit each party to the achievement of partisan objectives by any and all means, while the latter bind the contesting parties to strive for their objectives solely by the means legitimized by the constitution.[6]

The prevalence of one or the other type of political ethics in a political system affects the functioning of democratic politics profoundly. Moreover, shifts in the balance between an ethics of constitutional means and an ethics of partisan objectives in any one segment of a political system is bound to influence the balance in others. This dichotomy was evident in all three Austrian political camps, and the resultant internal competition between those committed to one or the other type of political ethics kept Austrian democracy in a precarious state.

Tendencies toward an ethics of partisanship had in part been bequeathed by traditions of bitter political strife that had left their residue in programs, platforms, and polemics. These tendencies also fed upon the widespread poverty and economic insecurity that had followed the war and the disintegration of the empire.

Ethics of partisanship and political extremism had another source in the dubious legitimacy of the state. The First Republic of Austria is the only state in history upon which sovereignty was imposed by foreign powers against the expressed wish of its people and their leaders.

In view of all the political and economic problems that confronted the young Republic of Austria, it was doubtful that the new state could survive.[7] Nor did the Austrians have the will to survive as a nation. With the empire irrevocably gone, all parties endorsed a union with the German Republic of Weimar. In this spirit, Article 1 of the Constitution of the Republic of Austria stipulated explicitly that "Deutsch-Oesterreich," the German-speaking part of Imperial Austria that had become the Republic of Austria, was part of the Republic of Germany. All parties had endorsed Article 1 and it was passed by the assembled legislators with but one dissenting vote.[8] But when the peace treaty of Saint-Germain forbade Austrian unification with Germany, Article 1 of the constitution had to be revoked, and the First Republic of Austria was thus compelled to exist against the expressed wish of its people.

In protest against the ratification of the peace treaty, the German nationalists resigned from the government and rallied in the pan-German *Grossdeutsche Volkspartei*.[9] At the initiative of this party, plebiscites were held in several autonomous provinces of Austria with results that showed almost unanimous endorsement of unification with Germany. Thereupon the victorious Allies directed Austria, then in dire need of foreign loans, to abstain from further demonstrations against the terms of the peace treaty.[10]

Resigning themselves to their undesired independence, the Austrians gave to their political parties the loyalty citizens usually reserve for their country. Among all countries the world over, the First Republic of Austria remains unique in the extremely intense political involvement of its citizens. Political parties had their own flags, their own anthems, and even their own armed formations. Election days saw 90 percent of all enfranchised Austrians casting their ballots, and the daily lives of a large proportion of these voters were completely dominated by the framework of their political affiliations. Not only did they pay their dues to support the parties of their choice, but they joined social clubs whose members shared their political preferences. Even hiking clubs, glee clubs, and nurseries enrolled their members along ideological lines.

The spokesmen and leaders of the three camps were, on the whole, committed to parliamentary democracy and the maintenance of democratic parties. So too, most of the time, were the overwhelming majority of their followers until the early 1930s. But the pervasiveness of political associations in the lives of the Austrians kept the camps apart, and within the camps political ethics fluctuated. Ultimately, the devotees of ethics of partisanship—the ideological extremists—succeeded in setting the pace in all three camps and tensions escalated to the breaking point. An atmosphere of latent civil war found expression in countless clashes even before the two fateful civil wars of 1934 that marked the ultimate breakdown of democratic politics.

The polarization that led to this breakdown in Austria also brought the country's three ideologies into sharp relief. These ideologies are of special significance because many countries possess political movements committed to analogous ideologies. Variations of Socialist, nationalist, or religious movements often exist side by side, with resulting evolutions of ideological hybrids composed of these basic ideological ingredients. Almost all of these movements have, on occasion, been torn between a tendency toward uncompromising radicalism and a tendency toward moderation and cooperation. Thus the balance between ethics of partisanship and ethics of constitutional means so characteristic of Austrian politics in the twenties and thirties has its counterpart wherever political movements with strong ideological commitments participate in an unstable democratic system. Furthermore, the Austrian political camps gave expression to and developed ideological positions that are significant in their own right.

The Socialist Camp

The policies and programs of the Austrian Socialists reflect an ever shifting balance between ethics of partisanship and ethics of constitutional means that resulted from efforts to create a synthesis of moderate and radical positions. Efforts to create such a synthesis originated with the founding congress of Hainfeld, which brought together a radical faction and a moderate faction in the *Sozialdemokratische Arbeiterpartei*. This fusion, achieved at Hainfeld on 31 December 1889, set a distinctive stamp on Austrian socialism for generations to come. The Hainfeld program combined an unequivocal commitment to achieve, albeit in the remote future, partisan objectives of socialism with a highly qualified commitment to the constitutional means of parliamentary democracy.[11] Parliamentary democracy was explicitly endorsed as a means of somewhat doubtful value rather than as an end in itself. In this vein the program of Hainfeld states: "Without deceiving ourselves about the value of parliamentarism, a form of modern class domination... [the Socialist party]... fights for universal and equal suffrage... as a most important instrument for agitation and organization."[12]

The moderates were satisfied with the commitment to parliamentary democracy in spite of the hedging, because they were mainly interested in achieving such concrete reforms as a ban on child labor, the eight-hour day, a graduated income tax, the establishment of a Chamber of Labor, and above all else, universal and equal suffrage. The radicals were satisfied with the expression of distrust in parliamentary democracy. Radicals as well as moderates accepted the establishment of a classless society and collective ownership of the means of production as their ultimate goal.

Neither in Imperial Austria nor in the Second Republic of Austria did the Socialist commitment to Marxism affect concrete political action. Instead, the quest for a classless Socialist society on the basis of Marxist doctrine remained on a lofty level of sophisticated exegesis. In the First Republic, however, the policies of the Socialist party were influenced by Marxist ideological orientation. The synthesis of commitment to Marxism with participation in parliamentary democracy has since become known as *Austromarxism*. Austromarxism stands out as an effort to reconcile moderate Socialists with radical Socialists, as a principled synthesis of efforts for short-range reforms with aspirations for long-range objectives, and as an endeavor to establish harmony between theory and practice.

Austromarxism was of little consequence in the Second Republic of Austria, but its synthesis of Marxism with participation in parliamentary politics appears today in the practice of several left-wing Socialist parties. The policies and positions of several sizable parliamentary Communist parties hardly differs from those that evolved under Austromarxist efforts to reconcile revolutionary Marxist theory with practices that are necessarily geared to the give-and-take of parliamentary politics.

The Austromarxist synthesis has been articulated in numerous programs,[13] books, and debates,[14] notably in the Program of Linz of 1926 where it was stipulated that the Socialist society was to be achieved by rallying the majority of voters.[15] Recourse to radical means is, however, explicitly countenanced in case the bourgeoisie should not support the Socialist measures that a Socialist Parliament would enact:

But if, however, the bourgeoisie should resist social change which will be the task and objective of the state authority of the working class by such means of sabotage as systematic throttling of the economic life, armed rebellion, or conspiracy with foreign powers, then the working class would be compelled to break the resistance of the bourgeoisie by the means of dictatorship.[16]

The above paragraph expresses succinctly the duality of the Austromarxist approach: political power was to be won by obtaining a majority in Parliament, but the measures to be enacted by such a majority were expected to provoke resistance that would have to be broken by dictatorial force.

It is noteworthy that in the mid-sixties Communist parties that accepted revisionist positions endorsed by the Kremlin issued similar statements that combined commitment to the achievement of a Socialist society with commitment to democracy. The following is taken from a programmatic pronouncement of the secretary of the American Communist party,.issued in 1964:

Marxism-Leninism is a science that recognizes no contradiction between the struggle in defense of democratic institutions and democratic rights, and the struggle for socialism. It is our firm conviction that the masses of the working people are the bearers of the new socialist society that makes us uncompromising fighters for democracy. Democratic institutions are not obstacles on the path to socialism. On the contrary, these are the institutions which the people will use for the transition. Hence we want to preserve and extend them both for now and for the future.[17]

The Austromarxist synthesis was not limited to pronouncements and programs but extended to the day-to-day policies of the Austrian Socialist party in the twenties and thirties, where the duality of the commitments of the Austrian Socialists led to some apparent contradictions in their approach to the problem of revolution in theory, practice, and historical perspective. In 1919, while heading the coalition government of Austria, the Socialists effectively thwarted Communist efforts to foment a revolution.[18] A decade later the Socialists themselves discounted the significance of their antirevolutionary stand. At the annual party conference of 1932 the principal spokesman of Austromarxism, Otto Bauer, apologized to impatient young left-wingers for this and explained that unfortunate objective circumstances had rendered a Socialist revolution in Austria impossible at that time. These "unfortunate circumstances" included the country's dependence upon the "victorious capitalist powers" for badly needed essential supplies. The speaker mentioned as a further stumbling block the political strength of Austria's independent peasantry with its "decades of political training and organizations."[19] By so explaining why the time had simply not been "ripe" for a revolution, the Socialists also discounted the merits of their anti-Bolshevist stand in the eyes of the followers of the other two camps. Their use of revolutionary phraseology to justify their party's antirevolutionary action preserved a degree of unity within the Socialist camp but also brought closer together their opponents in the two anti-Socialist camps.

Yet the preservation of Socialist unity in Austria may be considered a major achievement of the Austromarxist synthesis. In all European countries, especially those bordering upon Austria, strong Communist parties competed with democratic Socialist parties for the allegiance of class-conscious workers. Throughout the twenties and thirties we find that the voting strength of the Czechoslovakian Communist party nearly matched the combined strength of the German-speaking and Czech-speaking democratic Socialist parties of this country, both of which were participating in coalition governments. In all Czechoslovakian elections in the twenties the Communists ran neck and neck with the party of the Czech agrarians, the strongest non-Communist party in the country, and continued to poll about 15 percent of the vote. In Germany, Communist voting strength increased from 3.3 million, or 10.6 percent of the vote, in May 1928 to 6.0 million, or 17.7 percent of the vote, in November 1932, while Social Democratic voting strength declined from 9.2 million, or 29.0 percent, to 7.2 million, or 20.4 percent.

In Austria, however, the Communist vote never exceeded 0.5 percent of the total vote, polling only twenty thousand votes in November 1930. By contrast, the vote of the Austrian Socialist party remained steadily at the 40 percent level throughout the twenties. In local elections held in many parts of Austria in the crisis year of 1932, the Communist vote nearly doubled its November 1930 figure but remained infinitesimal compared to the Socialist vote. While the Communist party remained the strongest party in Berlin from 1928 until 1933, the Communist vote in Vienna remained below the 2 percent level in April 1932, while the Socialist party polled about 60 percent.

The Austrian Socialists took pride in their achievement of "working-class unity" at home and even saw it as their sacred mission to advance such unity abroad, notably in their tireless efforts to bridge the gap between the Second, or democratic Socialist, International and the Third Communist International on a world scale.[20] It was this sense of mission that induced a certain ambivalence into statements about the Soviet Union by Austrian Socialist spokesmen, who would deplore the lack of freedom and democracy there while hailing the great achievements of Lenin's revolution. The tendency to explain away defects in the Soviet system became even more pronounced after the catastrophic defeat in the civil war of February 1934. The outlawed underground organ of the suppressed party gratefully acknowledged the generous acts of solidarity on the part of democratic Socialist parties from all over the world and proclaimed the affinity of revolutionary Austrian socialism with the Russian dictatorship of the proletariat: "Austrian socialism has become the natural link between the revolutionary socialism of the East and the democratic socialism of the West."[21]

Another, even more impressive dimension of the ideological unity that rallied moderates and radicals in one Socialist party was the extensive and all-embracing organizational party network whose size also reflected the high degree of political mobilization characteristic of Austrian politics. In a population of slightly over six million, with about four million voters, over seven hundred thousand people paid regular monthly dues to the Sozialdemokratische Arbeiterpartei. In Vienna alone there were four hundred thousand dues-paying members. A dedicated and well-organized staff of thousands of volunteers collected dues and saw to it that the members and their relatives turned out to vote or to attend rallies and meetings.[22]

The number and scope of affiliated organizations was likewise impressive. Socialist unions enrolled the overwhelming majority of Austria's one million wage earners. The Socialist party sponsored numerous educational and cultural societies as well as social clubs for activities of every kind. Also affiliated with the party was the atheistic *Freidenkerbund* (League of Freethinkers) which, in turn, influenced the way the party ran its nursery schools and helped to indoctrinate the party's scout clubs for teenagers. The party even ran its own burial society, which arranged for cremation, a way of burial not countenanced by the Catholic church.[23]

Of great consequence were the lending libraries set up by the Socialist party in a country where free public lending libraries, so characteristic of Anglo-

Saxon countries, were unknown. These libraries were part of a comprehensive program of adult education that contributed a great deal to the lives of the many working men and women who had received but eight years of formal schooling. The educational program of the party also familiarized Austrian Socialists with the values and traditions of free debate. It should be attributed to this tradition of open debate within the ranks of the Austrian Socialist party that Austrian workers proved not amenable to totalitarian appeals that were to be directed at them by Hitler's national socialism and by Stalin's communism.

Of special significance was the *Republikanischer Schutzbund* (Republican Defense League), the Socialist party's army of militant and disciplined volunteers. Though its main function was to maintain order at meetings and rallies, the Schutzbund was known to be armed, and it did fight the battles of the party in small skirmishes and in the civil war of February 1934.

Touching every aspect of its members' lives, the party and its affiliates truly constituted a state within the state. No other political party in any democratic country has ever achieved such a high degree of enduring voluntary participation. This is all the more noteworthy since the party, with its 40 percent of the vote, had remained in the opposition after its defeat at the polls in 1920. The party did control, through its elected representatives, the autonomous city of Vienna and numerous industrial municipalities, but this provided very little leverage in the form of patronage. Nor could the party offer any other form of material inducement to motivate such extensive involvement of the masses.

Dedication to unity for its own sake had initially caused the Socialist party to pursue a moderate policy while indulging in radical rhetoric. The threat of schisms on the Left, however, made it difficult for the party to depart too far from its rhetoric in political practice. We shall see how this dedication to unity affected Socialist policies in the fateful years of 1931 and 1932. These policies have as yet failed to receive the attention they deserve. They are of special interest in view of tangible alternatives that have been explicitly rejected.

The Two Anti-Marxist Camps

Throughout the twenties the two non-Socialist camps joined forces to such an extent that it was, at times, impossible to distinguish between them. Time and again the Socialists were confronted at the polls by anti-Marxist fusion tickets that rallied proclerical conservatives and anticlerical German-nationalists in order to forestall the specter of an Austromarxist regime.

It is noteworthy that the cooperation between the two anti-Socialist camps brought moderate conservatives together with the more moderate German-nationalists without ever obliterating their respective identities, while extremists in both camps fused completely for a while in the ranks of the paramilitary and avowedly fascist *Heimwehr*. Only with the beginning of the thirties did polarization set in within the anti-Marxist camps so that Austria was soon divided into three irreconcilably hostile camps. Before this three-way polarization actually took place, a last chance for cooperation between the moderates in all three camps appeared briefly and was deliberately rejected in the interest of maintaining unity within the camps themselves.

The Proclerical Conservative camp

In the conflict between good and evil, in which great advantage is given to evil by neglect, the Christian cannot be indifferent to so important an area of conflict as that of politics.— Eugene J. McCarthy, Commonweal, 1 October 1954.

The possibility of conflict between church and state is always present when the head of one is not the head of the other. For this reason clericalism versus anticlericalism has always been an issue in Roman Catholic countries. The question of clerical influence is likely to arise in questions regarding the school system and other matters where the private sphere and the public sphere overlap.

The proclerical *Christlichsoziale Partei* originated in Vienna and Lower Austria in the 1880s "as an expression of the discontent of the masses against the economic and social abuses created by Liberalism. Uncertain of its objectives, it comprised the petty bourgeoisie and those without property."[24]

Under the leadership of its founder, Karl Lueger, the Christlichsoziale Partei was anticapitalist, anti-Semitic, devoutly Roman Catholic, and loyal to the Habsburg dynasty and the Austro-Hungarian empire. Initially, Leuger's radicalism and his reputation as a populist demagogue led to the crown's refusal to accept him as mayor of Vienna until he had been elected twice consecutively. Soon the party was accepted as one of the bulwarks of the empire, and in 1907 its leaders entered the government of Imperial Austria. In Vienna the proclerical party lost to the Socialist, and in the small nonindustrial towns the anticlerical German-nationalists rivaled the conservatives for the allegiance of the non-Socialist voters. The Christlichsoziale Partei became the party of the devoutly Roman Catholic independent peasantry, thus enabling it to participate in every government of the First Republic of Austria. After the Socialists went into opposition in November 1920 the conservatives became and remained the major government party of he Republic.

The Christlichsoziale Partei maintained close relations with the Roman Catholic church and counted many members of the clergy among its leaders, most prominent among them Msgr. Ignaz Seipel, head of the government for more than half of the twenties. The coalition governments headed by the proclerical conservatives included German-nationalists for all but two months from November 1920 till September 1933. Only from September 1930 until

90   WALTER B. SIMON

November 1930 and from May 1932 until September 1933 did the conservative Christlichsoziale Partei share governmental responsibility with the Heimwehr. In September 1933, the Christlichsoziale Partei fused with the Heimwehr to form the *Vaterlaendische Front,* the party of the Dollfuss-
Schuschnigg dictatorship.

Scrutiny of the record suggests that large sectors of the proclerical and
conservative Christlichsoziale Partei would have preferred the preservation of
democratic politics. Of the three identifiable groups in the party, the two
major ones showed reservations about fusion with the Fascists. Many groups
among the Roman Catholic yeomanry, the mainstay of the conservative camp,
favored democracy. So did the small group of devoutly Roman Catholic
workers led by Leopold Kunschak, who was most outspoken in opposing
fusion with the Fascists and articulately in favor of preserving democratic
politics. Unsympathetic to a complete fusion, though willing to accept the
Fascists as allies, were the spokesmen of political Catholicism, among them
Schuschnigg, the subsequent chancellor, and Miklas, president of the Republic.[25] The leader of the Christlichsoziale Partei, Carl Vaugoins, is also on the
record as having made efforts to preserve at least the identity of his party
within the framework of the Vaterlaendische Front.[26]

In Imperial Austria and again in the First Republic the proclerical conservative camp was oriented toward the preservation of the established order of
things. In addition to its base among the Roman Catholic peasantry, the camp
rallied support among the small shopkeepers and craftsmen who had given the
party of Lueger its triumphant start in Vienna before the turn of the century.
Also of note was the small band of proclerical and conservative Roman
Catholic workers who played an important role through their resistance to the
party's drift toward the extreme right and oblivion before democratic politics
came to an end. After the establishment of the autocratic regime in which their
own political camp played a leading role, this group did provide labor with a
legal voice and continued to stand, albeit without telling effect, against authoritarianism in government. While the Roman Catholic workers were outnumbered among their peers by the Socialists, the devoutly Roman Catholic
academicians and intellectuals were outnumbered among their colleagues by
the German-nationalists.

Today, the record of the voluntary fusion of the proclerical conservative
party with the fascistic Heimwehr and the history of the subsequent authoritarian dictatorship constitute a source of mortifying embarrassment for Austrian
conservatives. Examination shows, however, that the other two camps bear a
fair share of responsibility for the disasters that were to disrupt democratic
politics in Austria, wipe Austria off the map completely for seven years, and
usher in ten years of foreign occupation. The disastrous foreign policy and the
oppressive domestic policies of the authoritarian regime from 1933 till 1938
have left conservatives in Austria with an unpalatable legacy. They had,

however, no choice but to yield to extremists in their camp when extremist radicals determined the policies in the two other camps.

The German-Nationalist Camp

When one talks about "nationalism" among Austrians, the qualifier "German" must be added to avoid confusion. Among Austrians it is understood that in Austria "nationalists" are actually German-nationalists who either reject their Austrian identity entirely or at least subordinate it to their encompassing German nationality.

German-nationalism in Austria, like German-nationalism in Germany or, for that matter, nationalism in general, gives expression to diverse and basically irreconcilable impulses. All ideological impulses seem to contain contradictory and mutually exclusive moral sentiments, but in the case of Austrian German-nationalism such dualism is pronounced with greatest clarity.

Originally, German-nationalism contained and inspired humanist and universalist values; cultivation of the cherished German cultural heritage was combined with respect for the national heritage of others. In Austria, as well as in Germany, German-nationalism was at one time a liberal force, the motive power behind the revolution of 1848 with its demands for constitutional government and individual freedom. In opposition to the tutelage of autocratic regimes, nationalism emerged in many places as a humanist force that afterwards shed its humanist impulses in order to advance chauvinist intolerance and imperialism. This development has been especially swift and far-reaching among the German-nationalists of Austria.

For nearly a century, Austrian German-nationalism has been characterized by an extreme chauvinism, intolerance, and ruthless expansionism that finally left its mark on world history through Hitler's nationalist-socialist regime. Yet the original humanist and liberal impulse, albeit hopelessly overshadowed and banished into marginal recesses, has never been extinguished completely. Occasional upsurges of liberal and humanist traditions have provided Austrian German-nationalism with a varied, fluctuating, and extremely complex history.

Furthermore, German-nationalist sentiments in Austria were at no time limited completely to the various German-nationalist parties but rather found repeated expression in the policies of the two major parties, at times even dominating the politics of the German-speaking provinces of Imperial Austria and the politics of the First Republic. Thus in Imperial Austria the Socialists often compromised their internationalism, and the proclerical conservatives the supernational position of their church, when they supported German-nationalist aspirations in the language question. In the First Republic of Austria all three political camps supported unification with Germany. The Socialists as well as the proclerical conservatives endorsed Austrian independence only after Hitler had come to power in Germany; before this they had accepted the Republic's imposed independence only under duress.

The various German-nationalist parties have differed a great deal among themselves and fluctuated widely both in their ideological commitments and in the size of their following, making German-nationalism the most volatile and unstable element in Austrian politics. By the 1880s the German nationalists in Imperial Austria had broken away from the liberal camp with which they had been indentified since the revolution of 1848, motivated partly by their anticapitalism but mainly by their unbending intransigence in matters related to the language policies of the polyglot empire. In the nearly completely German-speaking provinces that were to form the Republic of Austria, the greatest support for the German-nationalists came from students, the intelligentsia, and the anticlerical bourgeoisie. German nationalist parties polled most of their votes in small towns with little or no industry, in enclaves of Protestant farmers, and in the mixed-language area of southern Carinthia.

But although the German-nationalist parties were comparatively small in Imperial Austria as well as in the First Republic, their policies prevailed, after a fashion, in both, to the detriment of democratic politics. In Imperial Austria, the German-nationalists were strong enough in mixed-language areas and at the universities to impede all efforts to achieve harmony between the language groups by compromise solutions that would have given non-German languages a measure of recognition. It is noteworthy that in one of these mixed-language areas, the Sudetenland of Bohemia, there was a National Socialist German workers' party that as early as 1907 had a program containing the principal points of what was to become the program of Hitler's party and the basis for the policies of the Third Reich. A branch of this party appeared in the Republic of Austria in 1918 and competed with the Austrian branch of Hitler's party for two years after its establishment in 1926 before the two joined forces.

The bulk of German-nationalist support in the first thirteen years of the First Republic of Austria rallied under two parties committed to parliamentary democracy under the German republican colors of black, red, and gold, the colors of the German revolution of 1848. The urban Grossdeutsche Volkspartei represented the anticlerical intelligentsia, especially students and their professors, and found its principal support in nonindustrial provincial capitals and county seats as well as among the salaried petty bourgeoisie. The rural *Landbund* rallied the farmers in Protestant enclaves and their neighbors. The Grossdeutsche Volkspartei never ceased to make an issue of union with Germany (as a result of which the party itself at times lost nearly all of its votes since the cogency of this issue fluctuated). The Landbund, which concentrated its efforts upon the representation of agrarian interests and readily compromised on ideological issues, was willing to support the ratification of foreign loans even when they stipulated, as they invariably did, thanks to

French preoccupation with this matter, a clause that committed Austria to forgo unification with Germany, though this had already been prohibited by the peace treaty. Both parties were represented in all coalition governments with the Christlichsoziale Partei from November 1930 until May 1932; at that point the Grossdeutsche Volkspartei went into opposition over the ratification of the so-called Loan of Lausanne, which involved an Austrian reaffirmation of the injunction not to join Germany for another twenty-five years. The Landbund supported ratification of the loan and remained in the coalition government until September 1933, when the proclerical conservatives fused with the Fascist Heimwehr to install the authoritarian dictatorship.

The firm commitment of the two moderate German-nationalist parties to constitutional government and parliamentary democracy brought them into conflict with the Heimwehr, and in September 1930 both went into opposition against the coalition regime of the Heimwehr with the Christlichsoziale Partei. The fusion ticket of these two parties did very well at the elections held on 9 November 1930. Obtaining nearly 12 percent of the total vote and 19 of 165 members of Parliament, the two moderate German-nationalist factions replaced the defeated Heimwehr as the coalition partner of the conservative proclerical party.

Significantly, the fusion ticket of the two German-nationalist parties entered the elections under the designation *Nationaler Wirtschaftsblock und Landbund, Führung Dr. Schober.* Johann Schober had made a name for himself as chief of the Vienna police and then as a statesman of international caliber. Under his leadership a whiff of old-fashioned liberalism appeared once more on the political scene, and the success of his ticket at the polls was among the aspects of the political situation that appeared to give the harassed Republic a new lease on life. It is of interest that Schober's ticket had received the endorsement of *Die Neue Freie Presse,* the organ of the Jewish bourgeoisie of Vienna that had been the paper of the liberal party before its disintegration.

Subsequent local elections showed that the voters of Schober's fusion ticket defected to Hitler's party in such large numbers that by April 1932 nine out of ten of the party's urban voters had become National Socialist voters. The Grossdeutsche Volkspartei members of Parliament who had been elected on Schober's fusion ticket soon followed their voters and went over to Hitler's National Socialist German workers' party.[27] Thus the bulk of Austrian German-nationalists abandoned the German republican colors and went over to Hitler a year before he became chancellor of the Reich.[28]

Fascism

The pressures that came from across the border were ultimately decisive in putting an end to democratic politics in Austria. With the triumph of Fascism in Italy, antidemocratic forces in Austria gained a great deal of vigor, and Hitler's ascent to power in Germany made democratic politics in Austria altogether unworkable.

Mussolini's seizure of power in Rome contributed significantly to the polarization of Austrian politics. For one thing, the triumph of Fascist "law and order" over "the danger of red revolution" served to encourage the extremists in both anti-Socialist camps. Also, the Italian Fascist regime contributed directly and rather openly to Austrian right wing paramilitary organizations. Furthermore, the brutal oppression of the Italian Socialists stiffened the militant determination of the Austrian Socialists and made them more distrustful of Austrian conservatives, whom they perceived—not altogether without reason—as leaning toward the Fascists. It should also be kept in mind that before the emergence of Hitler's Third Reich as a major power Italy was by far the strongest neighbor of Austria.

The influence of Fascist Italy upon Austrian politics was compounded by its close alliance with the conservative-authoritarian Hungarian regime, which, in turn, had cultivated ties with Austrian ultraconservatives that dated back to the good old days of the Austro-Hungarian empire. The alliance of Italy with Hungary aimed primarily at achieving a revision of the peace treaties of Paris. The Hungarian regime refused to accept the allotment of formerly Hungarian territories on all four sides. Large parts of the new successor states of the defunct Habsburg monarch—Yugoslavia, Rumania, and Czechoslovakia— were constituted from territories ceded by Hungary, and the flags at half-mast on all new Hungarian borders testified to revisionist aspirations. The Italian regime aspired to recover from Yugoslavia the former Austrian Adriatic littoral province of Dalmatia that had at one time belonged to the Republic of Venice. The Austrians had little sympathy for Hungarian revisionist aspirations (especially since Austria's easternmost province, the Burgenland, was among the territories ceded by Hungary), and they had even less sympathy for the Italian claims upon Yugoslavia, since they bitterly resented Italy's wartime role and subsequent seizure of Trieste and southern Tyrol. Also, the oppression of the German language in southern Tyrol offended Austrian sensibilities.

All Austrians, regardless of political sympathies, despised the peace treaties imposed at Paris, and they did not think the state of affairs based upon them could endure. The right-wing proclerical conservatives and the right-wing anticlerical German-nationalists, much as they resented Italian denials of language rights to the southern Tyrolians, accepted Mussolini as a sponsor of their opposition to the order of things established by the hated peace treaties of Versailles, Saint-Germain, and Trianon. They also accepted Mussolini as their champion in the fight against the threat of red revolution and against what they despised as effete liberal democracy.

It is of general significance that the coalition of the two anti-Socialist camps went much further among extremists than among moderates. The moderate proclerical conservatives and the moderate anticlerical German-nationalists, both committed to the preservation of democratic politics, retained their separate identities while they worked together against the Socialists. Thus the agrarian Landbund, unlike the less moderate Grossdeutsche Volkspartei, never even entered fusion tickets with the proclerical conservatives. Among the anti-Socialist extremists, the proclerical Fascists and the anticlerical German-nationalists remained all but undifferentiated until the emergence of Hitler's party created an unbridgeable schism between those oriented toward Rome (or Mussolini and the Vatican) and those loyal to the cause of the Third Reich. Anti-Socialist unity most effectively overshadowed all differentiations among the paramilitary right-wing formations that intermittently clashed with the paramilitary formations of the Socialist Republikanischer Schutzbund. The activism of the avowedly antidemocratic anti-Marxists was motivated at least in part by their desire to conceal from themselves the existing fissures and budding conflicts within their ranks. It is quite possible that activist radicalism is often motivated by such a need to avoid confrontation with contradictions and latent conflict within the ranks.

In the Socialist camp, radical phraseology served to reconcile potential revolutionary dissenters with a basically moderate and reformist policy, while on the extreme right feverish activism served to reconcile ultraconservative, authoritarian proclerical Austrian patriots with anticlerical revolutionary pan-Germans who despised everything Austrian.

Throughout the twenties clashes between militant Socialists and militant right-wingers were the order of the day. These clashes took place on the outer margin of the political decision-making that was guided by democratic processes. The clashes, often involving the shedding of blood and not infrequently the loss of lives, provided an ominous background to acrimonious legislative debates over negotiable issues. There can be no doubt that the bloody clashes exacerbated tensions and rendered the issues at stake more serious than differences regarding the economic policies of such a small country warranted.

The policies of the country as a whole and of its nine autonomous provinces and over four thousand incorporated cities, towns, and villages were determined by democratic politics. There is no evidence that the decision-making process in the various legislative bodies of the Republic has ever been determined by violence in the streets. Ultimately, it was the tripartite polarization at the polls, engendered by influences from across the borders and exacerbated by tensions at home, that brought democratic politics to an end. Intermittent violence reflected and at the same time contributed, however significantly, to the ongoing polarization.

In the chronicle of violence, bloody 15 July 1927 stands out as the watershed in the development of Fascist influence in Austria. Its roots lay in one of the episodic armed clashes that were no rarity in the First Republic of Austria. In a small industrial town in the formerly Hungarian province of Burgenland, a long series of clashes between Socialists and their opponents came to a head on Sunday 30 January 1927 when members of a right-wing paramilitary organization fired on Socialists who passed their headquarters after an exchange of verbal threats, challenges, and insults. The shots killed a child and a crippled war veteran and injured several others. In July, a jury acquitted the accused, triggering a protest in Vienna that became completely unmanageable. A disorderly mob set fire to the Palace of Justice and to the publishing plant of the proclerical conservative daily, whose endorsement of the acquittal had appeared under a banner headline reading "Ein Klares Urteil." The police restored order with a maximum show of force, leaving close to one hundred dead (among them four policemen) and several hundred wounded.[29]

From that day on the Socialists were on the defensive. The spokesman of the party had to admit in Parliament that the party had lost rapport with its followers, and he pleaded in vain for amnesty.[30] Within the Socialist party the Left gained ground among the younger members, but in the country as a whole the initiative passed to the extreme Right, whose various paramilitary outfits rallied now in the avowedly Fascist Heimwehr.

In order to intimidate the Socialists, the Heimwehr, protected by large escorts of federal police, paraded through urban working-class districts that had long been Socialist strongholds. The Socialist leadership, afraid of another massacre, endeavored to restrain their followers with a minimum loss of face by drawing them to rallies held in other parts of the towns and districts in question. Their red flags and other party emblems showed the parading Fascists where the sympathies of the people in these districts lay. Those who had hated and feared the Socialists were, however, most favorably impressed by the capacity of the Heimwehr to intimidate the Socialists, and subsidies flowed freely from banks, industrial corporations, and finally from Fascist Italy. In 1929–30 the Austrian banks alone contributed to the Heimwehr a quarter of a million Austrian schillings a month (about fifty thousand dollars, a fairly sizable amount in impoverished Austria) through the offices of the federal chancellor Schober.[31]

The Heimwehr was composed of the most diverse elements, from devoutly Roman Catholic young farmers to rabidly anticlerical German-nationalist urban petty bourgeoisie, with numerous shades in between. Some favored the return of the monarch, others looked to Hitler, whose star was beginning to rise in Germany, and many more set their hopes on Mussolini. The feverish activism of the Heimwehr in the late twenties resulted at least in part from the necessity to avoid confrontation with the issues that threatened to split its ranks. In numerous armed clashes with the Socialists, the Heimwehr appeared clearly as the aggressor, and the leaders of the diverse factions boasted openly of their plans to take over the government by force in order to suppress the Socialists. On 18 May 1930 leaders of the Heimwehr publicly took the famous "Oath of Korneuburg," which contained the following pledge:

> . . . we plan to seize the power of the state and to remodel the state and the economy for the benefit of the whole people. . . . We reject western democratic parliamentarism and the party state. . . . We want to replace [Parliament] by the self-determination of the estates ["Staende"] and to provide a strong leadership for the state, not by representatives of the parties but from the leading persons of the big estates ["Staende"] and from the best and most able men of our movement. . . . Every comrade knows three powers: faith in God, his own hard will, and the word of his leader.[32]

Among those who took this oath were several proclerical conservatives whose commitment to parliamentary democracy is beyond doubt. Foremost among them was the leader of the Lower Austrian peasants, Julius Raab, subsequently head of the coalition government of Socialists and conservatives that guided the Second Republic of Austria for twenty-four years, including the decade under Allied occupation. This detail is significant as a characteristic instance of how moderates may be caught in spite of themselves in actions and commitments promoted by radicals. It is my contention that incongruities of this type should be noted rather than overlooked, and they should be examined objectively rather than exploited for facile criticism. The good name of Julius Raab and the memory of his accomplishments is not tarnished in any way by his unfortunate association with the lamentable Oath of Korneuburg, and a study of this matter should contribute to our understanding of politics.

At the time of the Oath of Korneuburg, misgivings about the Heimwehr had begun to develop in both anti-Socialist camps, especially among the moderate German-nationalists who finally broke over this issue with the proclerical conservatives.

From September 1930 till after the elections of 9 November 1930, the Heimwehr participated in a minority coalition with the proclerical conservative Christlichsoziale Partei against the opposition of the moderate German nationalists and the Socialists. The Heimwehr participated in the election under the designation *Heimatblock,* while some of its units in Vienna and Lower Austria fused with proclerical conservatives to form the ticket "Christlichsoziale Partei und Heimwehr." The Heimatblock polled 6 percent of the total Austrian vote and elected 8 of Austria's 165 members of Parliament. Soon after the elections its ministers resigned from the government. It is characteristic of the fissions within the Heimwehr that its ministers in that short-lived coalition regime were to go different ways. Prince Ruediger von

Starhemberg, vice-chancellor and minister of the interior, was to become once more vice-chancellor in the authoritarian regime of Dollfuss in 1934 and had to go into exile when Austria became part of Hitler's Third Reich in 1938. Franz Hueber, brother-in-law of Herman Goering, and minister of justice in the coalition government from September until November 1930, became once more minister of justice on 11 March 1939, when the National Socialists took over Austria, and he then flourished with the Third Reich.

Soon after the elections of November 1930 the Heimwehr began to disintegrate. For a while its leaders continued to threaten that they would emulate Mussolini's March on Rome with a similar march on Vienna, but their increasing isolation from the moderates in both anti-Socialist camps rendered them ineffective. In the meantime, the ranks of the Heimwehr dwindled with the emergence of Hitlerism as a major political force in Austria. The disintegration of the Heimwehr in the spring and summer of 1931 accounts for the phenomenon that democratic politics in Austria actually took a new lease on life even while Austria's economic situation deteriorated. To be sure, the Heimwehr succeeded in making headlines when some of its units staged an uprising in upper Styria the Sunday of 13 September 1931 and in a revolutionary declaration announced the impending march on Vienna and a Fascist takeover. The government forces were very slow in moving against the rebels, but when two unarmed Socialist workers were shot in one of the industrial towns in the disaffected area the Socialist party presented the government with an ultimatum demanding the immediate suppression of the rebellion lest the Socialist party deploy its own armed units. Thereupon the rebels surrendered to the government forces without a further shot being fired, and the leaders of the rebellion were all acquitted in jury trials three months later. When soon after the Styrian Heimwehr and the leaders of this comic-opera rebellion went over to Hitler's National Socialists, the brief respite granted to democratic politices by the disintegration of the Heimwehr came to an end.

Radicalization and polarization did not follow a straight line at all but proceeded in a complex zigzag of a kind easily overlooked in summary historical accounts. Our purpose here will be to throw these patterns into bold relief as an antidote to the mechanistic determinism that presents past developments quite mistakenly as having been inevitable.

Economic Distress

The precarious state of the economy was a source of discontent and unrest that occasioned and compounded political strife throughout the history of the First Republic of Austria. It is, however, of consequence that political tensions did not parallel economic distress. The economic situation affected the political but it did not determine it.

The postwar inflation that reduced the currency to one fifteen-thousandth of its original value wiped out savings, retirement plans, and insurance policies. At the same time, the transfer of German-speaking civil servants and teachers from formerly Austrian parts of the defunct empire to the territory of the Republic, especially to Vienna, deprived the middle class—robbed of their savings by the inflation—of opportunities for employment as well. Thus the members of the older generation faced poverty upon retirement and the members of the young generation found it difficult to get work.

In 1926 the government suspended the acceptance of new candidates for the judiciary and for administrative positions, thereby blocking access to careers that had previously absorbed about two-thirds of all law graduates.[33] The depression worsened the employment prospects for university graduates considerably, and detailed statistics show that from 1930 to 1934 students leaving the Austrian universities and faculties with final degrees outnumbered retiring practitioners several times over in the professions of law and medicine.[34] The same source states that

no detailed statistics could be obtained on the situation amongst arts and science graduates. All observers agree, however, that it is tragic. . . . In so far as these faculties prepare primarily for the teaching profession their graduates are suffering acutely from the economy measures affecting schools . . . even for the year 1932 . . . there were no openings for teachers of mathematics, physics, and modern languages. The combination of economy measures and of an increasing number of students with a degree seeking employment has made the teaching profession one of the most overcrowded of all careers.[35]

The economic condition of Austrian labor was also distressing. From the stabilization of the currency in 1922 until the beginning of the depression in 1929 the proportion of unemployed continued to hover at the 10 percent level.[36] The percentage of unemployed workers then went from 12.3 percent in 1929 to 15.0 percent in 1930, to 20.3 percent in 1931, to 26.1 percent in 1932, and 29.0 percent in 1933.[37] The production index of 1932 was 60 percent of 1929 levels.[38] During the same years the number of suicides in Austria increased from 2,434 in 1929 to 2,605 in 1930, to 2,775 in 1931, and to 3,972 in 1932.[39]

The increasing unemployment hit the young especially hard. Here we have no reliable statistics because those figures we have were compiled from the rosters of employment, from labor exchanges, and from insurance rolls. It is, however, a matter of record that apprenticeships for teenagers became virtually nonexistent, while the completion of apprenticeships frequently led to the dead-end of permanent unemployment. Graduates from schools that prepared students for entry into colleges and universities received upon graduation letters of congratulation from the various professional societies with the advice not to prepare for entry into their respective professions because these were already hopelessly overcrowded. In the meantime, bankruptcies of business establishments and the failures of banks and insurance companies often wiped out modest savings that had been accumulated since the stabilization of the currency after the inflation.

The Brief Respite

The initial effect of the world depression on Austrian politics was a temporary relaxation of tensions. Though it was followed by greatly heightened political tensions, this short hiatus in political strife should warn scholars against excessive reliance upon economic determinism. In the dramatic course of Austrian history crucial choice points have been overlooked because these were marked by a short interval of undramatic relaxation of tensions. This is understandable because the relaxation was necessarily undramatic. Also, a brief interval of genuine cooperation between the major parties bore fruit of enduring value. This suggests that an experiment in closer continuing cooperation between the major parties, proposed by the leader of one of them, might have changed the course of events that ultimately led to the breakdown of democratic politics.

The relaxation of tensions and the increased vitality of democratic politics hardly appears in those chronicles that fail to go below the surface. Violent clashes continued with no real letup while Fascist militancy became, if anything, more strident.

In the meantime, the right-wing extremists were temporarily paralyzed by internal dissensions. The economic crisis continued to worsen. An effort to rally the moderates of all three camps to establish a coalition government failed, and the two antagonistic extreme antidemocratic right-wing movements that emerged from the schism were to triumph in succession, one under the sponsorship of Fascist Italy and the other as vanguard of National Socialist Germany. Yet there was an instance of cooperation between the three camps that demonstrated their prevalent commitment to democratic politics, a commitment that was endorsed effectively by the voters at the polls.

The revision of the constitution. The outcome of the struggle over revising the constitution is testimony to the vitality of democratic politics in the First Republic of Austria.

In 1929 latent civil war, marked by intermittent armed clashes, threatened to erupt into open civil war over the issue of constitutional reform. Initially, spokesmen of the extreme Right enjoyed the support of the entire anti-Socialist camp for their proposed revisions, which were designed to undercut the position of Vienna as autonomous federal province and to undermine the

Socialist position in numerous other ways. But with well over one-third of the seats in Parliament, the Socialists were in a position to veto changes in the constitution by constitutional means. The Heimwehr and its allies hoped to circumvent Socialist parliamentary veto power by submitting the proposed constitutional changes to a popular referendum. The Socialists made it clear that they would meet with force any attempt to impose constitutional reform by such unconstitutional means as a popular referendum.

Johann Schober, leader of the two moderate German-nationalist parties that were to fuse temporarily under his leadership, who was at that time federal chancellor of the Republic of Austria, also opposed the referendum as unconstitutional. Thanks to his good offices, leaders from the moderate factions of all three camps, the Socialists included, succeeded in working out a revision of the constitution that was acceptable to all parties represented in the Austrian Parliament at that time.

It is significant that the constitution enacted by the representatives of all three political camps in 1929 was reenacted in 1945 as the constitution of the Second Republic of Austria and has been in force since then except for constitutionally enacted amendments. The successful constitutional reform of 1929 certainly indicates that cooperation between the three political camps was possible in spite of the tensions between them. The endurance of this constitution as basic law of the Second Republic of Austria testifies to the political acumen of the leadership of the three political camps during the time of the strife-torn First Republic. The men who represented their parties in working out the constitutional reform do not stand out in history. Their names have been overshadowed by those associated with more dramatic developments and events. Their work did not endure at that time even though it had received the overwhelming endorsement of the Austrian electorate.

The elections of 9 November 1930. The results of the elections held on 9 November 1930 appeared to have revivified democratic politics. The outcome certainly did not suggest that these were to be the last free nationwide elections in Austria for many years to come. Endorsed by the electorate were, above all else, the constitutional reform enacted in the preceding year and beyond that, the regime that had prevailed from November 1920 until September 1930 when the proclerical conservatives accepted the Heimwehr as coalition partner in place of the moderate German nationalists.

Throughout the twenties the German nationalist moderates had worked closely with the proclerical conservatives to contain the Socialists, to oppose Socialist economic programs, and to advance a conservative economic policy that involved the solicitation and acceptance of foreign loans, high protective tariffs, a turnover (or sales) tax on consumer goods, measures to cut the costs of welfare programs, and, as far as possible, a balanced budget and a sound currency. The anti-Socialist camps considered the Socialist economic policies in Vienna to be a program of taxing the rich in order to finance extensive low-cost public housing of good quality, a generous welfare program, and other features that made the autonomous province of Vienna into a miniature welfare state. Also, the anti-Socialist camps opposed the Socialists' legal support of the union shop or the "closed shop" that favored unionization. Furthermore, the Socialists backed legislation to protect the working conditions of those employees who, because of their comparative isolation, lacked real bargaining power, e.g., domestic servants, apprentices and journeymen in small shops and stores, and labor in agriculture and forestry. Here the Socialists encountered the opposition of numerous small-scale employers who provided the backbone of the anti-Socialist parties. The issue of rent controls stirred similar opposition from landlords. These differences regarding economic policies motivated formation of fusion tickets between proclerical conservatives and anticlerical German nationalists but they did not undermine democratic politics as such unless the conflicting parties undergirded their positions in ideological terms.

The enduring class character of the lineup of political forces in the First Republic is reflected by the relatively unchanging composition of the parliaments elected by the Austrian votes in five elections (as tabulated in table 1). These parliaments reflect the popular vote fairly well since they were elected by a system of proportional representation that gave slight advantages to the larger parties.

Thus, in November 1930 the three major parties elected 157 out of 165 members of Parliament and received 90 percent of the votes cast in an election in which over 90 percent of those entitled to vote actually cast their ballots.

Table 1. Composition of the Parliament of the Republic of Austria

Year	Socialist	Proclerical Conservative	Moderate German-Nationalist	Other	Total
1919[a]	72	69	26	3[b]	170
1920	69	85	28	1[c]	183
1923	68	82	15	—	165
1927	71	73[d]	21[d]	—	165
1930	72	66	19[e]	8[f]	165

[a]Without the Burgenland ceded by Hungary in 1920.
[b]One Liberal, one Zionist, and one Czechoslovakian.
[c]One Liberal.
[d]In 1927 the anti-Marxist fusion ticket of Die Einheitsliste elected seventy-three proclerical conservatives of the Christlichsoziale Partei and twelve members of the pan-German Grossdeutsche Volkspartei, while the agrarian Landbund elected nine moderate German-nationalists.
[e]Nationaler Wirtschaftsblock und Landbund—Fuehrung Dr. Schober, the fusion ticket of the Landbund and Grossdeutsche Volkspartei.
[f]The (Fascist) Heimatblock, ticket of the Heimwehr.

These three parties had founded the Republic in 1918 and had recently reaffirmed their joint commitment to ethics of constitutional means and democratic politics by their cooperation in revising the constitution. The Socialists had held on to 42 percent of the vote and had increased their representation in Parliament from 71 to 72. The fusion ticket had likewise done well with 12 percent of the votes cast and the election of 19 members of Parliament. Only the proclerical conservative party had suffered significant losses, and with 36 percent of the vote and 66 seats in Parliament it had become the second strongest party.

Among the avowed enemies of parliamentary democracy the Communists had received about twenty-thousand votes or barely 0.5 percent, in contrast with the 13 percent of the vote polled by the Communist party in Germany two months earlier. The Austrian branch of Hitler's National Socialist party polled slightly over one hundred thousand or not quite 3 percent of the votes cast and likewise remained without representation in Parliament. The Heimatblock polled slightly over two hundred thousand votes, or about 6 percent of the votes cast, and elected 8 members of Parliament, whereupon its ministers resigned from the government in which they had served for just over two months. Soon after the elections the Heimwehr and its political agent, the Heimatblock, began to disintegrate. Even its 8 representatives in Parliament separated and went off in different directions.

The proposed all-party coalition. The establishment of a Fascist party with its own electoral ticket strengthened democratic politics even before that party disintegrated because the defection of the Fascists from the established parties strengthened the moderate wings in both anti-Socialist camps. Then the disintegration of the paramilitary Fascist Heimwehr and its party, the Heimatblock, relaxed tensions further.

Msgr. Seipel, leader of the Christlichsoziale Partei, who had already been chancellor for nearly half of the Republic's brief existence, intended to use the respite to bring together all the forces that wanted to preserve democratic politics. He invited the Socialists and both moderate German nationalist parties to form a national coalition that could cope with the crisis. Though himself once an implacable foe of the Socialists and a sponsor of the Heimwehr, Seipel in the spring of 1931 no longer feared the Austrian Socialists and their version of Marxism. It is probable that he had begun to appreciate that the Socialists employed their radical oratory primarily for the benefit of potential left-wing defectors while their policies sustained democratic politics. Also, Seipel was becoming disenchanted with capitalism. In this vein he stated in June 1931 that he had hoped at one time that reliance upon international capitalism would rehabilitate the political and economic conditions in Central Europe sufficiently to facilitate resistance against the threat of communism. Seipel acknowledged this to have been an error and felt that a position was called for from which communism and capitalism could be opposed simultaneously.[40] This change of heart, occasioned by the collapse of the capitalist economy, contributed to Seipel's readiness to welcome the Socialists as a coalition partner.

It was obviously clear to Seipel that the lull in tensions resulting from the disintegration of the Heimwehr was not going to last. The economic crisis worsened all over the world and made itself felt in Austria with disastrous results.[41] Those looking for work were nearly as numerous as those able to hold on to their jobs, and in many small industrial towns the whole labor force was out of work with no prospect of employment in sight. The plight of the young, who had nothing to look forward to but protracted unemployment, became a particular source of serious unrest and an explosive threat to democratic politics. Many young people lost hope and became apathetic. Others swelled the ranks of militant extremist organizations, who offered them a sense of belonging, a source of self-respect, and hope for a better future.

In addition, Austrian politics had previously been affected by developments in Germany, and there democratic politics collapsed under the tidal wave of extremism. The vote of Hitler's party had grown from 800,000 or 2.6 percent of the total in May 1928 to 6.4 million or 18 percent in September 1930. Elections held in several German states and municipalities in the spring of 1931 left no doubt that the National Socialist party had become the strongest in Germany. In one legislative body after another democratic politics broke down when the antidemocratic parties rallied majorities. The National Socialists and the Communists were not able to work together, but their majorities kept democratic institutions from functioning.

The two moderate German-nationalist parties, at that time still united under the leadership of Johann Schober, were prepared to join an all-inclusive coalition. They shared with the proclerical conservatives the conviction that only a broad coalition of all parliamentary parties committed to democratic politics could hope to cope with the mounting crisis and its political consequences.

The Socialists refused to accept Seipel's invitation to enter a coalition government. This refusal appears as the one deliberate step at a clearly identifiable turning point in Austrian history; and that refusal as well as other Socialist policies in the fateful years 1931 and 1932 deserve a great deal more attention than they have so far received—especially in view of the tangible alternatives and fatal consequences.

The significance of the motives behind the Socialist rejection of the coalition offer transcends the scope of our study of Austrian politics because these motives also bear upon the relations between moderate and radical wings within organizations and political parties in general. It seems that the motive of preserving unity of the ranks as an end in itself often inspires radical oratory that may well impede cooperation with political opponents even when such cooperation would be in the best interests of the moderates of both antagonistic camps. The Socialists refused to participate in the coalition in order to preserve the cherished unity of their party. This action facilitated the takeover of political initiative by the extremists in the other two camps as well.

At the subsequent annual congress of the Austrian Socialist party the decision was explained in terms of Austromarxist theory:

Comrades, I have to warn against taking this path [that of entering a coalition government] no less emphatically than against the other of attempting a revolutionary coup.

The mere entry of several Socialists into a government, such as Dr. Seipel had in mind when he made us this offer a few months ago after the fall of the cabinet Ender, changes nothing in the power relationships between the classes.

We would encounter in the government the same resistance, the same bourgeois sabotage, that we now encounter in Parliament.

No, comrades, the mere entry of Socialists into the government at this time in which the disintegration of the capitalist system is approaching would bring us into great peril; in this government we would just have *to participate in administering the affairs of collapsing capitalism* [italics in original text to indicate enthusiastic applause from the delegates] and we would be in no position to really serve the interests of the working class and the ideals of socialism.[42]

It is obvious that the Socialists were motivated by their fear that entry into a coalition government would split their ranks and jeopardize the Austromarxist unity that meant so much to them. This preoccupation with unity is discussed by an American academic observer who may be considered the principal apologist of Austromarxist policies, Charles A. Gulick. In his defense of the Socialist rejection of Seipel's invitation, Gulick states explicitly that participation in unavoidable economy measures would have compromised the party before the electorate and "perhaps even split their party."[43]

The refusal of the Socialists to join a coalition government on the basis of Socialist principles appears in an odd light in view of the success of the Socialist-conservative coalition that governed the Second Republic of Austria from 1945 until 1966 under the Constitution of 1929, a constitution that itself had been conceived and enacted by a coalition effort accomplished by the Socialists with the parties of the two other camps.[44]

Austrians of all three political camps are now burdened with an *unbewaeltigte Vergangenheit*, a past they cannot cope with. Austrian Socialist historians and historians sympathetic to Austrian Socialism simply ignore the matter of the rejected offer.[45] This omission makes it possible to free the Socialists of even a small share of responsibility for the breakdown of democratic politics in Austria and places the whole burden upon the record of the conservatives.[46]

It is probably true that Socialist participation in a coalition government would have split the ranks of the party because this would have led to the breakaway of radical left-wingers, especially among the young. The other coalition partners would undoubtedly have been confronted by protests from the extremists within their respective camps. Developments would ultimately have depended upon the capacity of such a coalition government to cope with the economic crisis.

This is not the place to speculate on the unorthodox economic measures Seipel's all-party coalition regime might have undertaken to cope with the impact of the world-wide depression upon Austria and what measures the Socialist ministers might have sponsored. (It is, after all, probable that such a regime would have had the means for unorthodox economic measures, since its stability would have assured it access to credits in Western countries.) This is, however, the place to take a critical view of the Socialist quest for unity between moderates and extremists as an end in itself. The implications of such a quest are of consequence for political moderates everywhere.

It is, of course, impossible to predict to what extent Socialist participation in such a coalition government might have compromised the Socialists with their voters, as Gulick fears that it might have. We know for certain, however, that the young radicals who would have gone over to the Communists would undoubtedly have come back. This we may assert with a high degree of assurance because Socialists who went over to the outlawed Communist party after their own party had been outlawed did not accept the tutelage of the Kremlin for long, having become accustomed to thinking for themselves and to speaking their minds freely in the best tradition of Austromarxism and democratic socialism. In the words of Otto Bauer:

. . . comrades attracted by the revolutionary character [of the Communist party] re-fused to forgo the right to think critically and to criticize the Soviet Union and the party line. . . . they were soon repelled by the Communist party and attracted to the revolutionary Socialists. [Under the impact of civil war, dictatorship and suppression the Austrian Socialists who refused to become Communists called their underground organization "Revolutionaere Sozialisten."][47]

The acceptance of unity as an end in itself, long characteristic of Austrian socialism, was articulated effectively by Otto Bauer at the annual congress of the Socialist party in Linz in 1926: "A hundred times better to go the wrong way united . . . for mistakes can be corrected, than to split for the sake of the right way!"[48] This pronouncement, received with thunderous applause by the delegates, was quoted again and again in order to inveigh against the feared schism between the Left and the Right that had immobilized Socialist labor in so many countries, especially in Italy and in Germany. Thus the Austromarxists appear to have pursued what they sensed to be the wrong way in the expectation that mistakes in policy could be corrected with greater facility than rifts in the unity of their party.

A coalition of the three parties would have brought together the moderates of all three camps and would have rallied them against the extremists of all three camps in a joint undertaking to preserve democratic politics. When the great coalition failed to materialize, a realignment of political forces led to a new constellation that left Austrian politics split into three hostile camps, each irreconcilably antagonistic toward the other two. This development rendered democratic politics in Austria unworkable.

The realignment of political forces. It was to be expected that the growth of Hitler's National Socialist party in Germany would enhance the appeal of his party in Austria. The political composition of the Austrian electorate suggested, however, that the potential for growth was much smaller for Hitler's party in Austria than it had been in Germany. The increase in National Socialist votes in Germany had come primarily from former supporters of Protestant agrarian and middle-class parties and from former nonvoters.[49] In Germany, the total vote of the two Marxist parties and the total vote of the two proclerical Roman Catholic parties had actually increased while the National Socialist vote increased from 0.8 million in May 1928 to 6.4 million in September 1930 and to 13.7 million in 1932. In Austria voter participation had always been at the 90 percent level, compared to the 70 percent level in Germany. Thus Austria did not possess a sizable reservoir of nonvoters. Also, in Austria the proclerical conservatives shared with the Socialist Austromarxists over 80 percent of the votes cast. Considering how well the proclerical parties and the Marxist parties had been able to hold their own in Germany, this too indicated that the potential for growth was smaller for the Austrian National Socialists than it had been for their counterparts in Germany. The provincial and municipal elections held in most of Austria from the country's last parliamentary elections in November 1930 to the last municipal elections in April 1933 left, however, no doubt that Hitler's party had become a mass party in Austria as well.

The provincial and municipal elections in Austria in 1931, 1932, and the spring of 1933 do not provide us with a complete picture of party strength at any one time for the country as a whole. Yet these elections, held at different times in different places, do provide a fairly reliable picture of the changes in the political alignment of the electorate.

There was, first of all, a steep drop in voter participation immediately after the national elections of 9 November 1930. All parties represented in the Austrian Parliament suffered losses. Losses by the two major parties, the Socialists and the proclerical conservatives, tended to be minor compared to those of the moderate German nationalist Grossdeutsche Volkspartei and of the Fascist Heimwehr. At first Hitler's National Socialists registered only minor gains, but later, in the fall of 1931, throughout 1932, and in the spring of 1933, voting participation recovered and went even beyond the 90 percent level, and they became Austria's major third party. They not only attracted the defectors from the Fascist Heimwehr and from the two moderate German-nationalist parties but they also took votes away from the two major parties.

The municipal elections held in Innsbruck in May 1931 and April 1933 reflect this trend with concrete precision: voting participation went from 91 percent in November 1930 to a record low of 75 percent in 1931 and then to an all-time high of 93 percent in 1933, while the National Socialist vote rose from 794 votes to 1,196 and then to 14,996. In the same elections the moderate German-nationalist vote dropped from 9,742 to 5,063 to 828. The results of the Innsbruck elections in 1930, 1931, and 1933 (see table 2) show clearly that the bulk of the new National Socialist voters were not defectors from their former parties to Hitler. Their losses had rather increased the nonvoters.

Of special interest are the elections held in Klagenfurt, capital of Carinthia, in 1931 and the subsequent mayoral elections by the city council. The latter provide a revealing instance of collaboration between the Socialists and the proclerical conservatives. Incidentally, Klagenfurt already had a strong Austrian pre-Hitler National Socialist party that was absorbed by Hitler's party when the Austrian branch was set up (see table 2). The city council elected on 8 February 1931 became deadlocked when the Socialist, conservative, and National Socialist councillors could not summon the needed majority for a mayoral candidate. In the municipal elections of 31 May 1931 the National Socialists emerged as the second strongest party in the city council, overtaking the proclerical conservatives by additional gains primarily from the disintegrating Fascist party. It is of historical interest and of some significance for our discussion that the city councillors of the conservative Christlichsoziale Partei then helped elect the candidate of the Socialist party as mayor of

Table 2. Election Data for Upper Austria, Klagenfurt, and Innsbruck

	Upper Austria		Klagenfurt			Innsbruck		
	9 Nov. 1930 [a]	19 Apr. 1931 [b]	9 Nov. 1930	8 Feb. 1931	31 May 1931	9 Nov. 1930	17 May 1931	23 Apr. 1933
Socialist	134	128	5.1	4.1	4.5	13.4	12.0	9.9
Proclerical conservative	218	240	3.6	3.5	3.5	8.1	9.9	9.4
Fascist	40	19	1.3	1.5[c]	—	3.5	—	0.8
Moderate German-nationalist	72	51	3.7	1.7	1.9[d]	9.7	5.1	0.8
Nazi	12	16	1.9	3.0	3.7	0.8	1.2	15.0
Communist	2.2	3.7	0.2	0.4	0.4	0.1	0.4	0.5
Frauenpartei	—	—	—	—	—	—	0.742	—
Other	—	—	—	—	0.2[e]	—	—	—
Total votes cast (in thousands)	478	458	15.8	14.3	14.3	35.7	30.1	36.8

[a]National elections.
[b]Diet elections.
[c]Fusion of Fascists and a minor party.
[d]Fusion of moderate German-nationalists and a minor party.
[e]Splinter group, apparently Fascist.

Klagenfurt. It is noteworthy that the proclerical conservatives, when compelled to choose between a Socialist and a National Socialist, preferred a Socialist. Therefore, the mayoral elections in Klagenfurt support the view that Seipel's invitation to the Socialists to join a coalition had been made in good faith.

The revealing "moment of truth" in the rising tide of national socialism in Austria came with the provincial and municipal elections held in about three-fourths of Austria on 24 April 1932. These elections showed that Hitler's party had absorbed over 90 percent of the vote of the predominantly urban moderate German-nationalist Grossdeutsche Volkspartei, most of the urban vote and a large part of the rural vote of the Fascist Heimwehr, a large part of the agrarian and moderate German-nationalist Landbund, as well as votes from the two major parties. The elections held in the early part of 1931 had all shown a steep drop in voter participation. In the elections of 24 April 1932 voter participation had nearly returned to November 1930 levels. In the latter part of 1932 and in the spring of 1933 voter participation reached a record high.

On 24 April 1932 Austrians cast their votes in elections in Vienna, Lower Austria, Styria, Carinthia, and Salzburg. Cited here are merely the results of the elections in Vienna, where the National Socialist vote increased from 27,000, or not quite 3 percent of the votes cast in November 1930, to 201,000, or about 18 percent, while the number of votes cast was 35,000, or 3 percent below 1930 levels. The bulk of the National Socialist gain came from the Heimatblock, which had received 26,000 votes in 1930 and did not put up a ticket in 1932, and from the German-nationalists, who had polled 124,000 votes in 1930 as part of Schober's fusion ticket and who now polled 8,000 votes as the Grossdeutsche Volkspartei. The Socialists held their own fairly well, their vote dropping from 700,000 to 680,000, while the Communist vote increased from 10,000 to about 20,000. The decline of the proclerical conservative Christlichsoziale Partei from 283,000 to 234,000 accounts for the remainder of the increase of the vote of Hitler's party in Vienna. It is noteworthy that in Vienna as a whole, as well as in twenty of Vienna's twenty-one districts, the National Socialist vote of April 1932 may be figured directly from the election data of November 1930 by adding the 1930 vote of the National Socialist party to the vote then polled by the Heimatblock and by Schober's German-nationalist fusion ticket plus 15 to 20 percent of the vote polled in 1930 by the Christlichsoziale Partei. The only exception to this is the first district of Vienna, where the National Socialist vote in April 1932 remained below what Schober's German-nationalist fusion ticket had polled in November 1930. It appears that in 1930 the latter, endorsed by the liberal *Neue Freie Presse,* had obtained the vote of the Jewish bourgeoisie. Over nine-tenths of Schober's other voters went over to Hitler.

In Austria, unlike Germany, the National Socialists also took votes away from the Socialists and from the proclerical conservatives. These two suffered losses only where they had been weak all along and did well in their own strongholds. Thus the Socialists held their own in Vienna and in the industrial centers and suffered heavy losses in the Tyrol, Vorarlberg, and Salzburg, while the conservatives held firm in the countryside where they had always been dominant but suffered heavy losses in Vienna, industrial towns, provincial capitals, and county seats where they had always been weak. This attraction of Hitler's party for former nonvoters and voters of minor parties suggests that the mass vote of Hitler's party constituted a nonspecific expression of protest rather than a commitment to a program or an ideology.[50] This, in turn, lends support to our thesis that the breakdown of democratic politics in the First Republic of Austria was not at all inevitable.

The lack of firm ideological commitment among the bulk of National Socialist voters is also confirmed by the instability of the vote in the party's strongholds even while Hitler's party increased its vote by leaps and bounds all over the country. Of the nine communities in which the National Socialists had polled more than 20 percent in 1927 (when the National Socialist vote in all of Austria reached a bare 0.8 percent under the designation *Voelkischsozialer Block)*, there were four in which they polled less than 10 percent in 1932 when National Socialist voting strength in local elections in most of Austria exceeded 20 percent.[51] Thus Hitler's party was losing votes in established strongholds even while his party experienced election victories all over the country hardly equaled in elections anywhere.

This is not the place to devote a great deal more space to election results, but as a curiosity of some importance the vote in the military barracks of Vienna on 24 April 1932 is worthy of note: here the Christlichsoziale Partei polled 2,043 votes, the Socialists 1,705 votes, and Hitler's National Socialist party 1,860 votes.[52] It should be added that the peace treaty of Saint-Germain permitted Austria a volunteer army of thirty thousand men. In 1919–20 a Socialist minister had done his best to fill the ranks of this army with Socialists; later the proclerical conservative minister of the army did his best to recruit men of his own party. The vote in Vienna's military barracks indicated that the minister had been fairly successful in ridding the army of Socialists, but the high proportion of Hitlerites was probably a bequest from the period during which the anti-Socialist paramilitary organizations had rallied German-nationalists and proclerical conservatives indiscriminately.

The elections held on 24 April 1932 in Vienna, Lower Austria, Styria, Carinthia, and Salzburg left no doubt that the Parliament elected on 9 November 1930 no longer represented the political alignment of the voters. The results of these elections as well as of previous local elections suggested that new elections would return the Socialists with somewhat less than 40 percent of the vote, the proclerical conservatives with about 30 to 35 percent, and the agrarian Landbund with about 5 percent. The National Socialists were bound to poll well over 20 percent of the vote.

In response to the elections results the Socialists demanded the dissolution of the Parliament and election of a new one that would represent the voters.[53] Their demand was accompanied by indications that the Socialists would not consider entering a coalition government. In the words of Otto Bauer:

What matters most, however, is that we take into account in all political decisions and considerations the novelty of the situation. The petty bourgeoisie and the proletarian masses which had been following the old bourgeois parties are in motion, stirred by the crisis of capitalism. They may fall for the lures of fascism. They may be won over to us.

If we appear to the masses as co-partner and as sharing the blame [for the state of affairs] of the bourgeois world, then we shall merely push them to fascism and thereby strengthen the Fascist danger. The more resolutely we give expression to the mood of rebellion which has taken over the masses, the more sharply we differentiate ourselves from the capitalist world, the more resolutely we fight against capitalism, its government, its parties, its whole economic, political, and ideological system, the more resolutely we show the masses the great aim of Socialist revolution as a goal to fight for, the greater the part of the masses now in motion we shall attract.[54]

It is very difficult to infer from Socialist pronouncements what developments the Socialists anticipated or hoped for. They refused to indicate what they themselves might do in a Parliament in which none of the parties held a majority. It seems that they hoped to compel the National Socialists and the proclerical conservatives to form a poorly integrated coalition regime so that they might then attract defectors from both of these antagonistic camps after the inevitable failure of their government to cope with the crisis of capitalism. But this is mere inference. We have no Socialist pronouncements on what was to happen in a Parliament that reflected the three-way split that divided Austria's electorate at that time.

The realignment of voters soon affected Parliament even without new elections. The representative of one wing of Schober's moderate German-nationalist fusion ticket, the Grossdeutsche Volkspartei, went into opposition after refusing to support ratification of the Loan of Lausanne, a loan that was to commit Austria to pledge once again that no attempt would be made to move in the direction of union with Germany for another twenty-five years. With this intransigent stand the moderate pan-German members of Parliament narrowed the gap between themselves and the National Socialists to whom their voters had already defected.

The agrarian Landbund, however, remained in the coalition government and compromised its German-nationalist commitment by endorsing ratification of the loan. Inasmuch as the Socialists were adamant in their opposition to ratification of the loan, the defection of the Grossdeutsche Volkspartei left the government without a majority in Parliament. The government considered ratification of the agreement to obtain this loan essential for Austria's economy.

By that time, the summer of 1932, the Heimwehr had disintegrated altogether. Nearly all of their urban voters and many of their rural voters had gone over to Hitler's National Socialists, and many of their paramilitary units had joined the SA or the SS, the paramilitary organizations of Hitler's party. The eight members of Parliament elected on the Fascist ticket likewise failed to stay together. Only three of them went over to Hitler, but the remaining five, who had next to no following among the voters, were to play a decisive role in the breakdown of democratic politics in Austria. It mattered little that they had no followers among the electorate as long as they held the balance of power in Parliament. Only with their support was the proclerical conservative party able to forestall the quest for new elections demanded by Hitler's National Socialists in the streets and backed in Parliament by the Socialists, the pan-Germans, and the three Fascists who had gone over to the National Socialists. They were also badly needed to provide the parliamentary majority for the ratification of the Loan of Lausanne. As the price for their support the Fascists exacted the Ministry of Interior, which controlled the state executive, including the federal police of Vienna, and the ministry of commerce.

Even with the support of the five Fascists, the new government, formed in May 1932, was in a precarious position because of its small margin. Time and again the government was saved from disaster because accidental death or illnesses among members of Parliament resulted in providential tied votes or in one-vote majorities needed to save the regime. The Loan of Lausanne, for instance, was ratified on the basis of a one-vote margin that came about because a fatally ill supporter of the government died in time to have his successor sworn in to cast his vote for the government while a member of the opposition fell ill at an opportune moment. Several votes of no confidence initiated by the Socialists, by pan-Germans, or by Fascists-turned-Hitlerites failed because of tied votes. In the meantime the economic depression worsened and local elections continued to register sizable gains for the National Socialists.

In the fall and winter of 1932 Hitler's party suffered serious setbacks in national and local elections in Germany, and it seemed for a short while that the German National Socialist party was on the verge of disintegration. Had Hitler's party in Germany actually fallen apart, his party in Austria would undoubtedly have fallen apart too, and Austrian democracy might have had another chance. When Hitler came to power in Germany on 30 January 1933 the fate of democratic politics in Austria was definitely sealed.

The final stage.   In the late twenties and early thirties democratic politics broke down in many European countries and were threatened in most others. The triumph of Hitler in Germany cast further doubt on the survival of democracy long before his armies crossed many European borders. This was especially true in Austria, where the victory of Hitler's National Socialist party in

Germany doomed democratic politics even while Hitler's effort to gain power in Austria at that time failed.

In the spring and summer of 1933 the Austrian Hitlerites made a concerted effort to take over political power by force with the moral and financial support of the new regime in Germany. In reprisal for the deportation of German National Socialist agitators, among them a minister of Bavaria, Germany imposed a travel ban designed to injure Austrian tourism, which depended upon German tourists and played a tremendous role in Austria's weak economy. At the same time the Austrian National Socialists engaged in sporadic but intensive terrorism, using explosives that caused extensive property damage as well as injury and death. Most of their attacks were directed at supporters of the government, some at randomly selected Jews. The practice of depositing explosives in telephone booths also inflicted injuries randomly among the general public. National Socialist terrorism reached its peak in June 1933 when Storm Troopers tossed hand grenades from a roof into a marching formation of Roman Catholic athletes. The government proclaimed martial law and reintroduced the death penalty, abolished in 1919, and thus ended the situation in which the terrorists had operated without fear of reprisals since they did not expect to serve the jail sentences handed down to them. In the spring and summer of 1933 the Austrian National Socialists had been certain of instant victory, but the reintroduction of the death penalty and the ban on their party caused terrorism to decline considerably. The outlawed party continued, however, to function underground, thanks to a hard core of enthusiastic and dedicated young people, predominantly students, and the backing of the German Reich.

Although the failure of the efforts of the Austrian National Socialists to take over the government in the spring of 1933 and the subsequent suppression of their party postponed by nearly five years the day on which Austria was to become a part of Hitler's Third Reich, democratic politics were doomed. None of the three camps commanded a majority of the voters, and the fissures between them had by that time become too deep to permit any cooperation. In all three camps the initiative was with the extremists, and efforts on the part of moderates to break down the barriers piling up between the camps were stymied. The constellation of political forces simply rendered democratic politics impossible.

In March 1933 an intramural crisis paralyzed the Austrian Parliament. During a vote taken by the members of Parliament a Socialist committed an error when he cast his ballot. In the ensuing altercation, the speaker of Parliament as well as the first and second deputy speakers resigned from their posts. The government chose to interpret this development as an indication that "Parliament had eliminated itself," since it was without a speaker. From then on the government legislated by emergency decree on the basis of a defunct wartime authority of dubious legality. Among the first of these emergency decrees was the dissolution of the Republikanischer Schutzbund, the paramilitary organization of the Socialist party, followed by the outlawing of the Communist party and, soon after, also of the National Socialist party.

The details of the issues involved in the dissolution and elimination of the Austrian Parliament in March 1933 have been examined minutely by numerous chroniclers, but these details appear to be of little consequence in the general scheme of things. It actually matters little whether Parliament had eliminated itself by its own incompetence, as claimed by the government, or whether it had been the victim of a diabolical Fascist intrigue, as claimed by the Socialists. Nor does it really matter to what extent the government did or did not act illegally when it began to legislate by emergency decree on the basis of a provision promulgated during World War I. In historical perspective the legality of this provision is largely irrelevant, since the political constellation of that period precluded any "democratic solution" of the crisis. Clearly, the authority of the government to govern by emergency decree rested not upon legal claims of dubious validity but upon brute power. The extreme polarization in Austria's tripartite political alignments had, however, created a power vacuum that invited authoritarian intervention.[55]

A few moderate conservatives continued their efforts to bring the moderates from all three camps together, but they had next to no influence upon the government. It had become a willing captive of the authoritarian and pro-Fascist wing of the conservative proclerical camp, which had long admired Mussolini's regime of law and order. The government soon endorsed the program of the Heimwehr, which called for an "authoritarian" regime and explicitly discounted parliamentary democracy and democratic politics.

The German-nationalist camp had become identified with national socialism a year before Hitler became chancellor of German; a handful of urban pan-Germans remined faithful to the German republican colors and ideals even after Hitler had come to power in Germany. Their refusal to accept national socialism was, however, of no consequence whatever in the course of events. We find in this group a few men of outstanding integrity, intellect, and courage, but their number was very small.

Of some consequence was the moderate German nationalist agrarian Landbund, which continued to rally a fair following in and around Protestant farming communities to its German republican colors of black, red, and gold. The Landbund had readily accepted the ratification of the Loan of Lausanne despite its clause accepting Austria's imposed sovereignty, and its ministers remained in the coalition goverment all through the spring and summer of 1933. The sincere dedication of the Landbund to democratic politics brought it into conflict with the Heimwehr, represented in the government by the minister of interior and the minister of commerce, which led to the resignation of its ministers. Except for a brief spell of two months in the fall of 1930 the Landbund had participated in every Austrian government for thirteen years. The small but compact party had always been concerned primarily with agrarian interests. Its base of support had always been among a few Protestant farming communities but it also traditionally received a great deal of support from the surrounding Roman Catholic farmers. The Landbund in no way added to the drama of turbulent partisan conflict but appears to have contributed considerably to the effectiveness of Austria's democratic politics.[56] The withdrawal of the Landbund from the government in September 1933 marked a further step toward the total eclipse of democratic politics in Austria.

In the German-nationalist camp and in the proclerical conservative camp the developments in Germany in particular and the world-wide trend away from democratic politics in general put the extremist radicals in the ascendancy and inspired them with hopes for the immediate realization of their aspirations. In the Socialist camp both the extremist radicals and the moderates were in despair.

The impact of the catastrophe that had struck the German Socialists demoralized the Austrian Socialists, and in the new constellation of forces they were no longer able to hold their own. From 15 March 1933, the day Parliament was suspended, until 12 February 1934, when their party was outlawed and civil war broke out, the Socialist leadership tried desperately to contain government-sponsored aggression against the party and to restrain their followers from ill-considered action that had no chance of success. During that period the moderate leaders would probably have succeeded in convincing the Socialist party to accept almost any compromise with the conservatives, but the moderate proclerical conservatives were in no position to offer one, because they had lost all influence upon the course of events. The initiative in the proclerical conservative camp had passed beyond recall into the hands of the antidemocratic extremists who meant to put an end to democratic politics, to organized labor, and to the Socialist party in Austria.

The suspension of Parliament and the outlawing of the Republikanischer Schutzbund were followed by major infringements upon the constitutional rights of free speech, free press, and free assembly, which the Socialists had won in hard struggles before the turn of the century. The Fascist minister of the interior deputized members of his Heimwehr as auxiliary policemen and empowered them, as members of the executive forces of the state, to provoke and terrorize the Socialists.

In an effort to contain government terror and provocations within limits, and primarily to restrain radical youth who were spoiling to meet force with force, the Socialist leadership stipulated, at an extraordinary special convention in the fall of 1933, the conditions under which a call for a general strike, and with this a call to arms, was to be issued:

1. If the government imposed a Fascist constitution in violation of the constitution of the Republic;

2. If the government disposed of the constitutionally established and freely elected administration of the city and province of Vienna in order to install a government commissar;

3. If the government dissolved the Socialist party;
4. If the unions were dissolved or their administration taken over by a union sponsored by the government.[57]

The government refrained until February 1934 from taking any of the four steps that would have called forth massive Socialist resistance. They employed instead what has since become known as "salami tactics," a strategy designed to whittle down the position of the opposition in slices too small to motivate militant resistance. Specifically, the government forces went all out to raid Socialist stores of military equipment. The Socialist leadership could not bring itself to call for armed resistance over a few rifles and machine guns—which was the typical yield of such raids. Also, they continued to hope that moderation might yet prevail in the conservative camp because indications abounded that the majority of the conservative supporters were in favor of reconciliation with the Socialists. The leadership of proclerical industrial labor openly called for such cooperation in order to resore democratic politics and safeguard Austrian independence. Those in a position to determine policy preferred, however, to rely upon the guarantee of support from Fascist Italy, and under these circumstances they systematically undercut Socialist positions in order to prepare the ultimate blow. The Socialists were completely stymied by the fact that even a success against the Austrian Fascists would only bring them face to face with the National Socialists, who enjoyed the backing of Hitler's Germany. Furthermore, the forces of the government could count upon ample support from Italy and Hungary. The Socialists were fully aware of the hopelessness of their situation.

Unceasing provocations continued to goad the young Socialists into action, however, against the counsel of their leaders. Young Socialist spokesmen mocked their leaders with ironic references to the government arms raids that were slowly denuding the party of its secret arsenals: "Genossen, wir muessen mit geistigen Waffen kaempfen, denn andere werden wir bald keine mehr haben!"[58] Eager for action, they cited Karl Marx's dictum in reference to France after the collapse of the revolution of 1848: "Better an end with terror than a terror without end."

In the first week of February 1934 the Socialists suffered further humiliation when raiding parties of the Heimwehr, now deputized as auxiliary policemen, simply occupied and appropriated Socialist party headquarters in rural areas, where their party had always been weak. At the same time the homes and offices of Socialist leaders were subjected to extensive searches for hidden arms, and numerous Socialist leaders were placed under arrest.

On Monday 12 February 1934 a unit of the outlawed Republikanischer Schutzbund resisted on its own initiative a raid on the headquarters of the Socialist party in Linz, provincial capital of Upper Austria, which also had a sizable Socialist working-class population. Within a few hours, warfare spread spontaneously across the country and a general strike was called. The strike turned out to be fairly ineffective, but for several days the armed forces of the government, supported by paramilitary organizations of the government party, battled the Socialists in Vienna and numerous industrial towns throughout the country with tanks, artillery, and flamethrowers. The core of government strength was the volunteer army of about thirty thousand and the federal police force of six thousand in the city of Vienna. We only have rough estimates regarding the size of the paramilitary units involved.

Although the oppressive measures instituted by the Austrian dictatorship against the defeated Socialists appear comparatively mild when contrasted with those imposed by totalitarian dictatorship, the actions taken by the government fell far short of civilized standards of justice. The hangings of nine Socialists after summary court-martial proceedings have remained without moral or legal justification. Among the victims of the hanging courts was a member of Parliament who had returned to his constituency only after the fighting had broken out in order to be with his embattled constituents. Similarly unforgivable was the case of a man, injured in battle, who had to be carried to court on a stretcher and was carried to the gallows the same way. The evil memory of these nine hangings foreclosed any possibility of reconciliation between Austria's two major parties when Fascist Italy reneged on its pledge to preserve an independent Austria.

By September 1933 the proclerical conservative Christlichsoziale Partei had voluntarily dissolved itself in order to merge with the Fascist Heimwehr to constitute the Vaterlaendische Front. After the suppression of the Socialist party in February 1934 the Vaterlaendische Front became the party of the dictatorship. It should be noted that this party was itself pluralist in structure, since its constituent parts never completely surrendered their identities. Also, the regime itself became a great deal milder in its oppression of oppositional organizations and soon tolerated publications and organizations that expressed opposition views and rallied adherents of the two camps whose political activities had been suppressed by emergency decree. Numerous superficial observers of the Austrian scene, among them many Austrians, have long viewed the comparative tolerance of the Austrian dictatorship as a sign of weakness. The dictatorship was indeed weak, rent by inner dissensions, confronted by opposing camps that clearly numbered the majority of the population among their sympathizers, and increasingly hard pressed from across its borders. The internal pluralism of the political camp that supported the dictatorship and the dictatorship's tolerance for oppositional activities are, however, characteristic of authoritarian regimes in general.[59]

In July 1934 the Austrian National Socialists attempted an armed coup, but the dramatic occupation of the chancellery by 144 Storm Troopers wearing uniforms of the government executive (of which a fairly large number of the participants were indeed active members), while another troop of 14 men occupied the radio station, was thwarted. It then took the army and the paramilitary organizations of the government several days to suppress the fighting in the provinces. The Italian army massed units on the border, ready to march in case Germany should provide substantial support to the National Socialist rebels, who were getting a great deal of encouragement from the German broadcasting stations along the Austrian border.

Austria remained under an authoritarian dictatorship for another four years. Under comparatively mild police supervision the National Socialists, the Socialists, and the Communists were able to set up rather sizable underground organizations. Although the underground did not affect Austrian politics directly, it was able to infiltrate legal organizations that the government tolerated as "safety valves." The network of underground organizations that distributed illegal literature and held clandestine meetings during that period was probably as extensive as the network of organizations of all kinds that encompassed the lives of Austrians from the cradle to the grave during the First Republic of Austria while democratic politics prevailed.[60]

Throughout the mid-thirties the power and prestige of Hitler's Germany grew tremendously. Also, Mussolini's Fascist Italy moved closer and closer to Germany and eventually became the ally and junior partner of Hitler's powerful Third Reich. A conference between Hitler and the Austrian dictator, Chancellor Dr. Kurt von Schuschnigg, on 12 February 1938 in Berchtesgaden led to something of a false dawn. In compliance with Hitler's request, Schuschnigg took two Austrian members of Hitler's National Socialist party into the government and granted amnesty to the National Socialist prisoners. He went further, however, and pardoned all political prisoners—Socialists and Communists included—and took a man known for his Socialist affiliation into the government. For about two weeks it seemed that democratic politics were to be revived in Austria, but Schuschnigg's efforts to rally Austrians to the defense of the independence of their country came to nothing. The gestures toward the Socialists had come too late. Also, it did not help matters that Schuschnigg had been minister of justice in February 1934. Worst of all, reliance upon Mussolini's support had reduced Austria to a political pawn of Italian power that was now readily surrendered to Hitler.

On the evening of 9 March 1938 Schuschnigg, in a surprise move to thwart Hitler's aspirations and to legitimate Austrian independence, set the date for a plebiscite on Austrian independence for 13 March. A German ultimatum was followed by the triumphant entry of German troops, and to the frenzied cheers of Austria's German-nationalists, Austria became an integral part of Hitler's Third Reich.

Even though democratic politics broke down in the First Republic of Austria, the tradition of free debate and inquiry nourished by them did bear fruit. While a sizable proportion of Austrians had been enthusiastic supporters of Hitler's regime, resistance was a great deal stronger in Austria than in Germany. Among the thousands of Austrians who suffered under the National

Socialist regime because of their opposition to Hitler were Austrians from all three political camps. The success of democratic politics in the Second Republic of Austria is due to the accomplishments of democratic politics in the First Republic, as well as to the lessons learned from its collapse.

NOTES

1. Richard Charmatz, *Oesterreichs Innere Geschichte von 1848 bis 1907* (Leipzig: B. G. Teubner, 1911).
2. Robert A. Kann, *The Multinational Empire* (New York: Columbia University Press, 1950), vol. 1, pp. 95–108.
3. Adam Wandruszka, "Oesterreichische Politische Struktur," in *Geschichte der Republik Oesterreich*, ed. H. Benedikt (Vienna: Verlag fuer Geschichte und Politik, 1954), p. 291.
4. See, for example, Wilhelm Emanuel Ketteler, *Soziale Gerechtigkeit* (Munich: Deuerlein, 1950); August Maria Knoll, *Der Soziale Gedanke im Modernen Kapitalismus: Von der Romantik bis Rerum Novarum* (Vienna and Leipzig: Reinhold Verlag, 1932); idem, *Katholische Gesellschaftslehre: Zwischen Glaube und Wissenschaft* (Vienna, Frankfort, and Zurich: Europa Verlag, 1966); and idem, *Das Ringen um die Berufsständische Ordnung in Osterreich* (Vienna: Osterreichischer Heimatdienst, 1933). See also the references to Carl von Vogelsang in Friedrich Funder, "Vaterland," *Reichspost,* 11 February 1937; and E. Kogon, *Katholisch-Konservatives Erbgut* (Freiburg: I. Br., 1934).
5. Walter Goldinger, "Der Geschichtliche Ablauf der Ereignisse in Oesterreich," in Benedikt, *Geschichte.*
6. Walter B. Simon, "Politische Ethik und Politische Struktur," *Koelner Zeitschrift fuer Soziologie und Sozialpsychologie* 2, no. 3 (1959): 445–59.
7. Siegmund Schilder, *Der Streit um die Lebensfaehigkeit von Oesterreich* (Stuttgart: F. Enke, 1926).
8. Goldinger, "Der Geschichtliche Ablauf," p. 95.
9. To avoid the confusion of variant translations, the names of political parties will be retained in their original language except where there is a precise equivalent in English.
10. See Otto Bauer, *Acht Monate Auswaertige Politik* (Vienna: Brand, 1919); Friedrich Kleinwaechter and Heinz von Paller, *Die Anschlussfrage* (Vienna and Leipzig: Wilhelm Braumueller, 1929); and Anton Rintelen, *Erinnerungen an Oesterreichs Weg* (Munich: Verlag Brueckmann, 1941).
11. Ernst Winkler, *Die Oesterreichische Sozialdemokratie im Spiegel ihrer Programme* (Vienna: Verlag der wiener Volksbuchhandlung, 1964).
12. Ibid., p. 29.
13. Ibid.
14. Norbert Laser, *Begegnung und Auftrag: Beitraege zur Orientierung im zeitgenoessischen Sozialismus* (Vienna: Europa Verlag, 1963).
15. Winkler, *Die Oesterreichische Sozialdemokratie,* pp. 37–59.
16. Article 3, section III of the Program of Linz, ibid., p. 34–59.
17. Gus Hall, *Which Way U.S.A.? The Communist View* (New York: New Century Publishers, 1964), p. 10.
18. Ernst von Streeruwitz, *Springflut ueber Oesterreich* (Vienna and Leipzig: Wilhelm Braumueller Verlag, 1937), p. 213.
19. Otto Bauer, "Faschismus, Demokratie, und Sozialismus" (speech before the annual meeting of the Austrian Socialist party, Vienna, November 1932. *Protokoll des sozialdemokratischen Parteitags* (Vienna: Verlag der wiener Volksbuchhandlung, 1932), p. 34.
20. Otto Bauer, "Diktatur und Demokratie," in *Bolschewismus oder Sozialdemokratie* (Vienna: Verlag der wiener Volksbuchhandlung, 1920).

21. Otto Bauer, editorial in *Arbeiterzeitung*, 25 March 1934. This paper, a fortnightly, was published in Brno, Czechoslovakia, by the exiled leadership of the Socialist party and smuggled across the border in tens of thousands of copies for distribution by the party's underground network.

22. The party organization of the Socialists, with its mass membership, was revived after 1945 and persists to the present, further evidence of the high degree of mobilization in Austria's traditional three political camps even in the remarkably harmonious political climate of the Second Republic today.

23. Most of the Socialist leaders had severed their ties with the Catholic church and were officially registered as *konfessionslos*, i.e., without religious affiliation.

24. Friedrich Funder, *Von Gestern ins Heute* (Vienna: Verlag Herold, 1952).

25. Irmgard Baernthaler, "Geschichte der vaterlaendischen Front" (Ph.D. diss., Oesterreichisches Institut fuer Zeitgeschichte, Vienna, 1964).

26. Anton Staudinger, "Bemuehungen Carl Vaugoins um Suprematie der Christlichsozialen Partei" (Ph.D. diss., Oesterreichisches Institut fuer Zeitgeschichte, Vienna, 1969), pp. 172–82.

27. Franz Langoth, *Kampf um Oesterreich* (Wels: Welsetmuehl Verlag, 1951).

28. The German-nationalist camp remains today a most fluid and volatile force in Austrian politics. Nazi tendencies still exist side by side with traces of genuine liberalism. This camp also continues in its tendency to rally to leaders who appear as strong personalities without regard for their political views. Thus the German-nationalists rallied behind the moderate statesman and faithful civil servant Dr. Johann Schober in November 1930 only to go over to Hitler within seventeen months. After the war the "third camp" reached its peak in the Second Republic when it rallied the voters to its presidential candidate, Dr. Breitner, a former president of the Austrian Red Cross with a reputation as a humanitarian. The Austrian German-nationalists are also flexible in their acceptance of leaders from across the border in what they consider "their country." While Germans had at one time to choose between Bismarck and Kaiser Wilhelm II, the Austrian German-nationalists admired both simultaneously, and they ignored Bismarck's injunction that they should be above all else loyal Austrians. Judging from the press of the "third camp" in present-day Austria, the German-nationalists looked with pride upon the advances made by the Federal Republic of Germany under the leadership of Adenauer, and it appears likely that the upsurge of the Austrian Socialist party at the polls in March 1970 was occasioned to some degree by the victory scored at the polls by the German Socialists in the preceding fall elections. The Austrian German-nationalist camp has, then, always been somewhat enigmatic and unpredictable. It is, however, highly significant for our study that as late as November 1930 most of this camp endorsed parliamentary democracy and constitutional government. The prevalence of political forces in favor of democratic politics at that time supports the thesis that the collapse of democracy in the First Republic was not inevitable.

29. Violent clashes were especially frequent where Socialist industrial towns were surrounded by anti-Socialist rural communities.

30. Otto Bauer, *Der Blutige 15 te Juli* (Vienna: Vorwaerts Verlag, 1927). This is the text of a speech before the Austrian Parliament on 26 July 1927.

31. Franz Winkler, *Die Diktatur in Oesterreich* (Zurich and Leipzig: Orell Fuessli Verlag, 1935). The author was vice-chancellor until September 1933 and one of the leading members of the Landbund.

32. Charles A. Gulick, *Austria from Habsburg to Hitler* (Berkeley and Los Angeles: University of California Press, 1948), pp. 894–95. Gulick is probably the foremost spokesman and advocate of Austromarxism.

33. Walter M. Kotschnig, *Unemployment in the Learned Professions* (London: Oxford University Press, 1937), p. 107.

34. Ibid., pp. 108–9.

35. Ibid., p. 109.

36. *Wirtschaftsstatistisches Jahrbuch, 1929/1930* (Vienna: Kammer fuer Arbeiter und Angestellte, 1930), p. 83.

37. Kurt Rothschild, *Austria's Economic Development between the Two Wars* (London: Frederick Muller, 1947), p. 52.

38. Ibid.

39. *Statistisches Handbuch fuer die Republik Oesterreich* (Vienna: Statistisches Zentralamt, 1933), p. 24.
40. Ernst Karl Winter, *Ignaz Seipel als Dialektisches Problem* (Vienna: Europa Verlag, 1966), p. 64.
41. See above, p. 87.
42. Otto Bauer, "Die wirtschaftliche und politische Lage Oesterreichs," *Protokoll des sozialdemokratischen Parteitags, 13, bis 15, November 1931* (Vienna: Verlag der wiener Volksbuchhandlung, 1931), p. 29.
43. Gulick, *Austria from Habsburg to Hitler*, pp. 939–41. Gulick's defense of the Austromarxist rejection of Seipel's coalition offer is of interest as the one and only such effort undertaken on the Socialist side after 1932. The Austrian Socialists are repressing memories of the policies of their party during that period and do not care to be reminded (see 47).
44. Not to mention the recent Socialist minority government that depended for its survival upon the support of the *Freiheitliche Partei Oesterreich*, the present party of Austria's German-nationalist camp.
45. Thus we find no reference to the Socialist rejection of Seipel's coalition offer in the rather detailed account of developments in the First Republic of Austria by the Austromarxist historian Julius Braunthal in his *The Tragedy of Austria* (London: Victor Gollancz, 1948).
46. Austrian historians sympathetic to the Socialists likewise delete all references to Seipel's coalition offer. For example, Ludwig Jedlicka, "Das Autoritaere System in Oesterreich," *Aus Politik und Zeitgeschichte, Beilage zur Wochenzeitung Das Parlament*, 25 July 1970, pp. 3–115, in a fairly thorough account of Seipel's sponsorship of the Fascist Heimwehr, makes not a single reference to Seipel's role in the work on the compromise of the constitutional reform of 1929. Nor is there a single reference to Seipel's coalition offer, which would mar the presentation of Seipel as having held unswervingly to a strictly authoritarian position.
47. Otto Bauer, *Die Illegale Partei* (Paris: La Lutte Socialiste, 1939), p. 107.
48. *Der Parteitag von 1926* (Vienna: Verlag der wiener Volksbuchhandlung, 1926), p. 128.
49. Most of the analysts of the German National Socialist vote have come to the conclusion that the increase in the Nazi vote from 0.8 million in May 1928 to 6.4 million in September 1930 came primarily from former nonvoters.
50. Walter B. Simon, "Motivations of a Totalitarian Mass Vote," *British Journal of Sociology* 10, no. 4 (December 1959): 338–45. The actual election data have been taken from Vienna's *Neue Freie Presse* the day after the elections. Only the data of the Innsbruck elections, not recorded in the *Neue Freie Presse*, are taken from the Munich *Voelkischer Beobachter*, 24 April 1933.
51. Simon, "Motivations." p. 342.
52. *Salzburger Volksblatt*, 25 April 1932.
53. Otto Bauer, "Der 24 te April," *Der Kampf* 25 (1932): 192. *Der Kampf* was the monthly organ of the Austrian Socialist party.
54. Ibid.
55. The concept of a "power vacuum" was first applied to the collapse of democratic institutions in Germany where democratic politics were stymied when legislative bodies became paralyzed by avowedly antidemocratic majorities that would not and could not work together. See Karl Dietrich Bracher, *Die Auflösung der Weimarer Republik: Eine Studie zum Problem des Machtzerfalls in der Demokratie* (Stuttgart and Dusseldorf: Ring Verlag, 1957).
56. Winkler, *Die Diktatur*.
57. Otto Bauer, *Der Aufstand der Oesterreichischen Arbeiter* (Prague: Verlag der deutschen sozialdemokratischen Arbeiterpartei in der Tschechoslowakischen Republik, 1934), p. 13.
58. "Comrades, we have to fight with weapons of the mind and spirit since soon we will not have any others."
59. For a scholarly differentiation between "authoritarian" and "totalitarian" regimes, see Juan J. Linz, "An Authoritarian Regime: Spain," in *Mass Politics: Studies in Political Sociology*, ed. Erik Allardt and Stein Rokkan (New York: Free Press, 1970), pp. 251–83, 374–81.
60. For details on the Socialist underground organization, see Bauer, *Die Illegale Partei*, and Joseph Buttinger, *The Twilight of Socialism: A History of the Revolutionary Socialists of Austria*, trans. E. B. Ashton (New York: F. A. Praeger, 1953).

4.

The Lapua Movement: The Threat of Rightist Takeover in Finland, 1930-32

Risto Alapuro and Erik Allardt

Between the two world wars the right-wing or Lapua movement, which was opposed to the Finnish parliamentary political system, was relatively strong compared to similar movements elsewhere. It has often been stressed that a breakdown in the existing Finnish political system was a definite possibility in the years 1930–32.[1] Most of the features that are shown in this volume to be related to developments leading to a takeover apply to the Finnish case, i.e., the development of the Lapua movement. The situation in Finland was characterized by an emergent disloyal opposition, problems of public order, ambivalence on the part of neutral powers, and a narrowing of the political arena to a small number of participants across party lines or outside the parties, resulting in loss of power, power vacuums, and crises of resolution.

There was a partial breakdown of the existing parliamentary political system in that all public activities by the Communists were prohibited. The Communist party had been banned, to be sure, after the civil war in 1918, but up until the 1930s groups closely attached to the party had been able to participate in both party politics and the labor union movement. However, no takeover of the type that occurred in Germany, Italy, and several Eastern European countries took place in Finland. After the critical years of the early 1930s, the disloyal opposition of the Right fell into a peripheral position when a president was elected from the Agrarian Union and a coalition of the Agrarians and the Social Democrats in Finland's cabinet began.

The Lapua movement was never a political party, although it was close to and partly overlapped certain established parties. Also, the movement did not develop a distinct ideological profile, as did the Fascist-type parties in a number of countries at that time. These features seem in some respects to have enhanced and in others diminished the probability of rightist takeover in the Lapua years.

A third rather unusual feature in the Finnish case was the role of the Social Democrats. Their line was clearly and consistently revisionist and, for example, went along with the economic policy followed during the depression. This was probably very important in limiting polarization in the society and consequently decreasing the threat of a takeover.

In going back further, one may also emphasize the comparatively strong institutionalization of the existing political system and the impact of the civil war in 1918. The latter, in contributing to the unified bourgeois hegemony in interwar Finland, considerably affected the fact that in Finland the Fascist-type phenomena of 1930–32 were largely without an independent profile and that the interests of the crucial export industry came to be well represented within the existing political system during the depression.

The Civil War in 1918 and Structural Cleavages in Finnish Society

The best single point of departure for understanding the right-wing movement of the 1920s and 1930s in Finland, as in Germany and Hungary, is to be found in the structures and patterns emanating from World War I. In all these countries the bourgeoisie in the period between the world wars could remember a revolutionary attempt to take power, accompanied by a civil war. However, in Germany and Finland, unlike Hungary, the struggle did not result in a rightist dictatorship nor, for that matter, in a triumph for the revolution. As a consequence, there were dissatisfied groups within the bourgeoisies of these countries in the interwar years. In Finland, the crisis of the political system in 1929–32 was related in many ways to the division crystallized in 1918, although by no means predetermined by it. Of importance were both the structural cleavages due to the war in 1918 and developments preceding it, and the interplay of economic and political events in the critical years of the twenties and thirties.

The civil war in 1918 can be seen as a climax of a rapid mobilization of the working class and the rural proletariat and of a sudden change in the political system. Finland's transition from an estate-based system to universal suffrage in 1906 was unique in its suddenness and depth.[2] In the first general elections the Social Democrats gained 80 of the 200 parliamentary seats. In 1916 they gained the majority in Parliament with 103 mandates, and in 1918 the party led an attempt at revolution, suppressed only with difficulty by the bourgeoisie and the peasantry.

These developments were closely tied to developments in the Russian empire, in which Finland was a grand duchy until the end of 1917. The timing and thoroughness of transition to universal suffrage were largely due to the Russian general strike and attempt at revolution in 1905, and the outbreak of the civil war in 1918 was closely connected with the October Revolution of the previous year. The intertwining of radicalization within the Finnish social system and developments in Russia is of primary importance to understanding the structural conditions favorable to the Lapua movement.

The Bourgeoisie and Bourgeois Parties

Finnish linguistic nationalism, the so-called Finnocism, arose in the nineteenth century and became especially influential in university circles, in the church, and among the wealthy peasantry, while it was inimical to the Swedish-speaking upper class. By the end of the century the nationalist culture had been established as an important integrative value system in the country. This development was facilitated by the partial settlement of the cultural conflict within the upper classes due to the steady advancement of the Finnish among them, and by the easing of economic conflicts between the largely Swedish-speaking industrialist and merchant class and the Finnish-speaking wealthy peasantry. Also of immediate importance to the unity of the different upper-class groups were indications of the beginning of the all-Russian integrative efforts in the 1890s.

All these developments contributed to a culture with strong nationalist overtones, overtones approved largely in the different segments of the bourgeoisie and the peasantry. It may be noted that besides the Finnish nationalism there had also been a distinctly Swedish linguistic nationalist movement in Finland at the end of the nineteenth century.

These tendencies were strengthened, not surprisingly, by the enormous success of the Social Democrats after the introduction of universal suffrage in 1906. In the first general elections ever held in Finland, the Social Democrats gained a proportion of mandates equaled by no other European country at that time.[3] In the ten years from 1908 to 1918 the cultural controversies between Finnish-speaking and Swedish-speaking upper-class groups had clearly declined in importance, and nationalist cultural traits common to different bourgeois groups increased in importance. Significantly, the status of the church rose to a great extent.[4] In the years preceding the attempt at revolution there was considerable unity between elite groups, as has often been pointed out.[5]

This is somewhat different from the situation that usually precedes a revolution. No serious cleavages tore the elite, and in this sense Finnish society was not ripe for revolution.[6] But there were other significant factors. As is well known, the ultimate factor that precipitates a revolution is often the loss of unified control over the instruments of violence, particularly the army.[7] Due to Finland's position as part of the Russian empire, the dominant groups lacked an organized military force altogether; there was no army within Finnish society.[8] This was presumably an essential condition for the outbreak of the civil war. The Russian Revolution was not only an immediately precipitating factor. It also meant a sudden disappearance of the forces upholding authority in Finland. When the armed forces in Russia got out of the hands of the ruling groups, the consequences were apparent in Finland, which was totally dependent on Russia for the maintenance of its political and economic system.

The revolution in Finland was suppressed with great difficulty and with substantial support from German troops. It was also conceived differently by different groups in the population. On the Red side the war clearly was perceived as a class war, but among the Whites it was seen as a liberation war against Russian influence. The superimposition of national feelings on class conflict strengthened antagonisms and added to the cruelty of the revolution. Extremely bloody repression was practiced by the victorious Whites: 8,400 people were executed and about 10,000 people died of disease and starvation in prison camps.[9]

It can be argued that due to the civil war and developments preceding it, the bourgeoisie in Finland was more united after the war than is usually the case in postrevolutionary situations. The civil war was conceived as a national struggle by the victorious Whites, and throughout the 1920s and 1930s it was officially called the Liberation War. One telling feature of the situation after the civil war was the nature of the civil guard; unlike many armed unofficial groups elsewhere, it was a force supported by all bourgeois groups.[10] In contrast to the situation in Germany and Austria, all non-Socialist parties in Finland backed this one armed organization, which was also to become loosely tied with the state machinery. Its significance can be seen in the fact that in the early 1920s there were 100,000 armed men in the civil guard while the corresponding number in the army was between 20,000 and 25,000.[11] Another feature was the comparatively overwhelming domination of one nationalist organization, the Academic Karelia Society, among the students and the young educated class.[12]

This background presumably accounts for the fact that in Finland between the two world wars, a strong but very united nationalistic political culture existed—a more unified bourgeois hegemony than is found in most countries with a history of insurrections.

This cultural unity had consequences important for the development of the Lapua movement. Juan J. Linz states in his introductory essay that the legitimacy question is often tied more to symbolic problems than to conflicts of interest. In Finland's case one can assume that there were large segments of the bourgeoisie who would react similarly and sensitively to all threats against some symbolic national values. Second, it seems quite clear that symbolic conflicts between non-Socialist groups were extremely unlikely. Third, it can be assumed that in the event of a threat from the extreme Right, the borderline between a disloyal opposition and other bourgeois groups would be very vague—a trait that, according to Linz, is apt to increase the possibilities of success for the disloyal opposition.

The above statement hints at a considerable rightist potential in the bourgeoisie in the interwar decades. On the other hand, underscoring the cultural unity of different bourgeois groups is just another way of indicating the absence of a strong, clearly discernible reactionary group in the bourgeoisie. Certainly one central background factor contributing to this absence was the small size and relative weakness of the Finnish elite in the nineteenth century and prior to the civil war. Finland had no dominant landowning upper class in the first phase of its modernization, as did Germany and the Eastern European countries. In Finland the rising nationalistic movement in the nineteenth century had been associated with a quest for support from the wealthy peasantry. Presumably the flexibility of the upper classes after World War I was greater in Finland than in Germany and the Eastern European countries, where the oligarchic social structures existed until the recent past.

There are at least three developments generally related to this background and contributing to the viability of the parliamentary political system established after the civil war. One of them is the fact that the competitive political system had taken root long before the civil war; there was a clear institutional continuity. The same political parties and their corresponding social groups that had been important in the formative years 1906–17, when Finland was a grand duchy in the Russian empire, continued to be crucial after World War I.[13] The biggest of the bourgeois parties was the Coalition party, also called the Conservative party in the following pages. It was backed by the majority of the clergy and by many high-ranking civil servants. The commercial and industrial groups, especially the timber and paper concerns (the main export industry), openly supported it. Another clearly bourgeois postwar party was the Swedish People's party, representing not only the Swedish-speaking bourgeoisie but also other Swedish-speaking groups in the country. Unlike the small, liberal Progress party, these parties tried in 1918 to make Finland into a monarchy, an effort that failed only because of the German defeat in the war.

This initial situation for a parliamentary political system was quite different from the one that prevailed in the Eastern European countries. In Rumania and Poland the new constitutional forms remained in clear conflict with the oligarchic structure of society, and the old social relationships prevailed despite the new constitutions.

The other two important factors contributing to the viability of the political system concern the character of the Left and of the Agrarian Union.

The Working Class and the Social Democrats and Communists

The civil war, and the political mobilization that had developed rapidly and easily prior to it, had a great impact on the position and structure of the Left in

Finland in the 1920s and 1930s. The rapid electoral advance of the Social Democrats after the fundamental change in the political system in 1906 seems to have given some of their leaders a vested interest in the newly established political system. To be sure, explicitly revisionist ideas were not dominant in the party, but they did have a considerable number of supporters.[14] Indicative of the vagueness of ideological controversies within the Social Democratic party is the fact that the leadership had no defined or concrete revolutionary program. Political success seems to have fed the idea that revolution is predetermined, something that would come about through the necessity of nature.[15] In addition, there were nationalist elements in the party, which existed largely due to the strengthening of the all-Russian integrative efforts before and during the world war.[16] This nationalism reduced the gap between the bourgeoisie and a segment of the Social Democrats.

This was the internal situation in the Social Democratic party before the collapse of the Russian empire and before the dominant groups in Finland had lost the opportunity to invoke the armed forces. This sudden loss of the forces maintaining authority presented the revolutionary forces with an opportunity of the utmost importance. The revolutionary forces were undeveloped and weak and would hardly have provided a sufficient base for a serious attempt at revolution. Even revolutionary leaders admitted that the revolution was something of a surprise to the revolutionaries.[17] The bulk of the party leadership was drawn into rather than making the revolution. The revolutionary course was largely due to irresistible pressure from the masses, who were without food; and with the lack of armed forces to control the situation, conditions became rather chaotic in 1917.[18] Moreover, some active politicians in the party, among them several members of Parliament, dissociated themselves from the revolution and remained passive.[19]

The leaders of the defeated revolution founded the Communist party of Finland in Petrograd in 1918, and the revisionists who had kept at a distance from the revolutionary attempt carried on the activities of the Social Democratic party, participating in the general elections in 1919. So, in Finland as elsewhere, the Social Democratic party was divided after the Russian Revolution, but in Finland the gap was markedly increased both by the unpreparedness of party for revolution, which resulted in a deep cleavage within the party, and subsequently by the proximity of revolutionary Russia. The division between the Social Democrats and the Communists was to be reinforced by the division at the national level between Finland and Soviet Union.

Accordingly it seems justifiable to say that Finnish society was not ripe for a revolution when the favorable moment came. The aftermath of the revolutionary attempt was increased cultural unity among the bourgeois groups and a large and deep gap within the ranks of the Social Democrats. Presumably, this had a lasting impact on the nature of Social Democracy in Finland and its relations with Communists, not the least of it being in the critical years of the early 1930s.

The Peasants and the Agrarian Union

In addition to the bourgeoisie and the largely working-class Left, one must consider the peasants when analyzing the structural preconditions of the success and limits to success of the right-wing movement in the interwar period. The civil war and its preceding developments were also significant to the peasants, who were the rank and file of the White army. Going beyond its role in the critical juncture of 1918, the structure of the peasantry and the changes in its position seem to be of significance in its stand in the Lapua years. In Finland the peasants represented a stratum which had gained enormously from the democratization of the political system in 1906, and they developed into a mighty political force. In the first Parliament, elected in 1907, there were nine peasantist representatives out of two hundred; in 1916 the peasant party, the Agrarian Union, had nineteen seats; and in the first general elections after the civil war it gained forty-two mandates. It advanced further in the 1920s, being then the second largest or largest party represented in the Parliament. Thus, the position of the peasants in the Finnish parliamentary system clearly differed from the position of the peasants in the Eastern European countries.[20]

These differences probably reflect differences in the pattern of modernization and its structural consequences. Barrington Moore has argued that fascism was especially strong in those countries in which capitalism had developed in cooperation with the dominant landed upper class. In these countries—Poland, Hungary, and Rumania, for instance—there was a strong homogeneous elite. Therefore, the capitalist transformation could be brought into effect while maintaining intact the preexisting peasant society. In these labor-repressive systems, as Moore calls them, agriculture was adjusted to the market economy by preserving the traditional peasant society but by squeezing more surplus out of it. In these countries the peasants were still heavily tied to the traditional agrarian social structure during the 1920s and 1930s. The crisis of the market economy during the Great Depression hit them very hard and made them very susceptible to Fascist appeals. In these countries, unlike Finland, there was during the 1920s a relatively unstructured and unmobilized base that contributed to the weakness of the political center.[21]

Finland did not have a strong landed aristocracy in the initial stages of industrialization. The commercialization of agriculture did not occur through labor-repressive methods but essentially came about through reliance on the labor market. This, without doubt, contributed to the fact that in Finland the peasant stratum became a part of and a strong adherent of the parliamentary system.[22]

The Situation in the 1920s

It has been argued above that a considerable part of the cultural unity of the non-Socialist groups and the split within the Left were both ultimately connected with the international position of Finland. This connection became clearer still in the 1920s. The proximity of the Soviet Union preserved the close connection between internal and foreign policy questions in post–civil war Finland. For example, in justifying the civil guard, foreign policy and internal arguments were often given side by side.[23]

Within the Left this state of affairs probably deepened the gap between Social Democrats and Communists. In the early 1920s the left-wing Socialists and Communists tried to act within the Social Democratic party, but without success. Väinö Tanner was the leading figure in the attack on the left-wing representatives of the party. Under his leadership the party became in the 1920s an essentially reformist parliamentary party, consistently seeking cooperation with the centrist parties and displaying nationalist overtones. This can be seen especially in the sharp distinction drawn between "Russian" and "Western" traditions of the working-class movement.[24] The contrast was without doubt strengthened by the foundation of the autonomous Soviet Karelia on the Russian side of the Finnish border, headed by many central figures of the defeated revolution in Finland.

The left-wing Socialists formed a new party, which was connected with the Finnish Communist party in the Soviet Union. This party was able, with difficulty, to carry on its political activities in the 1920s and it had between eighteen and twenty-seven deputies in the Parliament while the Social Democrats at the same time gained between fifty-three and sixty parliamentary mandates. Left-wing Socialist representatives had central positions in the trade union movement.[25]

In discussing the developments in the non-Socialist groups, the strength of the civil guard has already been mentioned. Another organization, whose strength indicates the firm position of the bourgeois groups in the society, was the employer-financed strike-breaking organization, Vientirauha (Export Peace). It helped employers to win many labor conflicts, including the great dock strike that lasted from the summer of 1928 to the spring of 1929. The weak trade union movement was at its strongest in the late 1920s, due to the rapid economic growth of Finland in this decade. In explaining the small number of antiparliamentarian demonstrations among the bourgeois circles in the 1920s attention has sometimes been given to this economic growth.[26] This development, based mainly on the export of the products of the paper and timber industry forming 86 per cent of the worth of the exported goods in 1920–29, was of course extremely sensitive to changes in the international market, as would be seen at the end of the decade.

The Lapua Movement, 1929–32: Developments in the Political Arena

The Lapua movement in Finland from 1929 to 1932 was a disloyal opposition, according to the definition presented in Juan J. Linz's introductory essay. Its immediate aim was the destruction of "communism"—taken in a very diffuse sense—and the movement did not care about the rules of the political system in achieving its goals. Generally, the movement held the whole political system based on political parties in contempt, attacked it without scruples, and made demands contrary to the very essence of the party system.[27] Furthermore, on some occasions in those years a Fascist-type seizure of power by the movement and its supporters was not at all out of question. The most serious point appears to have been reached in the summer of 1930. By that time the Lapua movement had gone a long way toward provoking the disintegration of the political system, and the situation displayed many of the features typical of the period preceding the final takeover described by Linz.

The Rise of the Movement

The origin of the Lapua movement is usually dated from the end of 1929, when anti-Communist riots broke out, with farmers as the foremost participants. One cause of the riots was the depression, which had begun to hit the Finnish farmers in 1928. Thus, in Finland as elsewhere, the unsolved problems created by the depression formed a basis for the rise of the agrarian-based right-wing movement.

The strongest immediate support was given by the Coalition party. It is not surprising that within another political party, namely, the Agrarian Union, there also was immediate and substantial support for the movement. When the movement appointed its leaders in March 1930, among those elected was, in addition to two banking directors and two well-known industrialists, the chief editor of the leading Agrarian newspaper. The most visible leader of the movement, Vihtori Kosola, was a member of the Agrarian Union. Consequently, the rise of the Lapua movement might perhaps be characterized roughly by saying that there had been a certain potential for extremism in the Right after the civil war, but the crisis did not explode until there was also a popular movement and both these elements were linked together.

From the summer of 1929 to the summer of 1930 Finland had a minority government composed of the Agrarian Union and the liberal Progress party. From the end of 1929 on it constantly gave in to the demands made by the Lapua movement. The freedom to form associations was denied to Communists by law, and the government stopped all press activity among the Communists after riots and pressures. It summoned the Parliament to meet in the summer of 1930 in order to enact further laws aimed at suppressing Communist activity in correspondence with demands from the Lapua movement and in order to give exceptional powers to the president in cases of civil emergency.[28]

The Summer of 1930 and the Peasants' March

The influence of the Lapua movement reached its peak in the summer of 1930. During that summer and autumn three people were killed, and over a thousand members of local government bodies, Social Democratic party branches, public agencies, trade unions, staffs of newspapers, candidates and former members of Parliament, including the deputy speaker, and even the first president, K. J. Ståhlberg, were the victims of abduction.[29]

The moderate forces more or less withdrew from political responsibility. The sympathies of the president—traditionally a neutral power above the parties—toward the extraparliamentary forces contributed to this withdrawal. The political arena shrank to a very small group of people, and the crucial decisions were made in small circles of politicians and representatives of the Lapua movement. Such traits are a sign of the disintegration of the political system.

The situation developed during the summer of 1930 in such a way—under pressure of the continuing violence and disturbances of the Lapua movement—that the movement succeeded in getting its favorite candidate appointed to the position of prime minister. He was P. E. Svinhufvud, a strong conservative, who together with Mannerheim symbolized White Finland and the victorious Liberation War. It is obvious that in the beginning Svinhufvud was regarded within the Lapua movement as one of its own men. He had been chief executive—an office that preceded the office of the president—after the declaration of independence in 1917, and he had been a monarchist in 1918. As a symbol and figurehead of victorious White Finland he had enormous prestige. Svinhufvud offered two seats in the cabinet to the movement, but apparently because of internal conflicts it was not able to accept this offer. His cabinet arranged for the arrest of all Communist deputies, and with strong pressure from Svinhufvud and the Lapua movement all the anti-Communist laws proposed earlier were forced through. This was effected by insuring a sufficiently large non-Socialist majority in the Parliament through new elections, held under heavy pressure from the Lapua movement, while the government hindered Communists and related groups from running for office.[30]

Some conclusions on the strength of the Lapua movement during the election campaign can be drawn from the election results in table 1. The increase in the total vote was considerable but benefited essentially the non-Socialist parties, particularly the Conservatives. The vote gained by the Social Democrats in 1930 was no larger than the total vote for the Left in the previous year, and it resulted in just seven additional mandates. This change had no impact on the course followed by the Social Democrats. To be sure, they firmly opposed the demands of the Lapua movement, but basically their efforts during the years 1929–32 were concentrated on the defense of the existing political system, an approach markedly different from the Communists' line.[31] It was not until the next general elections in 1933, when the total vote again dropped somewhat, that they were able to increase considerably the number of Social Democratic mandates.

In the summer and fall of 1930 the disloyal opposition in the form of the Lapua movement had gone far toward achieving a disintegration of the political system. The culmination of its efforts was probably reached in the summer of 1930 when twelve thousand members of the Lapua movement, mainly farmers, marched on the capital, apparently inspired by the famous march of the Fascists to Rome in 1922. The Peasants' March, as it was called, was carried out under the auspices of the civil guard, and Mannerheim, Svinhuf-vud, and the Agrarian president, Relander, were present at the main demonstration, listening to the demands of the movement.

Table 1. Results of the Finnish General Elections of 1929, 1930, and 1933

Parties	Distribution of Mandates and Popular Vote (in thousands)					
	1929		1930		1933	
	Mandates	Votes	Mandates	Votes	Mandates	Votes
National Coalition party	28	138	42	204	18	188a
Patriotic People's movement	—	—	—	—	14	
Swedish People's party	23	109	21	123	21	115
National Progress party	7	53	11	66	11	82
Agrarian Union	60	249	59	308	53	250
Social Democratic party	59	260	66	386	78	414
Socialist Workers' party b	23	128	—	12	—	—
Others	—	14	1	32	5	59
Total	200	951	200	1,131	200	1,108
National turnout		55.6%		66.9%		62.2%

SOURCE: Official election statistics.

[a]The semi-Fascist Patriotic People's Movement and the National Coalition party formed party alliances in almost all constituencies.
[b]Communists and left-wing Socialists.

There is some indication that support for the Lapua movement among the Conservatives began to decline after the prohibition of all activities of the Communists and related groups in the fall of 1930. The Lapua movement had raised Svinhufvud to prime minister in 1930 as their own man. But friction between him and the movement arose almost immediately after he assumed office. More distinct differences emerged in 1931 when Svinhufvud was elected president as the candidate of the Conservative party. The Lapua movement, to be sure, supported him strongly during the electoral campaign, and it is also evident that the civil guard exercised pressure on the members of the electoral college, and especially on the Agrarian electors, before the final vote.[32] But a consensus was forming among a group of Conservatives as to who constituted the disloyal opposition, and this divergence in the Coalition party surfaced in the so-called Mäntsälä revolt in 1932. In the general elections in 1933 the divergence became institutionalized with the founding of a new, semi-Fascist party (see table 1).

The Mäntsälä Revolt

The leadership of the Lapua movement gave its support to a revolt in Mäntsälä, a community in the vicinity of the capital, and attempted to mobilize large groups from the civil guard behind its demands.[33] Among these demands was a call for the resignation of the government and the establishment of a new, "unpolitical," "patriotic" government. The aim was apparently to make Mannerheim a leader of the state and to make the conservative industrialist, ex-general, and member of the leadership of the Lapua movement, Rudolf Walden, the prime minister. Many important leaders of the Conservative party, a large part of the leadership in the civil guard, including its commander, and many officers in the armed forces rallied behind these demands.

The Lapua movement failed, however, and a decisive factor in its defeat was undoubtedly the stand of both Svinhufvud and the commander in chief of the armed forces against the demands of the Lapua movement. At the decisive moment the Lapua movement could not mobilize the masses of the civil guard, in which rural elements constituted a clear majority of the rank and file. Also, the commercial and industrial elite had apparently withdrawn much of its support for the movement.[34]

Besides the disengagement of some important conservative factions from the Lapua movement after the anti-Communist laws had been forced through, the attitudes of the other bourgeois parties underwent marked changes as well. This was obviously of utmost importance during the Mäntsälä revolt but it was also significant earlier in 1930–32. As early as late 1930, the so-called lawfulness front had begun to emerge, numbering the Social Democrats, the majority of the Agrarian Union, the Progress party, and the majority of the Swedish People's party as its foremost supporters. This development certainly

facilitated Svinhufvud's independent policy toward the Lapua movement
from late 1930 on.

Political Parties and the Lapua Movement

The Non-Socialist Parties

One outstanding feature of the Lapua movement has emerged very clearly
in the above discussion. Unlike the rightist/Fascist disloyal oppositions in
most European countries betwen the two world wars, the Lapua movement
was not a political party. It might be characterized as a pressure group or
perhaps more appropriately as a faction overlapping certain parties, notably
the Conservative party and, to a lesser extent, the Agrarian Union. There was
also a minority group close to the movement in the Swedish People's party.
Differences in attitudes, however, began to crystallize in the course of the
movement; as stated above, acceptance and even enthusiasm was general,
although it was not the only reaction, in all bourgeois parties in the initial
stage of the Lapua movement.

The fact that the movement encountered positive response so rapidly in the
form of mass meetings all over the country at its inception has led some to
conclude, not without justification, that the initial riots ripened similar demands already nurtured among the Conservatives.[35] The movement encompassed well-known Conservatives, even though the visible leadership of the
movement displayed a clear rural image. Most of the leaders appointed in
March 1930 were members of the Coalition party and Agrarian Union. It is
also noteworthy from a comparative point of view that the Lapua movement
never had an anticapitalist ideology, not even of the type of the Fascist
movement in Italy. The basic outcome of the Lapua movement was a prohibition of all activities by Communists, along with the emasculation of the trade
union movement. The least one can say beyond reference to an important
symbolic change in the political system is that the outcome greatly benefited
certain rightist groups, especially in the business sector.[36] Furthermore, the
weakness and irresoluteness of the official peasantist leadership of the movement can be seen as one more indication of the lack of a distinctive ideological
profile in the Lapua movement.

Presumably, the close connection between the movement and the different
political parties, especially in the initial stages, is indicative of the relatively
strong cultural unity among the non-Socialist groups in Finland. On the other
hand, it has also been argued above that symbolic victories were important for
the Finnish right-wing movement. It seems that both Svinhufvud's appointment as prime minister and the proscription of Communists from any public
activity had just such a strong symbolic significance. Finally, the election of

Svinhufvud as president highlighted a development in which the political system acquired a more conservative flavor but during which the actual changes in the political system were nevertheless limited. Not until these features had become evident did the Lapua movement acquire a clearer fascistic tone.[37] In other words, not until the basic climate of the political system had become clearly conservative did boundaries within the political Right begin to crystallize. At this point the differences between conservatism and fascism began gradually to emerge.

While the Conservatives continued to collaborate with the Lapua movement after 1930, the Agrarian Union dissociated itself from it in the years 1930–31. Reference was made earlier to the strong and stable position of the farmers in the Finnish political system as compared with the situation of their counterparts in Eastern European countries, which was largely due to a different kind of adjustment to capitalism. In Finland the farmers were fully mobilized long before the thirties and had an institutionalized channel for expressing grievances caused by the depression and reacting to them. In some Eastern European countries, however, the peasants, strongly tied to the structures of traditional agrarian society until recently, were mobilized by the depression in a way benefiting distinctly fascistic parties.[38]

At the level of immediate political developments, the Finnish farmers were hit by the initial stages of the depression at least as badly and probably worse than other social groups. Information on the decline in the level of income of different social groups and on profit rates of agriculture makes understandable the agrarian enthusiasm in 1929–30 for anti-Communist outbursts with strong populist overtones.[39] On the other hand, the final establishment of Agrarian opposition to the Lapua movement and the simultaneous dissociation from collaboration with the Conservatives was apparently also a part of the reaction to the impact of the depression, which sharpened the conflict between agricultural and commercial-industrial interests. It has been pointed out that although the Lapua movement contributed substantial support for depression-hit agricultural production, it did not do so by relieving the indebtedness of farmers. The number of compulsory auctions of farms increased until 1933. This problem apparently had an effect on the course chosen by the Agrarians from 1931 on. It is not without importance, for instance, that in this year the first unorganized and transitory outbursts, the so-called "Depression movements," grew up. Their immediate cause was the problem of indebtedness, and they remained outside the Lapua movement.[40]

The Social Democrats

The cultural unity of non-Socialist groups as a limitation on the success of the Lapua movement has been emphasized above, but it certainly was not independent of the role taken by the Social Democrats. The latter concentrated lar contact with President Relander in 1930, and the party consistently avoided clashes with the movement on the most delicate occasions.[41] Perhaps more important still, the Social Democrats went along with an economic policy that was largely classically liberal in its orientation and was very painful to the working class.[42]

Their role was different in interesting ways from the role of Social Democrats in Spain and Austria in the critical years of the 1930s. In these countries the Socialists obviously accelerated or essentially contributed to the breakdown process by going further to the left in the period preceding the final takeover (see Linz's and Simon's chapters). Unlike Finland, in these countries the boundary between Communists and Social Democrats was unclear. The weakness of the Communist parties allowed the Marxists to stay within the Socialist parties and to consider the Communists as a minor ally rather than as a powerful and dangerous competitor. In Finland this possibility was excluded from the outset. There was an extremely wide gap between two working-class parties after the civil war, while the Communists were considered an enduring threat. As a matter of fact, the orientation of the Social Democrats toward the political center was strengthened considerably in the Lapua years.[43]

The Causes of Government Stability

The conditions and developments contributing to or hampering the success of the Lapua movement have been discussed above mainly at two levels. On the one hand, structural conditions deriving from the civil war and earlier developments have been considered. Undoubtedly they were significant in producing the idiosyncratic relationship between the movement and the political parties, and also, in part, the attitude of the Social Democrats. On the other hand, immediate developments in 1929–32 in the political and, to some extent, the economic arena have also been discussed. These different factors by no means predetermined the limits for the success of the Lapua movement and are certainly not exhaustive in explaining it. There was a real possibility of a rightist takeover at several moments during these critical years. But it remains important to note that certain features typical of the Finnish case, discussed here, decreased the probability of a takeover even in the situations most favorable for the movement.

In the foregoing discussion reference has been made to those dangers that, according to Juan J. Linz, tend to emerge when the boundaries between the conservative groups and the disloyal opposition become diffuse—when there is no consensus on how the disloyal opposition should be defined, when the conservatives begin to cooperate with the disloyal opposition, and when, finally, the disloyal opposition is given an opportunity to share legitimate power. For instance, the Nazi rise to power had all these traits: the upper-class conservative groups wanted to exploit Hitler, but the servant became the master when the opportunity came.

In Finland there were similar features. In the initial phases of the Lapua movement, which led to the prohibition of Communist activities and to Svinhufvud's rise to the position of foremost political personality, the movement had wide bourgeois support. But when the movement attacked a system in which the Communists were no longer a part and in which Svinhufvud was the main symbolic figure, it got support only from some of the Conservatives and a portion of the civil guard. Consequently, it failed to reach its objectives. It seems as if the comparatively strong ideological consensus in the Finnish bourgeoisie and the importance of symbolic victories had at first enhanced the possibilities of a takeover, but after certain processes had taken place, they decreased these same possibilities.

While in Germany the cooperation between the Conservatives and the Nazis led to Hitler's rise to power, in Finland the right-wing movement played out its role and could therefore be dispersed. Put in another way, the semiloyal groups in the Coalition party and the Agrarian Union were not coopted by the disloyal opposition but, instead, first coopted and then neutralized the latter.

In this characterization it is implicitly asserted that the goals of the semiloyal groups had basically been achieved and that, given the prohibition of Communists' activities and the attitude of the Social Democrats, i.e., given the lack of a defensive revolutionary mobilization of the working class, there was no need to count on the activated violence of the Lapua movement; the bourgeoisie was strong enough without its collaboration.

This assertion can also be put forward in economic terms. The fact that the commercialization of agriculture did not occur through labor-repressive methods but essentially through reliance on labor market already suggests (if we follow Barrington Moore) that Finland never developed problems as acute as those of Germany or many Eastern European countries, pushing their industrial and commercial groups to support a fascistic solution. At a more immediate level, we can start with the point made in the beginning of this chapter: in Finland the struggle in the aftermath of World War I eventuated in neither a victory for revolution nor a rightist dictatorship. Discussions of Fascist phenomena in interwar Europe often point out that in many countries the democratized political system from the 1920s on left the capitalists in control of the economy but at the same time afforded the working class a share in political power and the freedom to organize and agitate for the achievement of its own ends. Consequently, fascism, according to this interpretation, once it had proved its right to be taken seriously, came to be looked upon as a potentially valuable ally against both the workers within the country and the capitalists of foreign countries.[44]

It has already been mentioned that before the rise of the Lapua movement the trade union movement was clearly disintegrating. But it remained for the Lapua movement to strengthen and finally confirm this development. The wages of workers decreased in Finland during the depression more, for example, than in Scandinavia, and this was basically due to the weakness of the Finnish trade unions. In the mid-1930s wages generally were less than half the corresponding wages in Sweden or England.[45] On the other hand, it has been pointed out that the extremely rapid industrial growth in Finland between the world wars was largely due to this low level of wages, which allowed the export industry to maintain its ability to compete in the international market.[46]

Consequently, it is not inappropriate to say that the Lapua movement was an ally for the capitalists both against the workers in Finland and against the capitalists in the foreign countries. But it seems that the interests of the export industry in particular came to be very well accounted for in the framework of the existing political system. Therefore, the conflicts within the economy and the accompanying turmoil in the labor market and in the whole of society could never polarize the population in Finland as they did in Germany, where they contributed to the urgency of the search for an agent to restore order.

A Note on Legitimacy, Efficiency, and Effectiveness in the Finnish Case

The use of the concepts of legitimacy, efficiency, and effectiveness usually involves difficult conceptual problems. When these concepts are applied to Finland between the two world wars this difficulty seems to be particularly salient, since the basic issue, the perception of a Communist threat and its elimination, relates to the very nature of the democratic process.

As regards legitimacy it ought to be remembered that in the civil war of 1918 Finland had been sharply divided. For some groups, notably those who supported the Communists, the Finnish political system was not regarded as legitimate during the period between the two world wars. The Communists have not been discussed here because in a historical perspective they seem to have been too weak to threaten the system effectively. For political parties and groups with political significance, notably the bourgeoisie and the rural population, it seems reasonable to say that the prevailing political system maintained an image of legitimacy in spite of the threats from the right-wing Lapua movement.

Many of the incidents and cases described above testify to the existence of a clear conception of the system as legitimate. One could refer to the fact that the Lapua movement did not become clearly Fascist until a distinct boundary between it and the Conservatives had arisen. A belief in the legitimacy of the system seems to have existed, and this was presumably one of the conditions for avoidance of a fascistic dictatorship. On the other hand, there existed a definite threat to the system, a threat that was not averted until the government came to be considered efficient and effective. Evidently, legitimacy alone provides a rather tenuous basis for stability if efficiency and effectiveness are not guaranteed.

The issues related to efficiency and effectiveness, however, are also problematical in the Finnish case. The efficiency of the government was measured in terms of how well it could eliminate the perceived Communist threat. The problem lies in the fact that efficiency here is defined in terms of matters related to the democratic process itself instead of in terms of some independent goals such as standard of living, food distribution, housing, etc. In this chapter it has been shown that the government in the final phase was considered both efficient and effective in hindering Communist activities. In fact, by its own standards it clipped the wings of the Lapua movement. In succeeding, the government also, however, curtailed the democratic process, since the Communists were no longer granted the freedom of association and speech. This relates to the concept of legitimacy. The conception of the government as legitimate was probably not based on very strong beliefs in the democratic process but rather on the simple belief that the present system was the best for maintaining law and stability. The Finnish experience represents a strong case for maintaining an open and historically specific definition of the concept of legitimacy.

Analytically it seems possible to regard legitimacy, efficiency, and effectiveness as separate categories. In practice, however, this conceptual differentiation seems more doubtful. Both efficiency and effectiveness are, so to speak, component parts of legitimacy. A belief that an organizing political authority or a regime is good and should command the obedience of the citizens can hardly be sustained unless there are proofs of its goodness in terms of efficiency and effectiveness.

NOTES

1. E.g., Anthony F. Upton, "Finland," in *European Fascism*, ed. S. J. Woolf (London: Weidenfeld and Nicolson, 1968), p. 184.
2. See Stein Rokkan, *Citizens, Elections, Parties* (Oslo: Universitetsforlaget, 1970), p. 86.
3. See, e.g., Erik Allardt, "Institutionalized Radicalism and Decline of Ideology," in *Decline of Ideology?*, ed. Mostafa Rejai (New York: Aldine and Atherton, 1971), p. 119.
4. Eino Murtorinne, *Taistelu uskonnonvapaudesta suurlakon jälkeisinä vuosina* (Porvoo-Helsinki: WSOY, 1967), pp. 90–104, 222, 229, 231.
5. See, e.g., Juhani Paasivirta, *Suomi vuonna 1918* (Porvoo-Helsinki: WSOY, 1957), pp. 62–64.
6. See Barrington Moore's and Charles Tilly's analyses: Barrington Moore, Jr., *Reflections on the Causes of Human Misery and upon Certain Proposals to Eliminate Them* (London: Allen

Lane, The Penguin Press, 1972), pp. 170–75; Charles Tilly, "Revolutions and Collective Violence," in *Handbook of Political Science*, ed. Fred I. Greenstein and Nelson W. Polsby (Reading, Mass.: Addison-Wesley, 1975), vol. 3.

7. E.g. Moore, *Reflections*, p. 175.

8. The Finnish army had been abolished in 1901 by the grand duke, i.e., the tsar.

9. Jaakko Paavolainen, "Vuonna 1918 teloitettujen punaisten lukumääräongelma," in *Oman ajan historia ja politiikan tutkimus*, ed. Lauri Hyvämäki et al. (Helsinki: Otava, 1967), pp. 210–11; Jaakko Paavolainen, *Vankileirit Suomessa 1918* (Helsinki: Tammi, 1971), pp. 234–48. Different sources present different figures for the number of Reds executed. According to material collected by the Central Statistical Office the number executed was 4,870. See Tor Hartman, "Dead and Missing Persons in the Civil War in 1918," *Tilastollisia tiedonantoja, julkaissut Tilastollinen päätoimisto—Statistiska meddelanden, utgivna av Statistiska Centralbyrån 46* (Helsinki, 1970), p. 18. There are some uncertainties in all the estimates, but the figures given by Paavolainen are in all likelihood closest to the truth. The total population of Finland in 1918 was three million people.

10. On the civil guard, see Marvin Rintala, *Three Generations: The Extreme Right Wing in Finnish Politics* (Bloomington: Indiana University Press, 1962), pp. 147–55.

11. Krister Wahlbäck, *Mannerheimista Kekkoseen: Suomen politiikan päälinjoja 1917–1967* (Porvoo-Helsinki: WSOY, 1968), p. 119.

12. On this organization, see Marvin Rintala, "Finnish Students in Politics: The Academic Karelia Society," *East European Quarterly* 6 (1972):192–205, and Risto Alapuro, "Students and National Politics: A Comparative Study of the Finnish Student Movement in the Interwar Period," *Scandinavian Political Studies* 8 (1973):113–40.

13. Cf. Erik Allardt and Pertti Pesonen, "Cleavages in Finnish Politics," in *Party Systems and Voter Alignments: Cross-National Perspectives*, ed. Seymour M. Lipset and Stein Rokkan (New York: The Free Press, 1967), pp. 328–29.

14. Hannu Soikkanen, "Miksi revisionismi ei saanut kannatusta Suomen vanhassa työväenliikkeessä?" in Hyvämäki et al., *Oman ajan historia*, pp. 184, 187, 191, 196–97; John H. Hodgson, *Communism in Finland: A History and Interpretation* (Princeton, N.J.: Princeton University Press, 1967), pp. 5–19.

15. Soikkanen, "Miksi revisionismi," pp. 196–97.

16. Hodgson, *Communism in Finland*, pp. 15–16, 22.

17. E.g., O. W. Kuusinen, *The Finnish Revolution: A Self-Criticism* (London: The Worker's Socialist Federation, 1919).

18. See Hodgson, *Communism in Finland*, pp. 29–52.

19. Hannu Soikkanen, "Työväenliikkeen jakautumisongelma itsenäisyyden alkuvuosina," *Turun Historiallinen Arkisto* 15 (1960):266–67.

20. See, for example, Henry L. Roberts's illuminating account, *Rumania: Political Problems of an Agrarian State* (New Haven: Yale University Press, 1951), pp. 89–91, 337–38.

21. Barrington Moore, Jr. *Social Origins of Dictatorship and Democracy: Lord and Peasant in the Making of the Modern World* (Boston: Beacon Press, 1966), pp. 433–38.

22. Cf. Moore, *Social Origins*, p. 422.

23. It was of importance, for instance, that because of the outcome of World War I expansionist efforts to annex the eastern Karelia into Finland, which in 1918–19 had seemed real enough to many in the Right—especially in the Coalition party—remained unsuccessful in the end. The Treaty of Dorpat with Soviet Russia in 1921 confirmed the situation and was in the following years attacked by the Right. This component of irredentism and expansive nationalism parallels the case of the Versailles settlement for Germany in many respects, as has been pointed out by Marvin Rintala. See Rintala, *Three Generations*, pp. 99–100.

24. Soikkanen, "Työväenliikkeen jakautumisongelma," pp. 267–71; Ilkka Hakalehto, *Väinö Tanner, Taipumattoman tie* (Helsinki: Kirjayhtymä, 1973), pp. 56–68, 81–100.

25. Hodgson, *Communism in Finland*, pp. 121–29.

26. Jorma Kalela, "Right-Wing Radicalism in Finland during the Interwar Period," *Scandinavian Journal of History* 1 (1976):111–12.

27. See Rintala, *Three Generations*, pp. 165, 166, 183–86.

28. Ibid., pp. 167, 174–75.

29. On violence, see Upton, "Finland," pp. 200–202. On the stand of President Lauri K. Relander, see his diary: *Presidentin päiväkirja II. Lauri Kristian Relanderin muistiinpanot vuosilta 1927–1931*, ed. Eino Jutikkala (Helsinki: Weilin+Göös, 1968), pp. 450–54.

30. See Rintala, *Three Generations*, pp. 174–84.

31. Hakalehto, *Väinö Tanner*, pp. 103–4, 107–8.

32. Rintala, *Three Generations*, pp. 177, 189. See also Paavo Hirvikallio, *Tasavallan Presidentin vaalit Suomessa 1919–1950* (Porvoo-Helsinki: WSOY, 1958), pp. 62–63.

33. On the Mäntsälä revolt see Rintala, *Three Generations*, pp. 191–94.

34. Cf. Upton, "Finland," pp. 209–10.

35. Upton, "Finland," pp. 195–96; Kalela, "Right-Wing Radicalism," pp. 113–15.

36. Kalela, "Right-Wing Radicalism," p. 121.

37. See Upton, "Finland," pp. 203–4.

38. Cf. Moore, *Social Origins*, pp. 437–38, 448–50. Illustrative of the sharp difference sketched here is the rise of agrarian-based fascism in Rumania, which at that time was still, at least formally, a parliamentary democracy. See Eugen Weber, "The Men of the Archangel," in *International Fascism, 1920–1945*, ed. Walter Laqueur and George L. Mosse (New York: Harper Torchbooks, 1966), pp. 110–18.

39. A rough comparison shows that in the initial stages of the depression the decrease in income among the farmers was greater than among the workers, whose real income even rose in 1929. See Klaus Waris, *Kuluttajain tulot, kulutus ja säästäminen suhdannekehityksen valossa Suomessa vuosina 1926–1938* (Helsinki: Kansantaloudellisia tutkimuksia XIV, 1945), pp. 123, 134, 153. The profit rate in agriculture was at its lowest in 1929–30; see Kosti Huuhka, *Talonpoikaisnuorison koulutie* (Forssa: Historiallisia tutkimuksia XLIII, 1955), p. 191.

40. Paula Oittinen, "Pulaliikkeiden alueellinen levinneisyys" (Master's thesis, University of Helsinki, 1975).

41. Relander, *Presidentin päiväkirja II*, pp. 424–25, 507, 521.

42. See Kalela, "Right-Wing Radicalism," pp. 121–22.

43. Hakalehto, *Väinö Tanner*, pp. 115–16. That the stand of Social Democrats cannot alone explain the failure of the takeover becomes clear in a comparison with Germany, where the Social Democratic party was also strongly reformist. Other factors differentiating the Finnish and German situation, at least those sketched above, must be taken into consideration.

44. See, e.g., Paul M. Sweezy, *The Theory of Capitalist Development* (New York: Monthly Review Press, 1968), pp. 329–30, 334.

45. Carl Erik Knoellinger, *Labor in Finland* (Cambridge, Mass.: Harvard University Press, 1960), p. 85.

46. Wahlbäck, *Mannerheimista*, p. 80.

5.

From Great Hopes to Civil War: The Breakdown of Democracy in Spain

Juan J. Linz*

The death of Spanish democracy was the last in a chain of breakdowns in Europe that occurred in Italy, Portugal, Germany, and Austria. This circumstance accounts for many of the distinctive features of the crisis of the Spanish Republic between 1931 and 1936, including foreign intervention in the civil war. That the Spanish democracy survived the rise of fascism in other countries helps explain Spanish socialism's unique response. The Republic was the most short-lived and unstable of the European democracies that failed.[1] It is the only case in which the final breakdown led to a civil war, and Spain and Portugal are the only countries in which the regimes then established have survived until, respectively, 1976-77 and 1974.

In these two countries on the Iberian peninsula the army played a direct rather than an indirect role in the breakdown, which brings their experience closer to the Latin American pattern. The high level of political mobilization in Spain, however, contrasts with the Portuguese and even more with most Latin American cases, and in this respect it resembles European models. Perhaps more than in any other case except the Italian, deep social cleavage and conflict lay beneath the political crisis. Class, religious, and regional conflicts combined and interacted with unique intensity. Spain was the only democracy outside Eastern Europe in which regional, cultural, and linguistic cleavages played a role in the breakdown of democracy. Regional tensions were certainly important in the Austrian crisis, and to some extent in the German crisis, but they did not approach the effect of emerging peripheral nationalisms against an established state conceived by most Spaniards as a nation-state.[2] While religious issues and sentiment were relevant to the crises of Weimar and Italy, and were important in Portugal and Austria, they were never so bitter—so central—as in Spain.

*In writing this essay I have benefited enormously from the critical reading of Edward Malefakis.

The cumulative effect of the problems faced was staggering, but it is notable that major divisions over foreign policy and war responsibilities were not contributory. The colonial wars of the late nineteenth and early twentieth century in Cuba, the Philippines, and Morocco were a closed chapter except for the size of the officer corps and the divisions within the army residual from that time. The world depression had affected Spain, but the agrarian, mixed economy and relative isolation from world trade reduced its impact.[3]

The Republic was a new regime, but perhaps in contrast to the Weimar and Austrian republics, the legitimacy of the monarchy had been more seriously undermined in Spain, and the loyalty of the officer corps to the crown was less intense.[4] Let us not forget that Spain had had a republican regime in the nineteenth century, that dynastic wars had weakened the monarchy after its restoration, but above all, that the king's support for the dictatorship of Primo de Rivera in 1923, in breaking with constitutional rule, had alienated the political class of the Restoration. The army had not been fully sympathetic to the coup of 1923, had turned largely against the dictator because of his arbitrary policies in military matters, and ultimately contributed to his fall, which left the monarchy in an ambiguous position. A significant minority of the army had even conspired against the crown, and after the surprise success of Republican candidates in the municipal elections of 1931, the army stood passively by, large numbers of officers ready to recognize the Republic, while the king left the country. In contrast to the *Reichswehr*, the number of aristo-cratic officers was small. The supporters of the dictatorship were certainly not enthusiastic about Alphons XIII, who had abandoned their hero. The challenge to the legitimacy of the new regime did not arise out of loyalty to its predecessor, even though a small group of committed monarchists was to become a disloyal opposition. It was a sign of a past crisis that the monarchists formulated their goals in terms of instoration of an authoritarian monarchy rather than restoration of the liberal constitutional monarchy.

The new regime was the result of neither external defeat by a Versailles peace treaty nor violent revolution, but an incredibly peaceful transfer of power, smoothly worked out by the elites. If the new regime had not challenged many values and interests, a large number of conservative Spaniards would have been neutral to, or even welcomed, the change of regime, without having a clear idea of what it involved but without regrets for the one that had fallen. The overthrow of the monarchy was more the result of a vacuum of support than of the organized strength of its Republican opponents, who benefited nonetheless from a widespread and diffused feeling that a change was necessary.[5] Except for the Socialist labor movement, support for the Republic was more an expression of sentiment than of a long, continuous build-up of the strength of antimonarchist parties. For the Anarcho-syndicalist labor movement, the CNT (Confederación Nacional del Trabajo), monarchy or republic made little difference, since its opposition was directed against any bourgeois regime and ultimately against the state itself. It is important to keep in mind, in analyzing the accelerated crisis of the thirties, that the regime initially enjoyed a wide margin of legitimacy, and many of those who had not supported Republican candidates in the elections of April 1931 maintained an expectant, potentially favorable, or passive attitude that could have been used to assure compliance and even to build legitimacy.[6] At that time, the regime faced the active disloyal opposition only of the traditionalists, or Carlists, who had been a passive principled opposition to the liberal monarchy; the supporters of the dictatorship, which served the Republicans as a symbol of political degradation for the country; a small number of loyal monarchists; and the anarcho-syndicalist labor movement, which posed a more serious threat, but having been freed from recent persecution, was still in an expectant mood. It shall be our task to analyze how, in the course of five years, the supporters of a Republic which had been inaugurated so hopefully in April 1931 could become an embattled minority.

In a Europe where fascism and communism had been the leading oppositions to democratic regimes since the early 1920s, the first Spanish fascist group was founded only a month before the proclamation of the Republic, and the Communist party was a sectarian group with few members or followers.[7] Fascism would never achieve an electoral success comparable even to that of the Rexists in Belgium; nevertheless, in the spring of 1936, without a single deputy, it was to emerge as a powerful symbol. The Communist party would exercise considerable influence on the internal struggles of the Socialist party and, through the fusion of their youth organizations, control an important mass organization. Paradoxically, while fascism and communism were weak and were latecomers to Spain, the tensions that the struggle between them had created elsewhere had an impact in Spain that should not be underestimated. The case of Spain is a good example of how the process of breakdown in one country cannot be understood apart from the crises in other democracies in the same period of history. The weakness of fascism in Spain also must be taken into account to understand why the outcome of the crisis was decided by the army, and why the Italian and German models of pseudo-legal takeover of power in Spain did not hold. The CEDA (Confederación Española de Derechas Autónomas), though ambivalent about democracy even to the point of considering an unconstitutional takeover of power, would have attempted this only with army support, not through a combination of violent street action with legal parliamentary action at the elite level. It is an indication of the internal divisions within the army and the desire of many officers for disengagement from politics after the experience of the Primo de Rivera dictatorship that feelers extended in that direction, in late 1934 and before and immediately after the 1936 election, proved unsuccessful.

In the thirties, Spain, like the other European democracies in crisis, was characterized by an increased level of political mobilization, although this was not fully reflected in the rate of electoral participation, partly because of an active syndicalist abstentionism. But that mobilization had been achieved in a short time, rather than as a result of the slow, continuous organizational effort that had taken place in Germany, Austria, and even Italy. Consequently, the level of socialization in the ideology of different parties was lower, as was the degree of stability of loyalties and the discipline of the membership. This fact should be taken into account in explaining the instability of leadership, the bitterness of factional fights (particularly within the Socialist party), the incertitude of the leadership about followers' responses to their policies, and the movement of organized blocks of supporters to more radical positions, particularly in the spring of 1936. This higher level of mobilization differentiates the Spanish crisis from the Portuguese and accounts for the relatively bloodless and slow transition from the Republic to the *Estado Novo* in Portugal as compared to the revolutionary upsurges in October 1934 and in 1936 in Spain. Such rapid mobilization is particularly striking given Spain's economic underdevelopment and brings the Spanish case closer to the Italian between 1918 and 1923. The problems created by underdevelopment in these two countries partly explain the maximalist radicalization of the Socialist labor movement and the ultimate inability of the moderate Socialists to contribute effectively to the consolidation of a progressive democracy. In Spain, however, maximalist strength emerged only after 1933, even though its roots lay further back, whereas in Italy it appeared immediately after the war. Because of the internal divisions in the Spanish Socialist party, its support of the October 1934 revolution, its unwillingness to share the responsibilities of governing after the Popular Front electoral victory in 1936, and its extremist rhetoric and actions from 1933 to 1936, the PSOE (Partido Socialista Obrero Español), a factor of stability in the first period of the Republic, became a major, if not the decisive, factor leading to the breakdown. The similarities and differences in the response of Marxist-Socialist parties to democracies in crisis is central to our study.

The Spanish party system clearly fits the Sartori model of an extremely polarized multiparty system.[8] In terms of the number of parties, their centrifugal tendencies, ideological polarization not only between parties but within parties, and the politics of irresponsible outbidding, the system resembles those of pre-breakdown Italy and Germany. (For the party composition of the Republican legislatures and the vote in 1936, see table 1.) But in the Spanish case these characteristics were sharpened because of the initial constitution of the Republic and its interpretation by the Left Republicans as excluding the full loyalty of anyone to their right. This exclusivistic interpretation was applied even to parties willing to define themselves unequivocally as Republicans, resulting in the delegitimization of the old Radical party because

Table 1. Party Composition of the Legislature during the Second Republic (1931–36)

Party	Constituent Assembly Elected June 1931	Legislature Elected November 1933	Legislature Elected February 1936 Seats	% of Seats	Percentage of Vote, 16 February 1936 Election
Sindicalista	—	—	1	0.21	0.13
Bloque Unificación Marxista	—	—	1	0.21	0.17
Partido Comunista	—	1	17	3.6	2.5
PSOE	114	59	100	21.3	16.4
"maximalists"[a]			(49)		
Esquerra (Catalan Left; Companys)	37	22	36	7.6	4.1
Acción Republicana (Azaña)	31	5	—	—	—
Izquierda Republicana (IR)	—	—	87	18.5	13.7
Organización Republicana Gallega Autómata (ORGA)	18	3	included in IR		
Radical Socialista Independiente	2	2			
Radical Socialista	55	1			
Unión Republicana (Mtnez. Barrio)	—	—	38	8.1	5.9
Partido Federal	13	1			
Progresistas	8	3	6	1.3	0.9
Agrupación al Servicio de la República (Ortega y Gasset)	13	—			
Republicanos Conservadores	—	16	3	0.64	0.8
Derecha Republicana	14	—			
Republicano Liberal Demócrata	2	10	1	0.21	0.8
Partido Radical (Lerroux)	89	102	4	0.85	3.6
Centro (Portela Valladares)	—	—	16	3.4	5.1
Lliga Regionalista (Catalan Right; Cambó)	4	26	12	2.5	2.8
Partido Nacionalista Vasco	—	12	10	2.1	1.4
Minoría Vasco-Navarra (includes four Traditionalists)	15	—			—

Independents of the Center-Right and the Right	18	13	15	3.2	3.1
Agrarios	24	32	12	2.5	2.6
Acción Nacional	5	—	—	—	—
Acción Popular, CEDA, Derecha Regional Valenciana (Gil Robles)	—	115	88	18.7	23.2
Renovación Española (Calvo Sotelo)	2	15	included in Bloque Nacional		
Bloque Nacional (same)	—	—	13	2.8	3.8
Tradicionalistas (Carlists)	2	21	9	1.9	3.4
Nacionalista (Fascists)	—	1	—	—	—
Falange	—	1	—	—	0.08
Unidentified	3	5	2	0.42	5.6
Vacant seats	—	8	3	—	—
	469	474	474	100.25	100.08

NOTE: The party identifications in the 1931 legislature were very imprecise. The *Anuario Estadistico de España* of 1931 (pp. 487, 489) lists sixty-two members as having been elected on "different Republican lists" in the election of 28 June 1931 and the by-election in November. The *Lista de los Señores Diputados* published by the Cortes in 1932 does not give information on party identification. The sources disagree even on the number of seats in the 1931 legislature: the *Anuario Estadistico* gives 470; the official *Lista de los Señores Diputados*, arranged by districts, gives 469, but includes only 461 names; and Ramón Tamames, in *La República: La era de Franco*, p. 58, gives 484. We have opted to use the figure 469 from the *Lista de los Señores Diputados* of December 1932. On the basis of a variety of sources, party histories, etc., we have attempted to give a figure for each party, even when at any point in the legislative period some deputies changed parties. This explains the discrepancy between sources and with the data in table 22 in Linz, "The Party System of Spain," p. 260.

Table 1. (*continued*)

For the 1933 legislature we have used the information given in the *Boletín de Información Bibliográfica y Parlamentaria de España y el Extranjero* 1, no. 6 (November–December 1933): 1054–71, on party affiliation. It includes the names of 9 more deputies than does the *Lista de los Señores Diputados* of March 1935, which gives 455, but it is not complete. In the case of some deputies, party identification could be obtained from other sources, in order to complete the information, at the risk of some errors due to changes during the course of the legislative session.

Figures for the legislature elected in 1936 were taken from the official *Lista de los Señores Diputados* published by the Cortes in 1936, which lists the parliamentary groups. This list is dated June 1936 and therefore takes into account the results of the "second round" elections that took place in districts where none of the candidates had obtained the required minimum or where the first election had been voided. Since those elections were held after the Left had taken power in February 1936, they were particularly controversial. Some of the discrepancies between these figures and those given in other sources are due to this.

In the 16 February 1936 election, voters were basically confronted with two great coalitions: the Frente Popular and Frente Anti-revolucionario, except in some provinces where the Centro and the PVN ran their own tickets. It is therefore impossible to determine the number of votes the different parties would have obtained if competing with each other (as would have been the case under a system of proportional representation). Assuming that the placing of candidates of different parties on the coalition tickets reflects their appeal in each district, and considering the fact that the voter could split his ticket and give preference to one or another candidate, we have calculated the votes obtained by candidates of different parties compared to the total number of votes cast. Coalition discipline was generally high and probably benefited weaker parties represented on the coalition lists. There are also some missing data and contested returns. Therefore, these data should be considered as indicators of the approximate strength of parties in the electorate. In the comparison between votes and seats it should be kept in mind that the data on seats refer to the final composition of the chamber after the runoff, where required, and in the case of voided returns. Before the debate for admission of election certification, according to initial returns, the CEDA would have had ninety-six instead of eighty-eight deputies, the PSOE eighty-eight instead of one hundred, and the Izquierda Republicana seventy-nine instead of eighty-seven. The debate on the fairness of the election hinges on these highly controversial decisions by the legislature.

The figures for the 1936 vote have been calculated on the basis of the returns for different coalitions and candidates in Javier Tusell, *Las elecciones del Frente Popular* (Madrid: Edicusa, 1971), vol. 2, Appendix 1, pp. 265–97, in Juan J. Linz and Jesús M. de Miguel, "Hacia un análisis regional de las elecciones de 1936 en España," *Revista Española de la Opinión Pública*, 48, April–June 1977, pp. 27–68. Given the electoral law, the attribution of votes to parties rather than to large and heterogeneous coalitions required making certain assumptions and complex calculations presented in the article.

[a]The division of the Socialist (PSOE) deputies into "maximalists" and "moderates" was not institutionalized, but manifested itself in the 49 to 23 vote on the organization of the parliamentary group in March 1936 (Ricardo de La Cierva, *Historia de la Guerra Civil Española* [Madrid: San Martín, 1969], p. 678) and in the 49 to 19 vote in the caucus of 12 May against participating in any sort of government coalition (Stanley G. Payne, *The Spanish Revolution* [New York: Norton, 1970], p. 195).

of its collaboration with the Catholic CEDA. In contrast to the Weimar Republic, in which the constitution was a compromise between Social Democrats, Democrats, and the Zentrum, the Spanish constitution was drafted and supported by a much narrower coalition of Radicals, Left Republicans, and Socialists. But by the fall of 1933, the shift of the Radicals toward the right and the discontent of the Left Socialists under Largo Caballero would break even that relatively narrow coalition. This contrasts with the relative permanence, particularly in Prussia, of the initial Weimar coalition.

That the regional nationalist parties of both the Right and Left would make only a conditional commitment to the regime, and gave priority to their distinctive national interests instead, further complicated the definition of regime-supporting parties. With the exception of minor parties, all parties, even the less radical ones, were loyal to a democratic regime and constitutional procedures only so long as certain values they held higher than democracy could be pursued within the democratic framework. Even the system parties were unwilling to make a clear break with disloyal oppositions on their side of the spectrum.

It is difficult to say whether this basic ambivalence toward the central democratic regime was the result of ideological predispositions or to competition for the same social base in a very fluid and unstructured political situation. It could also be argued that it was a by-product of an electoral system that gave an inordinate advantage to broad coalitions and made it nearly impossible for those not entering them to aspire to a majority in Parliament. During three legislative elections and a number of regional elections in Catalonia, this contributed to distrust between parties that might otherwise have been closer to each other than to extremists on their own sides.[9] Hermens attributes much of the crisis of democracy in Europe to proportional representation;[10] but an electoral system that necessitated coalition with extremists and produced overrepresentation in Parliament of the winning coalition, led to a fragmented and polarized situation that was probably more dangerous to democracy than proportional representation would have been.[11]

There can be no question that Spanish democracy in the thirties faced economic and social problems that exceeded the resources of a liberal democratic regime, but the political leadership added to those problems others that were even more disruptive. In April 1931, however, the strictly political legacy of the past was less of a burden than the memory of Imperial Germany for Weimar or the ghost of the Habsburgs in Austria. In fact, the discontinuity of political development under the constitutional monarchy from 1876 to 1923 was in someways a disadvantage for the Spanish Republic. While in Germany and Austria the regime parties and their leadership represented a continuity of political experience acquired in Parliament and were stable organizations under the old regime, in Spain, except for the top leadership of the Socialist party and the Radical party politicians with municipal political experience, the elite consisted only of new men with little political or administrative experience who had not worked together in Parliament before. This applied to much of the leftist Republican leadership as well as to that of the new mass party of the Right, the CEDA.[12]

Paradoxically, some of the politicians most concerned with constitutional, liberal, democratic legality were men who had occupied legislative and cabinet posts in the liberal monarchy. The nonradical, almost loyal leaders of the Republic at the end of 1935 were a president of the Republic, Niceto Alcalá Zamora, two prime ministers, Chapaprieta and Portela, and a president of the chamber, Santiago Alba, all of whom had been cabinet members under the monarchy. In the spring of 1936, the less strident voices of the opposition were those of men linked by family and career to the old political elites, such as the bourgeois politicians of the Catalan Lliga. Many with political experience under the liberal monarchy made a better adjustment to the Republic than the newer leaders of the Right, who, after the 1931 debacle, had taken the place of the old oligarchic leadership. This raises an interesting question: does a newly established democracy really gain by eliminating from political life those who participated in the previous regime? Might not the new leaders of the same interests be more radical in their opposition than the old leadership would have been?

In terms of the main parties, particularly the system parties, and of political personnel, the republican regimes in Germany and Austria enjoyed greater continuity than did the Spanish Republic. This would explain their greater capacity for compromise, particularly between the social democrats and the Catholic parties, which for several years insured an apparent stabilization that has no equivalent in the Spanish case.

The Problems of Spain and the Crisis of the Republic

The breakdown of Spanish democracy could be viewed as the result of the serious and basically unsolvable problems inherent in Spanish society. It could be argued that the Republic could not overcome all these problems, which had to one degree or another led to the fall of preceding regimes. The argument would be that the structural problems of Spanish society were beyond the capabilities of even the most able democratic elite, and perhaps of any ruling elite. I would be inclined to reject this interpretation, stated in this way. Certainly previous regimes had experienced deep crises, but most managed to last longer than the Republic, and their breakdown cannot be directly and immediately linked with persistent problems in the social structure. The Isabeline monarchy fell in 1868 because of political and conjunctural factors; the First Republic, which was in any case an accidental and highly artificial creation, fell because of disunity within the small elite groups that genuinely believed in it. The most durable regime in Spain after 1800, the Restoration monarchy, survived serious crises for nearly fifty years. The pronunciamento of Primo de Rivera, triggered partly by the Moroccan War crisis (rather like the Fourth Republic's fall because of the Algerian War), ultimately brought it down, but its fall was not exclusively or even primarily due to the basic unsolved social and political problems which had so clearly manifested themselves in 1917. The same is true for the dictatorship of Primo de Rivera and the brief effort at reequilibration of the Restoration before the advent of the Republic in 1931. Certainly the deep crisis in Spanish society lay beneath all these breakdowns of political institutions, but the immediate cause was never a major mobilization of conflicting social groups, never a revolution or a real counterrevolution, and none of these crises of regimes divided society to the point of civil war.

The new regime, therefore, must have exacerbated the problems of the Spanish society to an impossible limit, certainly compounded by the European atmosphere in general. If we had asked various Spanish elites at different moments to name the basic problems that needed solution, their ranking of those problems and their confidence that solutions would be found within the framework of the established regime would have produced very different lists. If we remember, however, that agenda-setting is the result of a complex interaction between the decisions of the elite and pressures from the society, we might be able to understand better the accumulation of problems confronting the new rulers. When so many problems accumulate and find expression under conditions of political freedom, political leaders confront real difficulty in setting priorities among them, for different considerations produce very different outcomes. Regime institutionalization and regime stability might not always be given priority over the realization of other values. In order to consolidate itself, a new regime must do two things: implement policies that will satisfy a large number of potential supporters and link them to the regime, with negative effect on the smallest possible number of opponents; and follow policies that will satisfy the leadership of the coalition which installed the new regime, avoiding policies that would provoke dissent and splits in the coalition.

For the Spanish Republic these two goals were, to a considerable extent, incompatible. In the short run, the second seems to have taken precedence over the first, at the cost of the long-run stability of the regime. In addition, the first goal was unsuccessfully managed because of lack of resources, technical and administrative incompetence, and ideological preconceptions and rigidity.

The agenda of the new regime was dictated by a combination of pressures originating from the social structure (mainly the Socialist party and the labor movement, particularly the new agrarian socialism) and the ideological commitments of the participants in the pact of San Sebastian (largely derived from a conception of political problems that dated back to an older, radical Republican tradition). An agenda derived solely from the structural conditionings would have coped with its first problem, inequality in landownership, with a redistributive agrarian reform in the *latifundia* areas, yielding immediate benefits to tenant farmers, small farmers, and masses of farm laborers. A second problem, unemployment and underemployment, would have been handled next, probably with a large-scale public works program to create jobs. The first would have required a revolutionary will; it might have been possible to implement against the wishes of a relatively small group of noble and bourgeois landowners; additionally, if formulated in nonideological terms, it might have been acceptable to large segments of the population. A public works policy and government-sponsored or government-supported industrialization, however, was not feasible within the parameters of economic thinking at the time of the world-wide depression and the financial resources of the Spanish state. A third structural problem was posed by the popular demands for regional cultural and linguistic autonomy, particularly in Catalonia. A fourth major structural need that exceeded the financial capacity of the state was the rapid expansion and qualitative improvement of mass education. Fifth, these structural problems all demanded a thorough revamping of the fiscal system and reallocation of budgetary resources.

The agenda of the leadership of the Republican coalition coincided in part with the previous structurally determined agenda, but the Left bourgeois parties placed them in a different order and gave priority to other problems, chiefly the reduction and political neutralization of the army and the secularization of the society. Events made the Catalan problem more urgent. The central problem in the minds of the Republican policy-makers was to raise the educational level of the country, which led to an immediate effort to expand primary education in particular. However, these lofty ambitions encountered economic and technical difficulties compounded by the additional strain of attempting in a short period of time to replace the religious orders in the field of secondary education, where they had long dominated. Even the powerful personality of Largo Caballero could not place pro-labor and pro-welfare state policies on the agenda immediately, except for measures such as those on Términos Municipales and Jurados Mixtos, which gave labor unions advantages they had never before enjoyed and increased their size and bargaining power immeasurably. While agrarian reform was on the agenda from the beginning, serious efforts to legislate and implement a redistribution of rural wealth and power found little enthusiasm among the bourgeois Republican parties until later.[13] Even very secondary issues, like the responsibilities of the king and the Primo de Rivera dictatorship, absorbed considerable time on the agenda of the constituent Cortes.

The constituent period was the "honeymoon" of the new regime—a time that could have been used to promote policies creating a strong basis of support, particularly among the workers and peasants; clearly, the ordering of the agenda was not the best. Antimilitarism and anticlericalism received wide support among strata that resented the dominance of the military and the church in Spanish life. However, within the nonrevolutionary conception of the Republic held by its founding coalition, neither of these policies could really destroy or even seriously weaken the hold of the army and church over social power and influence. Both policies, but particularly anticlericalism, created deep resentments that mobilized large sectors of the population who had initially felt apathetic or expectant about the new regime rather than actively negative.[14] Once the immediate emotional gratification that those policies provided the regime-supporters had passed, they did not bring tangible benefits to the masses, and in fact appeared as only a bourgeois diversion from more immediate and pressing social demands. They did not serve to bring the Socialist working class, much less the masses organized in the CNT, into the bourgeois Socialist coalition. The way in which they were implemented, particularly through the retirement of officers at full pay and the proposed substitution of secular schools for the educational system of the religious orders, absorbed economic resources that might have been used to enact social policies benefiting the masses.[15] In addition, the bitter tenor that Azaña and others gave even to the necessary and acceptable army reform was perceived as ressentiment politics and alienated many officers who might have identified themselves with the new regime.[16] Many of the changes in this area, as in others, were more symbolic than pragmatic, creating discontent without benefiting anyone.

The same is even more true of many aspects of the anticlerical legislation and policies. The effort to secularize the society by decree inevitably mobilized a mass Catholic reaction against the new regime, particularly since these policies were accompanied by irresponsible acts by small groups, such as the burning of convents in May 1931, which the authorities were intially unable, or unwilling, to stop.[17] The high priority given to the secularization policy perverted what might otherwise have been an effective educational policy, and it interfered with attention to the Catalan and Basque problems. Catholic grievances were soon to be reinforced by the economic woes of the wheat-growing peasants of north-central Spain after ill-advised grain imports and an extraordinarily large harvest caused a fall in prices. In addition, certain provisions of the Agrarian Reform Law, such as the expropriation of many small and medium-sized land holdings under the *ruedos* provision and the inclusion in the inventories of expropriable land of properties in areas where agrarian reform would not be applied in the foreseeable future, reinforced peasant and small-town Castilian opposition. This opposition would manifest itself first in the April 1933 municipal elections and later in the November 1933 parliamentary victory of the Center Right.[18]

A less demagogic, cooler, and more pragmatic religious policy, taking advantage of compromise with the Vatican if not with the Spanish hierarchy, combined with the longer-range policy of secularization of education through the creation of an inexpensive and high-quality system, would certainly have created fewer opponents. A quickly and effectively implemented agrarian reform centered on a small number of very large landowners, both aristocratic and bourgeois, in areas of the country with serious unemployment problems and social discontent, would have alienated fewer people and gained considerable support for the regime. Ideological preconceptions, combined with lack of adequate information, legalistic constraints, bureaucratic inefficiency, and misconceptions, led the Republican leadership to miss these opportunities and contributed to the disillusionment of the Socialist leadership with the coalition, as well as the shift of the more conservative Republicans toward the right. Some particular aspects of the Socialists' policies in the agrarian labor field added to the growing discontent of the Anarcho-syndicalists.

Ideological rather than pragmatic policy formulation also prevented the regime from presenting those policies in a favorable light to those not directly affected by them, like the industrial middle classes. In the absence of any real commitment to create a socialist economy to substitute for the incipient capitalism of the industrialized regions, ideological debates about worker control and the rights of property could only create distrust of the regime. Agrarian reform should have been presented as an opportunity for industrial sectors to find new markets among the masses as they acquired a better economic position and improved buying power. If public secondary education capable of competing in cost and quality with that of the religious orders had been created, and if fair policies for institutional standards had been set up, the dominant position of the orders could have been displaced without creating the hostility that the outlawing of their teaching aroused.[19] Furthermore, the fact that such legislation could not be immediately implemented because of limited personnel and economic resources could only contribute to the discrediting of the regime.

The injudicious ordering of priorities and the ineffectiveness of the governments of the first bienio created immense problems and expectations that would remain unsatisfied. It also mobilized broad segments of the population, not just against the ruling parties, but against the regime, which those parties had identified with themselves by constitutionalizing what might have been ordinary laws. This meant that change required the mobilization of majorities sufficient to amend the constitution, not simple legislation. The search for such a qualified majority, together with the exigencies of the electoral law, pushed the possibilist sector of Spanish Catholicism into an alliance with the extreme Right. This alliance contributed to the division of those Republicans in the Radical party, who preferred to integrate the Right into the system and were opposed to some of the policies of the first two years, but would soon be disaffected by the revision of the anticlerical policies advocated by the Center Right with whom they had to cooperate to govern. The way in which the policy-making process was conceived by many Republicans, particularly Azaña, almost inevitably led to the splintering-off of the Republican parties more to the right and to the disappointment of the Socialist labor movement with the tangible fruits of the change of regime.

The regime-building phase of the Republic achieved placement of Spain's major problems on the agenda, and the good will of the Republican leadership during that period cannot be doubted. However, the specific formulation of those policies and the failures of their implementation, perhaps in part because of the personality of Azaña, left an unfortunate heritage: the mobilization of opponents, the disillusionment of a key supporter, the Socialist party, and the continuing and intensified hostility of the Anarcho-syndicalists. Only the Catalan policy worked out between Azaña and Companys, and crystallized in the *Estatuto* despite the opposition of Castilian intellectuals and nationalists, can be considered an important contribution to the stabilization of the regime. Even though the events of October 1934 endangered that solution, the relative stability of Catalonia in the spring of 1936 and the growing willingness of the Esquerra (the Catalan Left) and the Lliga (the Catalan conservative party) to play the roles of government and loyal opposition in support of moderate solutions in Madrid can be considered permanent fruits of those initial decisions.

Regional Politics and the Breakdown of Democracy

The peripheral nationalisms, particularly the Catalan, that have contributed to so many crises in modern Spain were also a factor in the crisis of the Republic.[20] Though not a major factor in the immediate causes of the military uprising in July 1936, they contributed to the alienation of the army and other sectors of the society from the regime. Franco propaganda during the civil war constantly referred to the struggle against the *rojo-separatistas,* or "reds and secessionists." The breakdown of federal or regionally decentralized democratic regimes, and of countries with cultural-linguistic minorities, is central neither to our model nor to the cases analyzed in this volume, even though it figured in the cases of the Weimar Republic, Austria, and to some extent, Argentina and Brazil. We shall, therefore, devote some attention to it here in an attempt to draw some general inferences.

The emergence of Catalan and, later, Basque nationalism posed a problem that appeared unsolvable to many Spanish politicians.[21] Decentralized, regional self-government was difficult to reconcile with the tradition of a unitary centralist state that had emerged in the eighteenth and nineteenth centuries. It was even more difficult to reconcile the idea of Spain as a nation-state with that of Spain as a multilingual and even multinational state. For most Spaniards, their country was a nation-state, but for important minorities on the periphery it was only a state compatible with a regional national identification. These two contradictory concepts of the state, complicated by the ambiguous demands of the regional political movements, erupted as inescapable problems after the proclamation of the Republic.

The repressive policies of the Primo de Rivera dictatorship against Catalan nationalism, and the democratization of what had been an upper-class bourgeois movement, led in 1931 to the proclamation of Catalonia as a state integrated in an Iberic Federation. One of the immediate tasks of the provisional government of the Republic, therefore, was to find a formula for bringing the Catalans into the regime. It was the great achievement of Azaña, against the opposition of the Right and of many Republicans, to find an institutional solution to the demands for regional autonomy in the Estatutos. The ensuing debates on the linguistic question, in which the prominent Castilian-speaking intellectuals intervened, aroused the Castilian Spanish nationalists. On the other hand, the anticlerical policy and the initial weakness of a nationwide Catholic conservative opposition helped to strengthen the Partido Nacionalista Vasco (PNV), which represented Catholic sentiment in the Basque country and had vain hopes for separate regulation of relations between church and state in that region. But Catalonia, thanks to the understanding established between Azaña and Companys, was to have an autonomous government in the *Generalitat*. In the Basque country, the disagreements between the Basque nationalists and the Carlists, and the lack of sympathy of the Left for their aspirations, which initially appeared as proclerical and hostile to the Republic, prevented the creation of an autonomous regional government.

Regional nationalism contributed indirectly to the crisis of the Republic by arousing the Spanish Castilian nationalism of the authoritarian Right, symbolized by Calvo Sotelo or Pradera, and shared by many supporters of the more moderate Right. Given the background of much of the officer corps, such sentiments must have been strong in the army. The weakness in Catalonia and the Basque country of the nationwide moderate Center-Right parties, the CEDA and the Radicals, deprived those parties of a solid base among the more modern, urban bourgeoisie and of the leadership such a base could have provided.

More directly, Catalan nationalism and the Barcelona rebellion contributed to profound crisis in October 1934. Companys's statement on 6 October represented a coup d'état by the head of the regional autonomous government and a break with the constitutional legality of the Republic. Let us quote him:

In this solemn hour in the name of the people and the Parliament, the government that I preside over assumes all the faculties of power in Catalonia, proclaims the Catalan State of the Spanish Federal Republic and, to reestablish and fortify the relationship with the leaders of the general protest against fascism, invites them to establish in Catalonia the provisional government of the Republic, which will find in our Catalan people the most generous impulses of fraternity in the common desire to build a Federal, free, and magnificent Republic.

The government of Catalonia will at all times be in contact with the people. We aspire to establish in Catalonia the indestructible redoubt of the essences of the Republic. I invite all the Catalans to obedience to the government and ask that no one shall disobey its orders.[22]

The coup d'état proclaimed a new regime, a Federal Republic in whose name Companys demanded obedience from the military authorities. Their refusal and their loyalty to the Madrid central government, plus Companys's failure to mobilize the Catalan population, quickly brought an end to the hopes of the rebellion.[23]

The October crisis in Barcelona in 1934 involves many of the variables of our model as well as others that are specific to the relationship between central and regional governments. In this last respect, the situation had analogies in Weimar. The coexistence of two governments, the regional one of the Generalitat and the central one in Madrid, the delegation of some of Madrid's powers to the Generalitat, with two parliaments, the national and the Catalan, created complex constitutional problems. In a fully consolidated regime, such conflicts between federal and state governments can be resolved by the decisions of the constitutional tribunal. This procedure was foreseen in the Spanish constitution of 1931, but because of its lack of tradition and the bias of its composition, the tribunal's decision on the competence of the Catalan Parliament to legislate on agrarian contracts lacked authority.[24] The effort to juridify a political issue, so characteristic of weak governments, backfired. In this case, the constitutional issue was complicated by the overlap between national and class cleavages. After the proclamation of the Republic, the Esquerra had become the dominant party in opposition to the traditional, bourgeois, conservative Lliga. While the November 1933 elections had brought to power Radical Republican minority governments with CEDA support in Madrid, the January 1934 elections for the Catalan Parliament had reaffirmed control by the Esquerra. Therefore, the central and regional governments came to represent opposing class interests. When the Esquerra-dominated Parliament enacted a rural tenancy law that favored the supporters of Companys and tended to expand Catalan autonomy, the Catalan landlords turned to the central government to question the authority of the Catalan Parliament to enact such a law.

The issue produced a mass mobilization in Catalonia, bitter debates in the Spanish legislature, the reenactment of the law after its constitutionality had been rejected by the Tribunal of Constitutional Guarantees, and actions by the Catalan authorities against the judiciary. Against this background, two other factors became decisive: the radicalization of the Esquerra youth organization, and the emergence of the Estat Català radical nationalist group under the leadership of Josep Dencàs, which, with its fascist characteristics and its representation in the Catalan government, exercised pressure on Companys. The central government was willing to compromise on the issue, a decision that contributed to its imminent fall. The growing polarization of Lliga and Esquerra interests led to the withdrawal of the Lliga from the Catalan Parliament. The result was a situation in which a powerful regional interest group could turn to the central government for support while the regional government transformed a local class conflict into a nationalistic issue.

At the same time, the generalized distrust of the CEDA and the reaction to its entry into the government of the Center Left, Republicans and Socialists alike, prompted Companys's ambiguous actions in October and the proclamation quoted above. The central government and many Spaniards saw in that proclamation an anticonstitutional act, if not secession. Even though it could also be interpreted as a defense of the Republican regime against a potential threat, Catalan nationalists hoped to use it to change the relationship between the Spanish state and Catalonia. In June 1934, during a parliamentary debate on the thirteen to ten decision of the constitutional court, Azaña stated that "Catalonia is the last rampart left to the Republic. The autonomous power of Catalonia is the last republican power standing in Spain."[25] The statement poses an important question for the analysis of crisis and breakdown of democracies, particularly since it often has been argued that a more strongly federal Germany would have been an obstacle on the path of Hitler to power. It is noteworthy that in the last phase of the *Machtergreifung* the Bavarian government entertained ideas similar to those of Companys in 1934. During the debate, Cambó, the leader of the Catalan Lliga, posed the problem in the following terms:

They speak always as if Catalonia has to be the bulwark of the Left in Spain and of the leftist orientation of the Republic. Within Catalonia parties have the right to express whatever sympathies they may wish; Catalonia collectively, and in its name, its government, has no right to make statements which might endanger the respect that the freedoms of Catalonia deserve of all those governing Spain. Catalonia, collectively, and specially the representative institutions of Catalonia, should not be the bulwark of anyone; they should only be the bulwark of Catalonia.[26]

Cambó rightly stressed how the combination of nationwide cleavages with center versus periphery cleavages threatened the consociational compromise achieved with the Republic. The regional government, by siding with the nationwide opposition and using powers delegated to it by the central government, broke with the consociational solution. The same would be true if the central government were to side with the regional opposition, as it did indirectly by taking the issue of legislative competence before the constitutional court. There is, however, a basic difference between the ill-advised transformation of the political conflict into a legal issue and the proclamation of a Catalan state in a Spanish federal republic by the Catalan regional government.

This crisis demonstrates many of the variables of our model. We find disloyal opposition to the Spanish state in the Catalan extreme nationalists of the Estat Català and other minor groups. Paramilitary groups, the *escamots*, emerged with their distinctive shirts and nationalist social revolutionary mystique. Semiloyalty to the 1931 constitutional pact of elements in Companys's party pushed him to his 6 October decision. The ambivalent relationship between a major party, the Lliga, and the interest group of the landlords, the Instituto San Isidro, prevented them from acting in a politically more constructive way. Azaña's presence in Barcelona made him suspect of semiloyalty, even though it seems clear that he disapproved of the proclamation. However, he did not communicate his knowledge of the intentions of the Catalanists to his political enemy, Lerroux, the head of the Madrid government, and this action would certainly not be covered by our strict definition of loyal opposition.[27] The destructive efforts of the Radical-CEDA governments to link Azaña with the rebellion later contributed to his leadership of a broad Popular Front coalition as well as to the hostility of many Republicans against those governments. This undermining of the personal legitimacy of potentially powerful and respected leaders, so characteristic of the crisis of regimes, was another result of the Barcelona rebellion. Perhaps the inevitable but politically unwise measures against Catalan autonomy, rather than against those responsible for the events, fanned the upsurge of nationalism there and made post-1934 reequilibration of the regime difficult by straining the relationship between Cambó and Gil Robles. Another consequence was the legitimization of the role of the army in deciding political crises, in this case under the intelligent and prudent leadership of a Catalan general in Barcelona, who in July 1936 would be put to death for failing to join the Franco rebellion. It is interesting to note that on 4 October Companys made an unsuccessful attempt to establish contact with the president of the republic, Alcalá Zamora (that is, in our model, with the neutral power) to try to prevent the formation of the new government.

The situation in Barcelona in 1934 exemplifies a special and complex pattern of semiloyal opposition: regional authorities acting beyond constitutional limits to defend a regime against what they perceive as its betrayal by the central government. In a real crisis, rather than a perceived crisis, such an act could serve to defend democracy; but when unjustified, as in this case, it serves only to deepen its crisis. Since the regional government represented a peripheral nationalism, such actions were inevitably perceived as a threat to the unity of the state. This analysis casts doubt on the thesis that the federal structure could serve as an instrument for the defense of democracy by creating regional bulwarks to serve as a basis for the reconquest of democratic institutions. On these grounds, a defense of democracy against Hitler on the basis of Bavarian particularism had little chance.[28] On the other hand, the different political alignments at the regional and national levels in a highly divided society are likely to create a constitutional crisis when the central government intervenes against the regional government, as in the action of the Papen government against Prussia. Those who place so much faith in regional autonomies as stabilizers of Italian democracy should not lose sight of these experiences. Certainly, in multinational societies, the defense of democracy by either the central or the regional government is not likely to help safeguard democratic institutions, since large segments of the population will perceive the conflict as one between nationalities.

It should also be noted that when the Esquerra deputies abandoned the Spanish Parliament to protest the decision of the constitutional court, the Basque nationalists also left their seats. In September 1934 they convened an assembly of municipal representatives to which the Catalans sent a delegation, but which was dissolved by the minister of the interior. The activities of the Catalans to create a coalition based on regional nationalism under the label "Galeuzca" was perceived by the Spanish Right as part of a conspiracy, especially after the Catalan rebellion converged with the Socialist revolution. Their perception was inaccurate but understandable, as it was a projection of their own conspiratorial activities. In 1934, the Basque nationalists, who had been courted by monarchist military conspirators in the first bienio, started their rapprochement with the Left, under the tactical guidance of Prieto. Their commitment to nationalism above all ultimately found them on a side where they did not belong in terms of class and religious outlook—a fact that ultimately embittered the Right against demands for regional autonomy and strengthened the authoritarian opposition to the Republic.

While the complex interaction between regional nationalism, class, and religious issues contributed significantly to the crisis of the thirties, in the spring of 1936 class and ideological conflict became dominant in the final breakdown. For, after the failure of the Estat Català group and in view of the unsympathetic attitude of the Right toward regional aspirations, the Esquerra and the Lliga in Catalonia developed relations that fitted the model of government and loyal opposition and made the region a focal point of relative stability.

Loyalty, Disloyalty, and Semiloyalty

In the Spanish case any attempt at meaningful delimitation of loyalty, disloyalty, and semiloyalty presents almost insuperable difficulties. The main actors do not include a mass Fascist party that explicitly rejects liberal democracy, or an electorally strong Communist party committed to revolution, but rather the Socialist party (PSOE) and the Catholic conservative party (CEDA), whose statements and actions could be characterized at one moment as loyal to democratic institutions and at the next as disloyal. The basic statements—and even more, the perceptions—of these major actors contributed to ambiguous decisions by parties that in other democracies would have been unambiguously loyal. Actions like the break with the institutions by Izquierda Republicana and Unión Republicana on 5 October 1934 can only be understood in that context. Suspicion of the intentions of the CEDA, within the frame of reference created by Hitler's *Machtergreifung*, and particularly the Austrian crisis in February 1934, explain Izquierda Republicana's revealing statement that "the monstrous fact of turning over the government of the Republic to its enemies is a treason. [We] break all solidarity with the present institutions of the regime and affirm [our] decision to turn to all means in defense of the Republic."[29] Such a statement would have been an appropriate expression of loyalty to democratic institutions in the case of a Fascist takeover. But the question here was the formation of a government, still under the leadership of Lerroux, a Radical party prime minister of Republican tradition, and concerned the appointment of three representatives of the CEDA (the largest party in Parliament, with 105 of 474 deputies) to the ministries of agriculture, labor, and justice. This crucial change in a fifteen-man cabinet took place in a parliamentary framework, not as a result of mass pressure on the streets, and two of the three CEDA ministers certainly could not be characterized as antidemocratic or even anti-Republican. In view of the public record after the October Revolution, but not perhaps if one takes into account the more informal feelers CEDA extended toward the army, the reaction of Izquierda Republicana must be defined as semiloyal.

This raises the question of "Loyalty to what?" If loyalty is defined in terms of the commitment to democratic institutions, it means loyal to whoever, under those formal procedures, is entitled to govern regardless of policies pursued, assuming, of course, that the government maintains respect for civil liberties, democratic processes, and the right to free elections. According to these terms, few political forces were unconditionally loyal, and even those coming closest to that standard acted toward democratic governments in ways that are at least dubious. For example, Lerroux, the leader of one of the great parties of Spanish Republicanism, conspirator against the monarchy, leading figure in the coalition governments of the first two years, was apparently not unaware of the sentiments that led to the Sanjurjo pronunciamento, but he only indirectly warned the prime minister, Azaña, of the growing danger.[30] Similarly, years later, Azaña, although he knew of the plans of the Socialists and the Catalan regional government, did not feel obliged to warn the prime minister, Lerroux, nor to publicly dissociate himself from his party's ambiguous support of Socialist revolution and Catalan rebellion.[31] An independent Republican and highly civil politician like Chapaprieta recounts in his memoirs that when asked for advice in March 1936 by the president of the Republic, he recommended appointing a new government (an act within his constitutional prerogative), which, with the support of the armed forces, would restablish order and authority.[32] He justified his position by arguing that the elections had given the Left only a small majority—he obviously did not take into account the dubious returns of the second round—and that a large number of the electorate had not cast their vote, so that one-third of the electorate was imposing its will on the rest of Spain. Presidential intervention would then pave the way for a new election. Certainly such advice ran counter to a strict definition of loyalty to parliamentary majority rule.

The definition of loyalty to the institutions of the new regime was even more restricted. Its founders were inclined to define as loyal only those who had participated in the establishment of the Republic; that is, those whose politics ranged from Radical on farther to the left. Irrespective of proper democratic behavior, the intention to modify the substantive content of the constitution was defined as disloyal. After 1933, the Socialist party defined as disloyal any party that advocated revoking or changing the policies enacted in the first bienio. Such positions tended to narrow the basis of legitimacy for the new regime.

The system of forces and parties will perhaps be more clearly understood if identified in terms of my definitions of loyal, semiloyal, and disloyal. The Anarcho-syndicalist CNT (Confederación Nacional del Trabajo) and the activists of the FAI (Federación Anarquista Ibérica) in control of the great trade union federation constituted a sincere disloyal opposition to a parliamentary regime, even under a Left-dominated government.[33] The CNT's antagonism to the Socialists and the actions of its followers, particularly the sporadic violence in the first bienio, provoked the regime to repressive actions like the events of Casas Viejas. These were cynically exploited by the opposition (including the Center Republicans) and contributed to Azaña's loss of prestige. The effect could be compared to that of the Spartakist and local Communist uprisings in the postwar years of the Weimar Republic.

The initially insignificant Communist party, the PCE, was a permanent disloyal opposition, which participated as a minor actor in the Asturian Revolution and afterward exercised an overt or covert influence on the maximalization of the Socialist party.[34] The fusion of the Socialist and Communist youth organizations in the spring of 1936 represented a major step in the polarization process and the centrifugal tendencies of the Left. Even though it had few adherents, nonorthodox communism in Catalonia—consisting of the Bloc Obrer i Camperol, the Partit Català Proletari, the later Partido Socialista Unificado de Cataluña (PSUC), the independent Communist leadership, and the Partido Obrero de Unificación Marxista (POUM)—assumed the role of a disloyal opposition combining nationalist and revolutionary appeals in Catalonia.[35] Those minor Catalan extreme leftist parties combined under competent leadership to create the revolutionary Alianza Obrera and played a role in the events of October 1934 in Barcelona, proclaiming a general strike and contributing to popular mobilization in support of the Catalan nationalists. Congruently with our model, the period after the November 1933 elections and even more after the October revolution strengthened centrifugal tendencies in the PSOE and the UGT (Unión General de Trabajadores, the Socialist trade union federation) that ranged from semiloyal to disloyal. In contrast to Germany, Finland, and even Austria and Italy, the line between a system-supporting Socialist party and the revolutionary opposition in Spain was continuously eroded. The competition between political movements on the left for the support of the working class and the context created by the rise of fascism brought the Socialists closer to the revolutionary, antidemocratic forces.[36]

On the other side of the political spectrum, the Traditionalists had always been a principled, disloyal opposition, even to the conservative liberal oligarchic monarchy.[37] Indirectly, they contributed much to the failure to integrate peripheral nationalism into the system. They also provided a historical ideological link for the turn toward authoritarianism of the Alphonsine monarchists.[38] In spite of equivocal appeals by the king for moderation, and the lack of cooperation of many monarchist notables and caciques willing to make peace with a conservative Republic, monarchism under the Republic underwent a process similar to that of the DNVP (Deutschnationale Volkspartei) under the leadership of Hugenberg. Hugenberg's Spanish equivalent, Calvo Sotelo, radicalized by persecution and intellectual contact with the Action Française during his Paris exile, became a pole of attraction to disloyalty and violence on the right.[39] Just as the Communists, orthodox and heterodox, represented a minority on the left, modern fascism was a minority force on the right, not comparable in strength even to the Finnish Lapua.[40] However, its presence in the heated political climate of the thirties contributed to the defensive violence of the Socialists and the retaliatory acts of Fascist violence; and finally to the exaltation of violence by its leaders, all of which fed into the process of breakdown of civil peace. Once again the boundaries between disloyalty and acceptance with reservations of the new regime by the Center Right, particularly the CEDA, were more blurred in Spain than in Germany, where the Zentrum and even the DVP (Deutsche Volkspartei) emphasized the distinctions between themselves and the NSDAP. That the supporters of Calvo Sotelo belonged socially to the same groups as many supporters of the CEDA, and thus did not represent a challenge to Catholicism, enhanced the ambiguity despite the disagreement of the CEDA and Calvo Sotelo about tactics. Participation in the Parliament and the government from 1933 to 1935 seriously strained the relationship between the Center Right and the extreme Right. In that period the Center Right began to move from semiloyalty to loyalty to the democratic regime.[41] However, as the Socialist party moved toward maximalist semiloyal, if not clearly disloyal, positions, and the CEDA faced the competition of the extreme Right and the Falange, particularly among its youth and student supporters, it could not avoid a turn to semiloyalty, even though some of its leaders expressed interest in last-minute reequilibration efforts.

It is difficult in our terms to define the Partido Nacionalista Vasco (PNV) as either loyal or semiloyal. Its actions, with minor exceptions, would place it in the loyal opposition, but the ambiguities of its nationalism, some of its organizational activities, such as paramilitary youth groups, its rhetoric, and its occasional withdrawals (*retraimientos*) from the parliamentary process led some participants at one point or another to perceive it as semiloyal. In Catalonia, minorities within the Catalan nationalist movement, particularly the fascistic activists of the Estat Català, can be considered another disloyal opposition; in 1934 they exercised a centrifugal attraction on the Esquerra, particularly its youth organization. Once more, the boundaries between disloyalty and loyalty, in this case to the Spanish state, were blurred. The effort to create paramilitary organizations and the rhetoric of violence was again present in a three-pronged attack against the conservative Catalans of the Lliga, the central government, and the CNT. If loyalty to the new regime were construed strictly and narrowly, the initial Catalanist interpretation of what the agreement of San Sebastian (on which the founding coalition of the Republic had been based) and the latter efforts to reinterpret the autonomy granted in 1932 could have been perceived by many Spaniards as semiloyal. However, until 1934 and again in the spring of 1936, the Esquerra could be considered one of the basic regime-supporting parties.[42] The same was true of the Lliga throughout the Republic, despite the belated rallying of Cambó to the monarchy in the period 1930–31, the temporary *retraimiento* from the Catalan Parliament dominated by the Esquerra, and local electoral coalitions with the extreme Right. Had it not been for a minority of extreme nationalists and the complexities of working-class politics in Catalonia, the two great Catalan parties, Lliga and Esquerra, could have been important regime-supporting forces. The Center Right, Radicals and CEDA, failed, partly under the pressure of the Castilian-nationalist-oriented Agrarians, in not working more closely with a regime-oriented party like the Lliga.

It is worth emphasizing once more that except for the Anarcho-syndicalist CNT, the openly disloyal oppositions in Spain were, almost to the end, weak in comparison with others in Europe. Neither communism nor fascism had a strong appeal to the Spanish electorate. Even the monarchists of Renovación were probably electorally weaker than the DNVP and were less well-connected with the industrial bourgeoisie, the army, and the bureaucracy. Their rhetoric notwithstanding, minority nationalist groups were less disloyal to the state than similar minorities in Eastern Europe. Ultimately, the breakdown of Spanish democracy must be blamed on the semiloyalty of parties that in other European countries tended clearly to define their allegiance to a democratic regime and their distance from disloyal oppositions, the Socialists, and the demo-Christians or Catholic parties. Blame also falls on the bourgeois Left, Center-Left and Center-Right Republicans, and the Esquerra, and this is the most complex problem. These parties, the regime's founding forces, acted, sometimes with the best intentions, in ways that contributed to the crisis of the regime. Their positions throughout those years would not have been called semiloyal; in retrospect, however, certain actions at some critical junctures, particularly in October 1934, could be defined as semiloyal to democracy, though not to the Republic as conceived by them, for loyalty to the regime established in 1931 is much more limited than loyalty to democracy.

The inability of Azaña and Lerroux, the two most outstanding Republican leaders, to continue working for the institutionalization of the regime, and the resultant fractionalization of the Center Republican parties, were both a sign and a cause of the crisis. It might be tempting to attribute that incapacity to personality differences, but that would be incorrect, since the policies of the Radicals and of the leftist Republicans (initially Acción Republicana, and later, Izquierda Republicana) represented two basic policy options. Azaña's was an effort to combine a bourgeois revolution with social reforms that would incorporate the Socialists into a democratic regime at the risk of losing conservative Republican support. Technical inadequacies, misjudgment in timing and priorities of reforms, pressure from sporadic violence of the Anarcho-syndicalists, the ressentiment policies of petit bourgeois politicians, and an ideological shift within the Socialist party all worked against the noble attempt.[43]

Lerroux, faced with Azaña's decision, the hostility those policies had created in a broad middle class that supported the Republic, and perhaps personally frustrated in his ambitions, attempted another strategy: the incorporation of the Catholic conservative masses, peasants, and middle classes into the Republic, luring them away from an ambiguous semiloyalty.[44] Though an inadequate solution to the social problems of an underdeveloped agrarian country, that policy, in view of the Socialists' tendency toward withdrawal from the responsibilities of the regime, represented a grand design in political terms. Its failure can be blamed on the disloyal revolution by the Socialists and the rebellion of the Catalan Generalitat, the semiloyalty of the Left bourgeois Republicans, the rigidity of the Right and of the interests it represented after 1934, and ultimately on the personal discrediting of Lerroux because of the corruption within the Radical party. The persistent veto of the neutral power of the president of the Republic, Alcalá Zamora, made Lerroux's design impossible. In a regime faced with unsolvable problems like conditional legitimacy, low levels of institutionalization of such conflict-solving mechanisms as a constitutional court, and disloyal oppositions engaging in violence or appealing to it, centripetal tendencies were bound to fail.

There was a third alternative in 1933, represented with more or less coherence by Gordón Ordás and Martínez Barrio. It was based on a broad centrist coalition of Republicans that would have isolated Socialists and clericals, pursued a policy of bourgeois political and cultural reformism, and de-emphasized the solution of pressing social problems.[45] Such a policy, which would have required a different attitude on the part of Lerroux and Azaña, might have been supported by the president and most of the army and have been able to face the opposition of the Right, but it would have encountered decided hostility from the working class, especially the Socialist party. Historically, it would have been a sterile solution, but it might have assured continuity of the regime at about the efficacy level of the Third Republic in France, given the social tensions. It would have been based on a solid core of parties loyal to a democratic regime and, with minor modifications, loyal to the constituent acts of the Republic in the fields of religious, military, and regional policy. Even some of the necessary social reforms would have continued at a slow pace. It would have been an embattled but persistent, if not stable, regime.

The great question that remains almost unanswerable and will be clarified only by more monographic research is why centrifugal tendencies rather than centripetal tendencies were reinforced in the major parties so that possible boundaries between disloyal opposition and conditional support of the regime became blurred. Paul Preston, polemicizing with Richard Robinson, has provided us with a good description of the strong semiloyaity in the CEDA that almost inevitably was perceived by the Socialists and many Left Republicans as a sign of potential disloyalty.[46] Stanley Payne, Edward Malefakis, and earlier, Salvador de Madariaga, have documented the radicalization of the Socialist party toward semiloyalty and even overt revolutionary disloyalty to a democratic republic. The problem is identifying the factors that led to those tendencies, their relative weight, and even more, their timing. Undoubtedly the mutual perceptions and misperceptions of key actors initiated a complex process of feedback that makes it difficult to place the blame on either side, even when the responsibility in terms of overt action of the maximalist Socialist leadership cannot be questioned.

If considerations of weight and timing are put aside, however, an enumeration of the most obvious factors is possible. Foremost is the accidentalism and consequent attentism toward democracy in both the Marxist and the Catholic ideological heritages. Democracy and a bourgeois parliamentary republic are of only instrumental value for a labor movement whose ultimate goal is a better society for the working class and can be abandoned for the dictatorship of the proletariat if perceived as necessary to achieve the goal. Only a full commitment to the long-run Marxist view of social development and the awareness of the limits for revolutionary action in a particular society can make a strictly Marxist view compatible with a negative integration into democracy. This accounts for the position of the only intellectual Marxist in the Spain of the thirties, Besteiro, who opposed participation in the Republican coalition government as well as the October revolution. The more pragmatic, "ouvrieriste" position represented by Largo Caballero allowed Socialist collaboration with the Primo de Rivera dictatorship, his acceptance of the Ministry of Labor in the bienio governments, and the maximalist turn after disillusionment with Republican and Socialist sponsored reformism. The ideological pragmatism that some would label opportunism and Prieto's realistic evaluation of the possibilities for reform and revolution were closer to the realities of the Spanish situation and to the traditional positions of Western European social democrats.[47] However, in the context of the thirties, given the rise of fascism, the unsolvable social problems, the rapid and massive mobilization of the working class, particularly by the Socialists in the countryside, and the competition with the Anarcho-syndicalists and orthodox and heterodox Communists, the appeal of such a position was limited. Besteiro's stance, in line with orthodox prewar Marxism, had been feasible in a stable nondemocratic regime like imperial Germany but was not politically viable for a democratic republic in a society like Spain.[48] In that context, the maximalist voluntarist interpretation of the ideological heritage appealed to most intellectuals in the party and to a large mass of new followers who had not been socialized in the social democratic tradition.[49]

A similar ideological ambiguity in the Catholic heritage operated on the right, compounded by both the Spanish and the international situations. The Catholic church as an institution sees itself as permanent and independent of political change, capable of compromise with any regime, as long as it is a powerful regime or one that respects the vital interests of the church. The stabilization of democracy in Europe, and the need to use its instrumentalities to defend the church's interests even in a hostile climate of bourgeois laicism and anticlericalism, led the papacy to formulate an accidentalist position toward changes in regime. This was quickly picked up in April 1931 by the lay leaders of Spanish Catholicism and was effectively supported by the Vatican, sometimes in conflict with certain leaders of the Spanish hierarchy, who were emotionally identified with the monarchy that had favored both them and the church.[50] This accidentalism was not easy to defend when faced with what many Catholics considered to be the outrageously anticlerical and even antireligious policies of Left Republicans in coalition with the Socialists. Certainly, there were strains of democratic commitment within the Catholic tradition. But the relative political neutralization of the church after the Restoration and the cultural isolation of Spanish Catholicism weakened those tendencies. The far-reaching secularization of the Spanish working class in the nineteenth and early twentieth centuries, and the complex interdependency between the church and the ownership class, had limited the strength of the Christian social movement except in some peasant areas. The sudden mobilization of the Catholic masses by the religious policies of the Republic became more defensive and therefore more conservative than either the Christian Democratic or Christian Social tendencies, and aroused the fear and suspicion of the Left Republicans and all working-class forces.[51] The emergence of a mass party without cadres socialized in the Catholic political and social ideology posed some of the same problems for the CEDA as did the expansion of the Socialist labor movement. The centrality of a single issue—the revision of the anticlerical policies—combined with the narrow-minded defense of the interests of a middle class insecure in its status and economic position, did not help to integrate the Catholic position into the Republic. The Catholic ideological tradition contained concepts incompatible with pluralist liberal democracy, such as corporativism, which in central and northern Europe, and even in France, nevertheless fused with secular non-Fascist intellectual traditions and practices but that in Spain were associated with the anti-revolutionary Carlist heritage and fascism. The example of Dollfuss's struggle with the Socialists in Austria made that ideological heritage particularly threatening.

These basic ideological ambiguities were reinforced by certain practical consequences of the electoral system: the disproportionate number of seats allotted to a relative majority; the need for a minimum quorum to qualify to obtain seats and to avoid a runoff in which divided opponents could unite to gain a disproportionate advantage; and the large districts that weakened the appeal of notables. These, combined with the parties' newness and uncertainty about their strength, obliged major parties to court minor parties by including their candidates in joint lists and to deemphasize the distinctions between allies, at least at the national level. In 1933, for instance, the Right maintained its ambiguity on the issue of monarchy versus republic. In parts of the country where it felt weak, it entered into alliances based on social conservatism with the clearly Republican Radicals, and in others, when more assured of victory, it emphasized its distinctiveness from the extreme Right.[52] Such ambiguity of electoral alliances in the campaign inevitably produced an image that justified accusing the Right of semiloyalty to the regime. These accusations gained strength through the later recriminations by the extreme Right when it felt betrayed by the Center's cooperation with Radicals and with the system generally.

Another effect of the electoral rules in the November 1933 elections was that their lack of cooperation weakened the representation of the Socialists and, particularly, the Left Republicans. This alone, even if no other reason had existed, would have precluded a post-election coalition between Center Right, Center Left, and Left Republicans of the type so well known in the Third French Republic.

In 1936 the same dynamics contributed to a popular front coalition that ranged from the Communists to the Center Left Republicans and forced the regime-supporting parties to appear to the electorate as though they had opened the door to semiloyal and disloyal forces.[53] This increased the difficulty of asserting their authority against their erstwhile allies. In turn the strains within the Right made the formation of joint electoral policies in 1936 difficult, thereby giving the Left an excess of confidence in its strength.

The electoral system had similar consequences for Catalonia's many parties. It forced moderate parties into alliances with nationalist extremists that allowed their opponents to question their loyalty to the Spanish state, or at least to the 1931 compromise on regional autonomy. It also obliged the Lliga to cooperate electorally with the nationwide parties on the Right that were hostile to demands for regional autonomy.[54] The system also tended to deprive parties appealing to the non-Catalan Castilian-speaking minority of a distinct representation. This created a false impression of unanimity in the support of peripheral nationalism.

On the basis of the experience of Germany and other democracies in crisis, Hermens has argued that proportional representation tends to make the fractionalization of parties permanent and permits crisis support for extremist parties to create patterns of representation in parliaments that soon become unworkable. In ways not yet fully clear, the Spanish system seems to have combined the disadvantages of extreme multipartisan, centrifugal polarization and confrontation of two major blocs, causing a bimodal distribution and the elimination of the Center, and assuring minor extremist groups of a disproportionate number of candidates because of the marginal utility of those additional votes. Unfortunately, the Spanish case was not included in the systematic analysis of the political and social effects of electoral systems, but as mentioned earlier, it should give pause to those who attribute too great a share in the breakdown of democracies to proportional representation.

During the course of the Republic, certain leaders were aware of the dysfunctional consequences of the electoral system, particularly the Lliga leadership and, judging by its programmatic statements, the CEDA.[55] But none of the major parties made a serious effort to reform the system. Hopes for a majoritarian victory became part of the maximalist syndrome and were incompatible with any centripetal and consociational tendencies characteristic of major parties.

Neither ideological ambiguity nor the ambiguous image and commitments fostered by the electoral system would have been so important if external events had not reinforced the fears of all major participants. Knowledge of semi- or pseudo-legal power takeovers in Italy, Germany, and Austria must have been an important factor in the defensive radicalization of the Socialists, the Esquerra, and the Left Republicans that crystalized in the October 1934 crisis. That changed European atmosphere also influenced the creation of a broad popular front, which finally included the Communists, despite their numerical weakness. The search for proletarian unity between Socialists and Anarcho-syndicalists, which would have been inconceivable in the first two years of the Republic, also reflected the changed climate. It also accounted for a certain mimicry of fascist styles by the CEDA's youth movement, the Juventud de Acción Popular (JAP), including provocative mass rallies.[56] The creation and success of partisan paramilitary organizations did not have roots in the Spanish past, but were a reflection of external influences. The violence of such organizations and the unwillingness of moderate leaders to dissociate themselves publicly from their activities became a major variable in the climate of distrust.

Counteracting these centrifugal tendencies and the semiloyalty, apparent or real, of parties and leaders would have required increased informal communication within the elite; this would have aided efforts toward political reequilibration of the type that operated in France in 1934 and 1958. However, the enormous discontinuity and inexperience of the political personnel of the regime precluded the establishment of such patterns before the critical years and even during the three legislative periods of the Republic (see table 2).[57] Of the 992 persons elected in those three legislatures, only 116 (11.7 percent) had been members of the lower house or the Senate between 1916 and 1923. In Germany in 1922, 27 percent of the elected officials had been deputies before 1918. Only 7 of the 105 PSOE deputies in 1931 had served under the monarchy, compared to the 48 veterans of the 108 SPD deputies in 1922. Again, in the 1933 legislature, only 10 of 105 followers of Gil Robles had pre-1931 parliamentary experience. This surely contributed to the lack of solidarity within the political class and the tense style of the parliamentary process. The electoral system reinforced those tendencies in the course of the five years of the Republic, since only 71 of the 992 deputies (representing 213 of the 1384 incumbencies) sat in the Cortes throughout the three legislatures. Six hundred seventeen of the 992 would meet their fellow legislators only during one legislative period. Despite the relatively similar quantitative

Table 2. Parliamentary Representation in the Three Legislatures of the Republic (1931, 1933, and 1936)

		Number of Deputies			
Legislature Elected	Elected to All 3 Legislatures	Elected to 2 Consecutive Legislatures	Elected in 1931 and 1936, but not in 1933	Elected to 1 Legislature	Total Number in Each Legislature [a]
1931	71	67	68	258	464
1933	↓	↓ 115	↓	197	450
1936	↓	↓	↓	216	470
Total	71 (7.1%)	182 (18.3%)	68 (6.9%)	617 (67.8%)	992
Total number of incumbencies held by those deputies	213 (15.6%)	364 (26.1%)	136 (9.8%)	671 (48.3%)	1384

[a]Based on 1384 seats. The deputies included in this analysis are only those who appear on the *Lista de los Señores Diputados* published by the Cortes in December 1932, March 1935, and June 1936. Those lists do not include all deputies, due to vacancies and contested seats. The actual number of incumbencies and individuals occupying them is therefore somewhat larger. For an analysis of those data see Juan J. Linz, "Continuidad y discontinuidad en la élite política española: De la Restauración al Régimen actual (Franco)," in *Libro homenaje al Prof. Carlos Ollero: Estudios de ciencia política y sociología* (Guadalajara: Gráficas Carlavilla, 1972), pp. 361–412. These data show the extent to which the crisis in the parties and the electoral system deprived the regime of a stable and experienced elite accustomed to working together in Parliament.

strength of the Socialist party representation in 1931 and 1936, only 29 percent of those elected in 1931 and 52.5 percent of the smaller parliamentary group of 1933 returned in 1936. This high turnover within the Socialist party reflects and in part explains the changed political outlook of the PSOE.

Our model emphasizes the significance of the questioning of the moral and political integrity of key leaders as a contributing factor to crisis and break-down. Certainly, in the case of Spain, this process affected two prominent leaders of the regime forces. This was exemplified by the hateful campaign against Azaña on the occasion of the Casas Viejas incident and later on the basis of his unproved participation in the Barcelona rebellion. The very early questioning by the new Republicans of Lerroux's role in opposition to the monarchy, combined with the suspicion of corruption surrounding him and his party, led many to push the old leader aside and ultimately brought about his painful downfall.[58] The animosity in the polemics within the Socialist party between Largo Caballero and Prieto after 1934, or within the Right between Calvo Sotelo and Gil Robles, and the widespread derision among all political groupings toward the president, Alcalá Zamora, were other instances in which the personal legitimacy of the leading actors was undermined.

Unfortunately, we know very little about the degree to which legislatures and leaders were prevented from taking responsible, system-oriented political action by their dependence on specific interest groups. How much truth is there, for example, in the often alleged role played by Masonry in producing splits and dissension within the Republican parties. Dependence on economic interests, particularly the large landowners, certainly contributed to the right-ward turn of the CEDA in May 1935; further, Gil Robles's refusal to support the tax reforms of Chapaprieta contributed to the disintegration of the last Center-Right governments in the fall of 1935.[59] The previously described role of the Catalan landlords in provoking the crisis of 1934 is another example.[60] In Spain, as in the other cases, the dependency of parties on special interest groups and the incapacity or unwillingness of the leadership to oppose them, sometimes against their better judgment, are both a symptom and a cause of the crisis.

In summary, at one point or another, and with varying intensity, the variables we have just discussed contributed to a situation in which few of the leaders of even the most system-oriented parties were willing to place the maintenance of the system ahead of their other commitments to ideology, interest groups, or personal vetoes.

The Role of the Neutral Powers: Defenders of the Constitution or Obstacles to the Democratic Political Process?

Our model illustrates how certain moderating powers outside or above parties—kings, presidents, and courts—become, in crisis democracies, independent influences rather than mere cogs in the democratic machinery. In

Table 3. **Cabinets of the Republic, 14 April 1931 to 19 July 1936**

				Ministers	
Period	Prime Minister	Date Constituted	Duration (in days)	Total Incumbents	Newcomers to Cabinet Level
I Provisional governments					
1	Alcalá-Zamora	14 April 1931	183	12	11
	Constituent Assembly election 28 June 1931				
2	Azaña Díaz	14 October 1931	63	11	1
II Left Republican-Socialist coalition					
3	Azaña Díaz	16 December 1931	543	11	2
4	Azaña Díaz	12 June 1933	92	11+1	4
Periods I and II			881	(average duration, 220 days)	
III Transition governments					
5	Lerroux García	12 September 1933	26	13	10
6	Martínez Barrio	8 October 1933	69	13+1	6
	Legislative elections 20 November 1933				
IV Radical party-dominated governments with CEDA tolerance					
7	Lerroux García	16 December 1933	77	13+2	5
8	Lerroux García	3 March 1934	56	12+1	3
9	Samper Ibáñez	2 May 1934	159	13	2
Periods III and IV			387	(average duration, 77 days)	
V Radical-CEDA governments					
10	Lerroux with 3 CEDA ministers	4 October 1934	181	15+2	9
11	Lerroux with "experts"	3 April 1935	33	13	6
12	Lerroux with Gil Robles	6 May 1935	142	13	7
13	Chapaprieta Torregrosa with Lerroux, Gil Robles	25 September 1935	34	9	2
14	Chapaprieta Torregrosa without Lerroux	29 October 1935	46	9	2
			436	(average duration, 87 days)	
VI Interim governments					
15	Portela Valladares	14 December 1935	16	10	6
16	Portela Valladares majority nonparty	30 December 1935	51	9	3
Periods IV, V, and VI—called "bienio negro" by its opponents			795	(the two black years) (average duration 79 days)	
	Legislative elections 16 February 1936				
VII					
17	Azaña Díaz	19 February 1936	47	13	7
18	Azaña Díaz	7 April 1936	36	13	
	Barcia Trelles	28 May 1936			
	substitute due to Azaña's presidential candidacy				
	Presidential election 26 April 1936				
19	Casares Quiroga	13 May 1936	66	13	—
Left-bourgeois governments after Popular Front election			149		
17–18 July—military uprising; One-day government of Martínez Barrios, 19 July 1936, first civil war government under José Giral					

NOTE: To summarize, during the period from 14 April 1931 to 18 July 1936 (1920 days), the Republic saw nineteen governments and eight prime ministers. The average duration of cabinets was 101 days.

studying a single case, it is tempting to attribute the impact of such offices to the personal idiosyncrasies of their incumbents rather than to structural factors. The personality of President Alcalá Zamora—his touchiness, his jealousy of other political leaders, his outdated political style, his personal preference for weak political leaders, and the role of his entourage—is a particular case in point.[61] The pattern of his relationship with parties, party leaders, Parliament, and extra-parliamentary opinion resembled that maintained by King Alphons XIII prior to 1923. Alcalá Zamora's dissolution of the legislature in 1933 and again on 1 January 1936, his efforts to influence the cabinet formation process, his selection of prime ministers in crisis periods, and his veto of certain leaders were certainly debatable aspects of the political process. Such actions were possible because of weakness or stalemate in Parliament, suspicion of the semiloyalty of parties and their leaders, his own sensitivity to opinion and other pressures outside of Parliament, and his use of information obtained informally. The president reacted to the unstable situation that had arisen by the summer of 1933 by broadening the interpretation of his powers and acting as an arbiter of legitimacy in the system, which led to the alienation and hostility of practically all major political forces and made his ouster before the expiration of his term an event regretted by few despite its ambiguous legality and serious consequences. In attempting to play his role as a defender of the constitution, he unwittingly contributed to a power vacuum and ultimately to breakdown.

The president's misinterpretation of his role in 1935, particularly in connection with the *straperlo* scandal, was manifest in his formation of governments that included his friends and excluded important party leaders, his persistent veto of Gil Robles, and the formation of the two Portela governments. (For data on cabinets of the Republic, see table 3.) The last of these, on 30 December 1935, included no representatives of any of the major parties, only individuals close to the president. It was similar in some respects to the Hindenburg presidential cabinets in that it was unable to present itself before Parliament and its purpose was to organize the elections in the vain hope of creating a new Center from above. All these were actions that contributed to the breakdown of parliamentary democratic government. The defenders of the president might argue that the potential semiloyalty or even disloyalty of Gil Robles and many others in his party justified the actions of the president as a defense of the Republican democratic government. Conversely, it could be argued that if that were true, Gil Robles had had ample time for a coup in the period between 6 May and 14 December 1935, when he was minister of the army.

A neutral power whose role during the Republic has not yet been studied is the Tribunal of Constitutional Guarantees; in addition, there is no analysis of the role of the judiciary as a whole in the handling of social unrest and political violence. Certainly, as noted first by La Cierva,[62] efforts to juridify political conflicts—the Catalan rural tenancy law, for example—and to reform the judiciary for political reasons—a policy advocated by the Center Right in 1935 and by the Popular Front in 1936—indicate that the crisis of democracy was accompanied by an increase in the political significance of the judiciary, and consequently of governmental efforts to exercise influence upon it.

Certain leading intellectual figures, particularly Ortega y Gasset, could also be considered to constitute a kind of neutral power. Written from a vantage point outside partisan strife, his brilliant critique of the Republic between 1931 and 1933 contributed to the alienation of many intelligent Spaniards from the system.[63]

In our model the neutral power of presidents or kings also plays a major role as well in the final power vacuum or crisis that legitimizes the transfer of power to antidemocratic forces, as with Hitler and Mussolini, or effects a reequilibration, as in the cases of Coty in France in 1958 and Svinhufvud in Finland. In Spain the situation was somewhat different. Perhaps it was in view of the role played by other presidents in Europe that the Republican-Socialist coalition decided to use its power in the legislature to oust Alcalá Zamora.[64] Politically, this was a paradox, since the new Left-dominated legislature existed only because of the presidential dissolution three months earlier of the legislature dominated by the Center Right. This decision was to be a significant factor in delegitimizing the regime. It must have been based in part on a fear that Alcalá Zamora might have legitimized a state of emergency, the formation of a provisional government, and the calling of new elections. The Left Socialists and Indalecio Prieto played a major role in this technically dubious and politically irresponsible act, perhaps in the hope that Azaña would move to the presidency. Prieto probably hoped to become prime minister in place of Azaña if the latter were elected to the presidency. But Azaña's election only served to neutralize the most prestigious and effective leader of the Republican Left, who enjoyed high personal legitimacy among the Socialists and other parties. Because the social democratic Prieto failed to gain the support of his party, having been vetoed by the maximalist followers of Largo Caballero, and given the fact that Azaña did not enthusiastically back him, the prime ministership went instead to Casares Quiroga, a close personal collaborator of the president who might have thought he would be just a presidential caretaker. There seems to be general agreement that Casares's was the kind of weak and ambivalent administration so often found in minority governments in the final stage of crisis. In contrast with other cases surveyed in this volume, and somewhat paradoxically, considering his previous, forceful role, in the tragic spring of 1936 Azaña had little effect on the political process, despite an eloquent speech in which he stressed a note of moderation and appealed for consensus.

The Intellectuals and the Republic

Students of the breakdown of the Weimar Republic have emphasized both how the thinking of different types of intellectuals contributed to its crisis by provoking alienation from the regime and how few and weak the so-called *Vernunftrepublikaner* were in German academia. They point out that experts in constitutional law helped to subvert the meaning of the constitution by interpreting it in a way that opened the door to authoritarian tendencies and questioned the role of political parties in a democracy. Right-wing literati added to the mood of crisis by formulating antidemocratic ideologies. Historians and educators contributed hypernationalism and the receptivity to *völkisch* ideas. On the left, literati and artists like Tucholsky did their share by ridiculing politicians and party officials, including the social democrats, and by keeping alive the radical utopian protests. In Italy, Salvemini, and before him, Mosca, have admitted regretfully that they had a share in undermining the Giolittian experiment in democracy with their critique of the failures of parliamentarism and their merciless exposure of the failings of the system. Like D'Annunzio with his rhetoric, the futurist intelligentsia did its share to create the climate in which fascism was born.

It would seem that in the Spanish case things were different. The Republic was often called a republic of professors. Rallied by the *Delenda est monarchia* of Ortega y Gasset, intellectuals of high and low standing played a decisive role in the crisis of the Primo de Rivera dictatorship and the fall of the monarchy. Many leading intellectuals and professors were to be found on the benches of the constituent assembly. According to the Right, the Institución Libre de Enseñanza was the moving force behind the new regime and was the source of its anticlerical policies.[65] Teachers and professors in public secondary schools were among the strong supporters of the new regime, in contrast to Germany, where the nationalist and *völkisch* inclinations of these groups made them pathbreakers of the Right and later often active supporters of the Nazis. In Spain, the right-wing intelligentsia was numerically small and few of its members enjoyed national prestige and influence. Ramiro de Maeztu, who had started as a radical in the milieu of the "98 generation," was not comparable to Mosca and Pareto, Maurras, Spengler, or Carl Schmitt, and was certainly no equal to Ortega or Unamuno. The young writers, journalists, and poets on the periphery of fascism were no match of those identified with the Left.[66]

Even so, intellectuals did not contribute to the consolidation of the Republic, and some of the positions taken by leading figures, largely against their intent, helped to alienate many Spaniards from the new regime. Their critique was often justified in substance, but its form must have contributed to the distrust and withdrawal of allegiance among the youth. None of them can be looked on specifically as a father of Spanish fascism, but some of their positions earned the sympathy of the Fascists, and some of their responses to the modern world and the Spanish situation helped the Fascists formulate their ideas. The Republicans, on the other hand, came to feel very ambivalent toward the intellectuals they had initially welcomed into their ranks as intellectual fathers of the new regime. It is no accident that few of the professors and leading intellectuals who sat in the Constituent Cortes returned either in 1933 or in 1936. Contrary to what might have been expected, the leading intellectuals of the older generation in 1936 were not ready to identify themselves with the Republic and its struggle against Franco. Some were even ready to accept a moderate counterrevolution, while others chose to stay or go abroad, rejecting both sides in the civil war. Among the younger generation, some took a decided stand on one side or the other, but this often led to a disappointing conclusion.

Turning Points

Continuing Crisis: Opportunity for Reequilibration?

The Spanish Republic started life with widespread support. Outside of Syndicalist CNT hostility in 1931, its only opposition was a disorganized and demoralized Right. Later it was to face not only guerrilla warfare by the disloyal opposition but semiloyalty from large parties and social forces that could have been integrated into the system. It would be challenged frontally twice before the final breakdown.

First was the ill-fated, poorly planned, and short-lived coup of 10 August 1932, the *Sanjurjada*, which was even more of a fiasco than the Kapp putsch and was defeated by the police without necessitating a massive general strike or the turning over of power to the army as an arbiter.[67] In fact, the period after the Sanjurjada represented one of stabilization of the system. The revitalized majority carried out the agrarian reform and other important constituent legislation of the regime, which had been floundering before the coup.[68]

The second and much more serious challenge to legal legitimacy was the proletarian revolution in Asturias and the ambiguous challenge to the authority of the Spanish state by the Catalan Generalitat in October 1934. Both were defeated by the government, which was able to invoke the support of the army without transferring power to it.[69] Why, then, did not the defeat of that revolutionary challenge lead to reequilibration of the system, once the temptation to use the crisis to establish an authoritarian rule had been rejected or proved unfeasible? One answer might be that the civil war of 1936 had really started in October 1934. After the major regime party, the PSOE, broke with legality and expressed its unwillingness to accept any system in which the Center Right would have a legitimate place, even though the latter had not used its power to establish an authoritarian corporative system, it was only a question of time before the Republic of 1931 would be declared defunct. A different perspective would argue that the defeat of the revolution provided a unique opportunity for a reequilibration and stabilization of the system, once revolutionary hopes, demonstrated to be weak in many parts of the country, had been defeated, and the bourgeois, conservative clerical forces had shown their unwillingness or inability to abandon Republican legality. From that perspective the period October 1934 to February 1936, particularly the year 1935, constituted an all-too-perfect example of the conditions that prevent successful reequilibration of democracies.

The crisis of the Center-Right coalition of Radicals, CEDA, and other minor parties in 1935 led to the premature parliamentary dissolution of 7 January 1936, and the subsequent election brought bipolarization to its height by destroying any workable Center. All in all, the political events of 1935 pinpoint some of the elements of our model: the role of the neutral powers, specifically the president of the Republic; the impact of the delegitimation of political leaders by scandals adroitly used; the interference of interest groups in the political process; and above all, a crisis in the efficacy of policy formulation combined with the dubious legitimacy of CEDA, the major party, in the eyes of a large part of the society, which was sustained by the moderating power of the president in his refusal to grant the premiership to Gil Robles, the CEDA leader. These were the difficulties the Spanish democracy faced in attempting reequilibration after a serious challenge to its authority; there were also others in the areas of repression, justice, and amnesty for its opponents.

The February 1936 victory of the Popular Front coalition under the leadership of Azaña can be seen in retrospect as the beginning of the end, given the ideological commitments, rhetoric, and actions of the maximalist leadership of the Socialist party and many of its followers, particularly after the PSOE refused to participate in the responsibilities of government and left it to the weak minority Left bourgeois parties. But the electoral victory can also be seen as a lost opportunity to reintegrate the Socialists into the Republican system and to take a more realistic attitude toward the Center Right. The latter had demonstrated between 1933 and 1936, and in the elections themselves, its strength throughout the country and its potential for disengaging itself from the extreme Right to participate in the system.

Under what conditions was reequilibration possible? When could the Republic have reaffirmed its democratic legal authority against the romantic revolutionary climate of the Left and the putschist conspiratorial climate of the extreme Right before the last desperate call of Maura and Sánchez Román for the Republican dictatorship had been made in June 1936?[70] To pose the question in these terms might sound unreal, almost ridiculous, but if we start to analyze the policies that might have led to the persistence of a democratic system from our basic heuristic position, and look at the critical junctures of March and April of 1936 in that light, the question is not so absurd.

As a good example of the problems in the study of crises and breakdowns of regimes, the point of no return might be placed in the first phase of the Republic, when its constitution created a "Republic for the Republicans" in which identification with democracy was possible only for those who accepted not only the institutions of democracy but also the laicism of the constitution. It was a period in which the regime-supporting forces permanently alienated the church, a large part of the officer corps, a diffuse Castilian nationalist sentiment, and important sectors of the landowning peasantry. On the other hand, these forces failed to make the "constituent reforms" that would have assured the loyalty of working-class Marxists and the poor peasantry and definitely linked the Socialist party and the Republicans of the Left in a firm policy of reformist social change. From that perspective, which emphasizes the structural, social, economic, cultural, and political problems, the Republic was doomed because it was not moderate enough on the religious issue or revolutionary enough on social issues to please the Marxists. Legions of sociological political analyses, particularly from the Marxist, and to some extent, the Fascist viewpoint, would see all liberal, democratic, and ideologically radical, but actually moderate, bourgeois reformist or revolutionary regimes of the twentieth century as doomed in advance.

Another point of view might argue that the cost in legitimacy and support resulting from the first bienio—under Azaña—would have been overcome with the incorporation of large part of the Right into the regime, after its electoral success in 1933. This was the perspective from which Lerroux entered into an electoral collaboration with the Right in 1933, governed with its acquiescence, and slowly aimed at obtaining its cooperation, bringing the Catholic Center Right into the government and into support for the regime.[71] From that point of view, the period 1933–35 can be seen as the reequilibration of the latent crisis provoked by the one-sidedness of the constitution-making period dominated by the Left Republicans and the Socialists and an effort on the part of the Radicals to prevent and undermine the disloyal opposition of the extreme Right. The latter found itself increasingly isolated and in the long run would have been unable to penetrate the masses of the conservative electorate. In this view, the crisis of October 1934 becomes the starting point of the breakdown, and the most central question is to account for the radicalization after 1933, and even before the election, of the Socialist party.

As noted before, overcoming the revolution of 1934 without a break in the essence of constitutional legality demonstrated the strength of the Republican regime and its symbols, and the legitimacy of the institutions, especially for the army. In that view, the crisis of December 1935 was a critical moment. It saw the premature dissolution of a parliament that still had the potential to produce majoritarian governments. Even if these had lacked popularity, encountered considerable hostility in the population, and demonstrated limited efficacy in solving the real problems of the country, in the long run they would probably have proved capable of gaining compliance. In contrast to most historians, with the exception of Pabón, we are inclined to pay special attention to that process of disintegration in the political mechanisms at the end of 1935 as well as to the president's blindness to the polarization that would inevitably accompany a general election held under the existing electoral law, given the repression of the working-class unrest and the economic conditions of the country at the time. Our argument would be that dissolution was not necessary and under the circumstances did nothing to reequilibrate, stabilize, and consolidate the regime as a political system. This is not to deny that the basic underlying problems of the country in the long run would not have been solved by the leadership of the Center Right, due to its sterility and narrow-minded selfishness. It is no accident that even Azaña, the great leader of the Republicans of the Left and of the Popular Front, should have confided to his diary in February 1936 a fear of victory.[72] As he foresaw, the democratic Left-bourgeois politicians would be exposed to overwhelming pressures by their maximalist and Communist allies, who were more concerned with achieving their demands than with the stability of the regime.

The acceleration of the crisis in the spring of 1936 makes it difficult to say at what point there was still a chance for reestablishment of public order that would have satisfied both the moderates and the military leadership. The latter was increasingly placing its hopes on a putsch aimed at stopping the mobilization of demands by the working-class parties and the increasing violence of many political organizations and individuals.

From the perspective we have taken, each of the situations, crises, and efforts at stabilization described can be seen as either an opportunity or an irreparable loss in legitimacy, efficacy, and effectiveness for the democratic Republican regime. All were steps in the loss of legitimate, authentic, and effective power, despite their appearance of having strengthened the regime in power by proving that it could defeat its opponents. The whole history of the Republic can be seen as a continuous decline, reflected in the increase in number and strength of disloyal and semiloyal oppositions ready to cooperate with disloyal positions rather than join in the effort to stabilize the regime. In that perspective the successful overcoming of the more acute crises constitutes only minor reversals of a downward trend.

There were, of course, critical junctures at which that trend could have been effectively reversed. At those points the regime could have defeated its opponents, functioned with a certain degree of efficacy by formulating some important policies and institutions (as it did after 10 August 1932), and reaffirmed the continuity of institutions without turning to extreme solutions. In that perspective, moments of crisis and stabilization appear more as part of a cyclical process. Indicators like the number of victims and the range and persistence of disturbance of public order reveal that the crisis increased in intensity and scope as the years passed. The cumulative memory amplified the propaganda which created an overwhelming fear of civil war, a readiness to preventive violence which only further fed the fear and led to ever more constant readiness to resort to violence by the other side. This vicious cycle led in the spring of 1936 to an atmosphere of undeclared civil war, attested to in statements by all the leading politicians. When the military uprising against the regime and the subsequent popular revolution by the working-class organizations occurred in July 1936, it was no surprise to anyone in Spain.

Perhaps more than any other, the case of the Spanish Republic exemplifies the risks that are run when a democratic regime is identified by its founding fathers with a specific political content rather than with a procedural system that legitimates decision-making in response to the changing will of the electorate. The constitutionalization of the ideology of the Left Republican-Socialist coalition, particularly laicization (Article 26, for example, prohibited teaching by religious orders), forced the opposition to make constitutional revision its program. The situation was reflected in the constant use of the term "republic" by the regime-maintaining parties and the relatively infrequent appeals to democracy or law. The expression "The Republic for the Republicans" reflects this emphasis on content rather than form. The Right's counterslogan of "Long live Spain" is another indicator.

It is interesting to speculate on how such a situation came about. One factor was central: the sudden installation of a new regime by a small conspiratorial group and the Socialist party after the disintegration of a dictatorship. This event, occurring in an underdeveloped, nonmobilized society, created an upsurge of support for the regime that was amplified by the electoral system and created overconfidence in its strength and unity of purpose, as well as dangerous ignorance and scorn for its conservative and clerical opponents. That opposition was able to organize its massive support, which, along with other factors, gave it and the Center-Right Republicans who were willing to collaborate an unexpected strength that could not be fully incorporated into the regime, given its identification with substantive content rather than a procedural framework.

There is a lesson in the Spanish case and in the Weimar Republic after its constituent election (which has some similar features): it is possible for new regimes to be built after a serious crisis by majorities which attempt a basic change in social structure and political outlook, even if they turn out to be temporary. But if the rapidly instituted changes remain more symbolic than real, they may outrage the temporarily weak opposition without satisfying the expectations of the supporters of the new regime. In this respect the failure of the Spanish Republic to effect agrarian reform rapidly, thereby disaffecting a small privileged stratum but benefiting large masses of landless persons, was particularly costly in legitimacy. A new regime based on a pragmatic consensus concerning institutions to serve as a procedural framework that left the substantive changes to the ordinary legislative process might ultimately have been more stable.

This points up a clear difference in the atmosphere surrounding the regime installation between post–World War II Italy or Germany and Weimar, and the Spanish constituent assembly. Perhaps the Italians who complained that the "Wind from the North" (the demands for basic reforms that arose in the more politically conscious northern Italy) was not incorporated into the constitution and protested that the Fascists' agreements with the church were constitutionalized in agreement with the Communists, should consider that this probably contributed to the stability of Italian democracy. The process of regime installation in the "North Italian" sense and in a democratic framework probably differs. An authoritarian regime can use the upsurge of support that might accompany its establishment to carry through decisive changes and destroy its opponent's basis of strength without long-run danger to stability of the regime. This is so because its unwillingness to share power with anyone in the first years gives the regime time to consolidate power and makes it impossible for opponents to recoup or realign their forces. A democracy, in which the constituent period is inevitably followed by elections, allows and almost encourages principled opposition to the newly installed regime and its content. Great political skill, which is not always available, is needed to distinguish the democratic institutional framework from the substantive content it has produced in the installation process. In Spain, many antidemocrats would not have been antidemocrats, but conservative or moderate Republicans, had the Constitution been shaped differently. This is especially important because many Republicans were not really democrats, but Republicans first of all.

The Aftermath of the 1934 Revolution:
The Failure of Reequilibration

It has been argued that the October 1934 crisis marked the beginning of the civil war, and that consensus within a democratic regime after that date was impossible. On the other hand, the outcome of that crisis could have led to the stabilization of the regime. This must have been the hope of many politicians of the Center Right and even of the moderate Right who assembled in the Cortes on 9 October to give a vote of confidence to the Lerroux government. Why was it inevitable that October should have poisoned the political atmosphere forever, particularly when, in spite of ambivalence toward the Republic and strong undercurrents of antidemocratic corporativism and authoritarianism, the CEDA and its leader could not bring themselves to use their popularity to establish a moderate authoritarian state with the collaboration of the army, as the clericals in Austria had done shortly before? In fact 1935 saw the incorporation of Catholic, conservative mass support of the CEDA into the Republic (even though not in the "Republic of the Republicans" enacted by the 1931 constitution) and increasing tension between Gil Robles and the extreme Right led by Calvo Sotelo and the few but noisy Fascist followers of José Antonio. Why did the second part of the "black two years," the *bienio negro,* lead to the bitterness of the Spain of 1936 and the recriminations that brought on civil war? Under what conditions would a reequilibration have been possible—granted that an immediate turn to an authoritarian solution had been ruled out?

No one ever questions whether the Left Republicans, and even more the Socialist party, could have reconsidered the positions they adopted in October 1934, or whether, as a loyal opposition, they might not have recognized a Center-Right government in the course of 1935. The question seems preposterous, considering the vengeful actions of the victors.[73] The Left Republicans and the Socialists certainly were not likely to put themselves in the place of the victors. Therefore, the question becomes, Why did the Center-Right government—which had all of the initiatives—ultimately fail? The literature has offered four basic explanations.

The answer provided by the extreme Right would be that the Center and the moderate Right did not use their power effectively to repress the disloyal opposition, specifically the responsible leaders of the Socialist party. This was the position of Calvo Sotelo, when he pointed out that the establishment of the Third Republic and the decades of subsequent stability in France were the fruits of the repression of the Commune.[74] Gil Robles rejected that position, and the government won a vote of confidence with the monarchists and traditionalists abstaining. Actually, such a solution was not possible because of the president's opposition and the probable lack of support among the centrist Radicals and other minor parties. But above all, repression was not feasible against popular mass party and trade union movements like the PSOE and the UGT. Reequilibration by outlawing and persecuting a disloyal opposition is possible only against smaller sectarian groups.

Another approach might have been generosity after victory: an effort to integrate the defeated into the system. This solution implies a different policy, at least toward those who had been caught in a semiloyal position by events not of their making. This would have meant a totally different attitude toward the unfairly and unsuccessfully persecuted Left Republican leader Azaña, who would, as a result, become the engineer of the Popular Front and its undisputed leader in February 1936. This might have worked, but Azaña's initial ambiguity in October, combined with hostility he had aroused during the first bienio and the personal antagonism between him and Lerroux, made such a farsighted and generous policy improbable. On the same political level, a more generous attitude toward the rights of Catalonia (as advocated by the

Lliga leadership), distinguishing the responsibilities of Companys from those of the Catalan people, might have been constructive. Unfortunately, Castilian-based Spanish nationalism had been aroused and could not overcome its distrust of Catalonia. In fact, in view of such predispositions, the response to 6 October in Barcelona was relatively moderate, as indicated by the increased transfer of functions to the Catalan authorities at the end of 1935 and the withdrawal of the anti-Catalanist, Royo Villanova, from the cabinet.

Indeed, a serious indictment can be made against the Center Right for its repression of the proletarian revolution, in both its legal and illegal aspects. The facts reveal the illegal, brutal behavior of government officials, the assassination of prisoners (particularly of a journalist who had reported brutalities), bad treatment of prisoners, delay in freeing those who had limited responsibility or were innocent, and unwillingness to discuss publicly the responsibility of those who had abused their authority and had been dismissed. All this proved an enormous advantage for the opposition, and would be used in the spring of 1936 to excuse revolutionary violence and threats of violence.[75]

The impolitic and unjust persecution of the Syndicalist CNT leaders, who had not participated in any way in the uprising, was particularly inexcusable. The issue of amnesty for those responsible contributed to a constitutional crisis within the cabinet and over the relationship between prime minister and president. While leniency ultimately prevailed for all top leaders, the execution of four relatively minor figures in the uprising, whatever their guilt in acts of violence, consumed political energies unnecessarily and aroused a moral reaction against the government. The rigid position in this case was particularly illegitimate in view of the amnesty granted participants in the putsch of August 1932 by the same parties.

Paradoxically, the nonavailability of the death sentence might have been an advantage for the democratic regime in crisis periods. It would have kept it from falling between the Scylla and Charybdis of appearing either too lenient, by giving in to humanitarian (as well as self-interested) demands for amnesty, or appearing too harsh, particularly toward the less prominent rebels (more easily established as responsible for more obvious crimes), while leaving the main leaders unpunished due to lack of evidence or broader political considerations.

It would, in fact, have been unrealistic to expect a generous reaction to a revolution, and this might not have changed the future behavior of the opposition leadership. The real hope for reequilibration, however, lay in government response to the grievances that had led to the revolutionary situation with a progressive and effective social policy. Let us note, however, that the main strength of the October uprising did not come from the most underprivileged sectors of the working class, and they would not have been the immediate beneficiaries of a more progressive policy. Nevertheless, the situation might have offered an opportunity to neutralize working-class opposition, if not to win its support. The main accusation against the governments between 1934 and late 1935, particularly those constituted after the fall in March 1935 of Giménez Fernández, progressive minister of agriculture of the CEDA, is that they did not enact progressive legislation on agrarian, labor, and tax problems. In fact, the parliamentarians of the coalition parties rejected even the most moderate reforms proposed by the governments which were, in principle, accepted by the leadership. An even stronger case can be made against the government's inability to check the reactionary response of employers and landlords against the defenseless working-classes and farmers, or at least its tolerance of such response. It is debatable whether this basically reactionary social policy was the result of the small size of the progressive wing of the CEDA, its lack of support from the leadership, or its inability to obtain parliamentary support. Contributing factors were that the CEDA did not have a significant working-class base in a Christian trade union movement and that social consciousness had not developed over time in Spanish political Catholicism.

Another significant aspect was the extraordinary venom and distortion in accounts of the Asturian revolution in the bourgeois press. This served to intensify the fears of the bourgeoisie and fuel their hatred against the defeated. That propaganda was to be first paralleled on the opposite side abroad and then at the time of the 1936 elections. Rigid censorship after October 1934 abetted this dual distortion.

The preceding obstacles to reequilibration, or at least to reintegration of the political system, were compounded by the internal crisis of a leading partner in the government coalition, the Radical party. It started with the replacement under pressure of two Radical ministers, by a vote of 161 to 13, on 16 November 1934. The decisive issues surfaced in 1935, however, when the infamous *straperlo* and Nombela affairs led to the incrimination of leading Radical party politicians, the resignation of Lerroux, exonerated of responsibility but affected by that of his political friends and relatives, and the resultant formation of two governments under Chapaprieta, a financial expert without party affiliation, on 15 September and 14 December. This crisis of confidence in a leading Center-Right Republican of undisputed legitimacy in the Republican system, and the weakness and corruption of his party, inevitably made the Center-Right CEDA, claiming 105 of the 238 deputies needed for a majority (particularly in view of the fractionalization of the other parties constituting it), the pivot of any parliamentary government.

Even admitting the lack of political generosity and flexibility, the failure of a progressive social legislative program to face the problems created by the economic crisis for the working-class and peasants, the inability to control the reactionary response of employers and landlords, and the crisis of confidence in and within the Radical party, we still can raise the question of whether dissolution was inevitable, necessary, or desirable, on 1 January 1936. This brings up one of the key variables in our model of the breakdown process in a crisis democracy: the role of the neutral powers. In this case the neutral power was the president of the Republic, Alcalá Zamora, with his unbreakable veto to a CEDA government, his readiness to appoint a government without representatives of the major parties that could not obtain parliamentary support and yet had the right of dissolution, and his effort to control the election under the mistaken illusion that it could produce a new Chamber with a new Center.[76]

If only structural, social, and economic dimensions of the crisis were emphasized, this point would be almost irrelevant. Sooner or later, the Center Right, dominated by the Right, would have failed and been replaced by a Popular Front type of coalition. From our perspective, however, the constitutional crisis of December 1935–January 1936 and the role of the president in it cannot be easily ignored. If we assume—and this is a difficult *if*—that the CEDA, with the cooperation of the Agrarios, the Lliga, minor parties of the Center, and the reconstructed Radical party, could have continued governing, even ineffectively, and maintained order without moving toward a dictatorship until the normal dissolution date in 1937, events could have worked out differently. The memory of revolution and repression might have faded, the impact of the scandals in the Radical party weakened, the economic situation improved, and the international tension in Europe might have contributed indirectly to recovery and unity. And what is perhaps equally important, a reform of the electoral law might have reduced the polarization of 1936. As we know from the Weimar Republic, anticipated elections in a society in crisis do not serve as an agent of reequilibration. Furthermore, the exercise of governmental responsibilities by the Center Right was deepening, and would have deepened even further, the personal and ideological conflict between Gil Robles and the fascistic monarchists who followed Calvo Sotelo, but an election under the law of 1931 inevitably brought them closer together and thereby exacerbated the polarized radicalization.

To explore even further the possibilities of reequilibration, let us ask whether the outcome would have been different if the CEDA leadership had been more enlightened. Certainly a more reasonable policy toward the Anarcho-syndicalists of the CNT, and even a somewhat Machiavellian tolerance for that union federation at a moment when its antagonists in the UGT were defeated, might have prevented an Anarcho-syndicalist turnout for the Popular Front against the formal declarations of its leaders. Even with such tolerance, the CNT could not have attempted any major or effective subversion. Another Machiavellian policy might have been to attract the PNV into the government's sphere of influence by facilitating Basque autonomy, ignoring the ambivalent role of the party in 1934, and rejecting the antiregionalist extremism of the Right. The Catholic Aguirre could have been a partner to Gil Robles as Companys was for Azaña, but unfortunately the Castilian Right lacked an understanding of the peripheral nationalists. An effort by the CEDA to penetrate the Catalan electorate was another folly of the times. Putting aside social reforms benefiting the working class, the regime might have pursued consolidation of its peasant and middle-class support. From that perspective, some of the economic measures affecting the civil servants were ill-conceived even when they were rational.

Assuming that the Center Right could have pursued a more generous policy toward its political and class enemies, would reequilibration of the system have been assured? Had the parties of the Republican Left, under the leadership of Azaña and his Izquierda Republicana—the Esquerra and the Organización Republicana Gallega (ORGA)—along with the Unión Republicana, led by Martínez Barrio, and other minor but prestigious groups, formed a coalition but refused to enter a Popular Front with the PSOE, the PCE, and other parties of the Left, there might be grounds for a positive answer.[77] Given the electoral law and the defeat sustained by both the Left Republicans and the Socialists in 1933, however, this does not seem plausible. Another possible consequence might have been the slowing down or the reversal of the radicalization of the working-class parties, particularly the PSOE, either by a change of view on the part of Largo Caballero or by a victory of his opponents within the party. Again, it seems dubious, in the context of the Europe of the thirties and in the presence of fascism, that the maximalist wing of the party could have changed gears or lost control (though the latter possibility cannot be ignored). After all, its radicalization began at the end of the Left Republican-Socialist coalition rule and was based on disillusionment over the possibility of reform, even with the collaboration of the bourgeois parties of the Left.[78] Excluding the possibility that a more enlightened policy might have prevented the formation of the Popular Front or a reversal in the ideological position and style of the PSOE, there would have been important positive consequences.

First of all, it would have tempered the political climate, lowered the intensity of class antagonisms, weakened the appeal of the amnesty issue, and reduced the distrust middle class sectors felt about the aims of Gil Robles. The Anarcho-syndicalists might have followed the traditional abstentionist posture and thereby weakened the Left electorally. It is difficult to say if it would have affected the vote for the Marxist parties, but it might have reduced the appeal to bourgeois voters of a Popular Front-type coalition. Even so, after the crisis of the Radical party, a Center coalition dominated by a Catholic party might have found it difficult to attract them. The scenario on the other side ignores the effect on the more rightist voters of a more progressive and moderate policy of the CEDA, given the competition of the extreme Right. Such a policy might have led to the loss of some votes and the defection of some of the CEDA deputies to Calvo Sotelo. It would have compounded the difficulty of any coalition for electoral purposes from the Center to the Right. A more generous policy toward Catalonia would certainly have benefited the Lliga and Cambó. Even when a different policy in 1935 would have reduced the polarization, and particularly its intensity, without a change in the electoral law, it is difficult to see how confrontation between these two blocs could have been avoided.

The real difference would have been that a more constructive policy, a less vindictive reaction, and support for the more progressive positions in the party (like those of Giménez Fernández) would have facilitated the cooperation of the CEDA with the Center parties, particularly the Lliga and the Basque PNV. Above all, it might have softened the distrust and hostility of President Alcalá Zamora toward Gil Robles.[79] A reduction of the tensions between those two men, as Chapaprieta and Cambó already knew, might have prevented the crisis at the end of 1935 and the premature dissolution of the Chamber. It is, however, unclear whether such reduction would have required Gil Robles to abandon, at least temporarily, his demands for the premiership and leadership of the party, if we assume that the conflict between the two men was more than political. If assumption of a more constructive position by the CEDA had reversed the presidential veto, facilitated Center-oriented coalitions, and isolated the monarchist anti-democratic Right, new elections might not have been called. Enough time would have been gained to heal the wounds of October, and time would have allowed the Socialist party congress to reverse the Largo Caballero line or a split between maximalists and reformists. Democracy would have been the beneficiary.

Violence, Disorder, and Regime Crises

The maintenance of public order and personal safety is a central function of any political system, though the threshold for tolerance of violence and the meaning assigned to it may vary. Obviously, violence, which in some countries is defined as common crime, acquires in others a political character because the violators of the law (and often the authorities as well) attach political significance to it. Rather than disengage themselves from the criminal acts, the leaders justify them in terms of social and political grievances and blame the government for having created the conditions that provoked them. It is not easy to say at what point the amount, intensity, visibility, and cumulative impact of violence transforms it into an unsolvable problem for the authorities. Any discussion of violence in a society in crisis is blurred by allegations and counterallegations as to who initiated it as well as exaggerations and denials of the evidence. In the present case, whether the acts of violence actually happened as they were described at the time is to some extent unimportant, since the reactions of the participants were more a function of their perceptions than of reality, and therefore absolute certitude about the objective facts becomes less central for the social scientist than for the historian. (See table 4.)

There can be no doubt that the Spanish Republic was characterized by a relatively high rate of social and political violence, that the October revolution and its aftermath represented a trauma that perhaps has no parallel in the other

Table 4. Deaths in Political Conflicts, 15 April 1931–17 July 1936

Year	Occurrences of Violence	Number of Deaths
1931	Incident with monarchists, anarcho-syndicalist violence	10
1932	Conflicts in the villages of Castilblanco and Arnedo between peasants and the police	9
	Sanjurjo pronunciamento (August)	10
1933	Anarchist unrest in Barcelona (January)	37
	Casas Viejas, Andalusian village uprising, and police repression	18
	Anarchist unrest and labor conflicts (December)	89
1934	National farm strike	13
	Falangist violence and counterviolence (June)	2
	Assassination of ex-director of security by Falangists	1
	Asturian Revolution	189
	(October)	

Deaths	Official Data	Data of Aurelio del Llano
Civilians	855	940
Police	144	168
Army	85	88
	1084	1196	1196

Estimated number of victims of repression	156–210; average: 183	
Barcelona and surrounding area	50	
Spain other than Asturias and Barcelona	42	
Total, October 1934		1471

Year		Number of Deaths
1935	Executions	2
	Varios incidents	43
1936	Fights and assassinations between 3 February and 17 July	
	Madrid	45
	Barcelona	3
	Seville, Malaga, and Granada	35
	Other provincial capitals	54
	Other cities	13
	Total urban centers	150*
	Rural towns in 13 agrarian reform provinces	34
	Villages in 13 agrarian reform provinces	32
	Rural towns in other provinces	25
	Villages in other provinces	28
	Total rural centers	119*
	Grand total for the period (can only be considered an approximation, subject to revision, probably upward)	1929

NOTE: Information on political violence, including number of incidents, the casualties, and even more, the responsibility for them and the political identification of the victims, is obviously a subject for bitter polemic, particularly in the case of the October 1934 revolution and its aftermath, and the period after the 16 February 1936 elections. The topic deserves monographic analysis. On the Asturian Revolution we give the official figures and those assembled by Aurelio Llano Roza de Ampudia in *La revolución en Asturias, Octubre de 1934* (Oviedo: Talleres Tipográficos Altamirano, 1935) that Díaz Nosty in *La Comuna asturiana* considers more accurate. And Díaz Nosty's rough estimate of casualties during the postrevolutionary repression. This table includes information from a variety of sources; for 1935 from *El Sol,* for the period 16 February to 17 July 1936 we have used the data collected by Edward Malefakis. We have coded all the crises of democracy in our study, and that the social tensions which accompanied it increased almost consistently throughout the period, particularly in the "tragic spring" of 1936.[80] Certain acts of violence acquired strong symbolic significance: the burning of convents in May 1931, less than a month after the proclamation of the Republic; the cold-blooded assassination of peasants in Casas Viejas by the police in January 1933; the outrages in the repression of the Asturian Revolution; and the chain of assassinations in Madrid in the spring of 1936, culminating in the death of Calvo Sotelo, one of the two principal opposition leaders, on 12 July 1936, in reprisal by policemen for the assassination of one of their comrades.

In numerous speeches, Azaña, and other political leaders as well, emphasized that fear had become a major political factor.[81] This is reflected in less easily measured results of nonfatal violence, like the burning of churches or attempts to do so, the destruction of property and crops, the intimidation of political opponents, and the brutality that characterized the agents of order. Nor is it possible to weigh the impact of structured violence in social relations, the refusal to give work to farm laborers or the expulsion of tenants with phrases like "go eat Republic" after 1934, and the threats against landowners and even wealthy peasants after February 1936. In a situation of crisis of authority, even the behavior of hooligans and common criminals takes on political significance, is justified in political terms, and is excused as a result of social injustice.[82] What strikes the reader of the political literature of the time—the newspapers and the speeches, even in Parliament—is the constant reference to the willingness to announce or encourage the use of force to achieve goals, the assertion of readiness to die for a cause, the frequent description of the situation as one of latent civil war. This atmosphere became intolerable and led participants to believe that the solution lay only in defeating and outlawing their opponents and establishing their own order.[83]

Could the leadership of different political forces have avoided the emergence of this climate of violence and diminished its political impact? Some violence could certainly have been avoided, while other events resulted from such deep-seated tensions in the society that they erupted beyond control of the leadership. At what point decisive action by the government could have

events reported in *El Sol,* the leading Spanish newspaper; for the extended periods of press censorship, we have used *La Prensa* and *La Nación* of Buenos Aires, both known for the quality of their reporting on Spain. The accuracy of the figures is almost irrelevant, since each side was ready to believe much higher figures, irresponsibly manipulated, in the absence of fully reliable information. Ramiro V. Cibrián has analyzed the data for 1936 in detail in an unpublished paper, calculating different indices and ratios that show the changes over time, the geographic distribution in relation to the strength or presence of different parties, and the different patterns of antireligious and other form of violence.

*Total number of deaths in the period 3 February to 17 July 1936 was 269. Among these, 57 were caused by the authorities. Gil Robles gives a higher total of 330 (La Cierva, *Historia de la Guerra Civil . . .* pp. 689–90).

prevented or stopped the cycle of violence is not easy to ascertain. There is no doubt that the political impact of the events could have been reduced by intelligent political and legal handling of the problem. The wave of church burnings in May 1931, for example, might well have been prevented by a quick show of authority, a course which the anticlerical members of the government opposed initially, even against the better judgment of a man like Prieto.[84] In other cases, greater concern for the rights of the victims, investigation of what had happened, and more honest, public disclosures of the acts of subordinates would have cleared the political air of suspicions, exaggeration, and distortion, and would have curtailed their political use in creating a climate of hatred and fear. One such case was Casas Viejas;[85] another, on a grand scale, the unwillingness of the Radical and CEDA governments in 1934 and 1935 to investigate responsible accusations against the army, police forces, and authorities in charge of the repression of the revolution in Asturias.[86] Even when the government indicated that it did not approve those acts, its persistent censorship of the opposition press both in that period and after the 1936 election contributed to the climate of suspicion and fear. Exploitation of embarrassing situations by the disloyal and even semiloyal oppositions in order to undermine the prestige of government leaders and ultimately the regime characterized the situation. During the parliamentary debate on Casas Viejas some extremely destructive phrases were coined about the government's performance during the first two years. In another context, we have noted the political importance of debates about persecution and amnesty of leaders and unknowns alike who were involved in revolutionary events and tragic violence, and the way in which these debates helped to delegitimize the political system, provide opportunities for intervention of the president's neutral power, and strain relationships within the political elite.

The Anarcho-syndicalists' revolutionary tradition provided the basis for both sporadic outbreaks of peasant violence and more-or-less uncoordinated local outbreaks, like those in January 1933 in Catalonia that produced thirty-seven casualties and the one in December 1933 that left 89 dead.[87] The participation of the Socialists in the government during the first years of the Republic and the hope for social reform kept strikes and other forms of conflict at a tolerable level, and the unfortunate events in Casas Viejas had already demonstrated the political dangers of any uncontrolled government response to anarchist violence. The Sanjurjo uprising in this period caused little bloodshed (ten dead and eighteen wounded), a fact that might have to be taken into account in understanding the pressures for leniency, the indignation of the Right at certain aspects of the punishment, and the later amnesty for those responsible. From a legal and moral point of view, this insurrection of the Right is no different from that of the Left in 1934, but the differences in the amount of fighting and bloodshed make the two difficult to compare.

The first massive politico-social action officially supported by the Left was the great rural strike in 1934, instigated by the Federación de Trabajadores de la Tierra in alliance with the Socialist party. In the view of the minister of the interior it represented a threat to the harvest.[88] The spring and summer of that year saw the first mass rallies of the European type: meetings were organized by the CEDA in El Escorial and Covadonga, which contributed so unfortunately to the fascistic image of the party among its opponents and provoked a preventive mobilization on their part.[89] This form of mass mobilization inevitably led to misunderstanding, in view of the events of the year before in Germany, Vienna, and Paris. The mass demonstration in April in support of the Generalitat in Barcelona had the same effect. It was during this period that the violence between Fascists and the Left began, which led to the assassination of a former Director General of Security. By the spring of 1933, the Socialist party had begun to organize its youthful militia, and in April 1934 it started talking about a revolutionary army.[90] Mass rallies, like that of the Alianzas Obreras in September 1934, those of the CEDA, and later of the Popular Front, contributed to the unrealistic sense of power among the leadership.[91]

It was, however, the Asturian Revolution that created the real trauma. Eleven hundred ninety-six people were officially listed as dead, and 2,078 as wounded, including 256 police and 639 military.[92] In addition, 100 participants on each side were assassinated outright or condemned with undue haste, though only four death sentences were actually carried out. There were all too numerous incidents of torture, mistreatment, and illegal executions reported by observers like Gordón Ordás, who were not sympathetic to the revolution; the government refused to investigate them. Estimates of the number of arrests all over the country ranged from 10,000 by La Cierva to 30,000 in the official account by the Communist party. If we consider the number involved in the struggle—4,214 from the local garrison of the army and police and a mobilized working class of some 30,000 individuals—we can sense the impact on public opinion. By contrast, the crisis in Barcelona had few casualties on the government side, 4 military dead and 26 wounded.

The post-1934 situation was unique in democratic regimes, for it involved a revolution and a confused attempt at secession (or at least, what was perceived as such) that led not to the establishment of an authoritarian regime but to continuation of democratic legal institutions using emergency powers of repression and allowing an election less than a year and a half later in which the disloyal oppositions won. The psychological impact on the counterrevolutionaries, who felt threatened by the electoral victory of their opponents and their desire to turn the tables, was a situation without parallel in countries with democratic regimes.

It should be noted that the Fascist party in Spain was unable to gain a mass following (or even to organize a significant number of activists of the storm trooper type). Certainly, the preemptive violence of the Left against fascism, the lack of sympathy of the Radical-CEDA governments for the new movement, and the lack of real support by the conservative interests who preferred to rely on the army, cut down Fascist violence and kept the size of the party insignificant by European standards.[93] In 1936 the only nonmilitary mobilized political threat came from the proletarian masses, mainly the Socialist party and its youth organization, which was soon to fuse with that of the Communists. They were confident that they had the strength to cope with any threat from the army, and in this respect the Spanish Socialists acted quite differently from their comrades in France as well as from the German social democrats who had joined the Reichsbanner against the aggressive Nazi squads.[94] The youth of the CEDA, the Juventud de Acción Popular, despite the ideological and symbolic ambiguities which gave it a pseudo-Fascist character, were not involved in street fighting and terror, even though the group had lost twenty-six members to violence before 1936. Other groups, like the Requeté of the Traditionalists and the Escamots of the Estat Català, acted as paramilitary groups with training by professional officers. The paramilitary forces of the Right were never of a size, organization, or discipline capable of threatening a government effectively. They became relevant only as auxiliaries of the army after the uprising in 1936, a factor that explains much of the later political development of Franco's Spain. Furthermore, the leaders of the Falangist party, including José Antonio, were under arrest from March 1936 on, and party activities were officially suspended.[95]

Little is known of the role of the civilian judiciary in handling political violence in those years, but there are indications that both sides of the political spectrum were dissatisfied and urged reform of the judiciary in order to gain greater political influence upon those decisions of which they disapproved.[96] This would seem to indicate that the Spanish judiciary probably was fairer during crises than its counterpart in Germany or even Italy. The increased tension of the period is reflected in the continuous growth of the police and security forces, which by February 1936 numbered some 34,000 Guardia Civiles and 17,000 Guardias de Seguridad and de Asalto, plus 14,000 Carabineros. This is in contrast to a total nominal army strength of 169,819 men in July 1936, (actually reduced by leaves, etc.) of which between 30,000 and 45,000 were in Africa.

There is no accurate information on the amount of violence and disorder in the spring of 1936.[97] According to accusations by the Right in parliamentary debate, 204 were killed and 1,057 wounded between the February elections and mid-May; in the following month another 65 were killed and 230 wounded. These figures would indicate that the high point of violence was in the period right after the election rather than in the late spring, but they do not jibe with the accelerated pace of violence and counterviolence between political groups in Madrid against prominent political figures and the leftist advisers of militias. In that context, the prime minister stated that the government was in belligerent opposition to fascism, a statement which can be understood only by realizing that the entire Right, including the CEDA, was labeled fascist by its opponents. Between the elections and mid-July 1936, the Right estimated the total number of deaths at 343. If correct, these figures contrast unfavorably with the 207 deaths reported in Italy in 1921 between 1 January and 14 May 1921, considering the populations of the two countries.[98] In summary, a figure of 2,000 killed in civil strife during the five and one-half years of the Republic does not seem an unreasonable estimate.

The social and political tension was manifest as well in the frequency and intensity of strikes. It is not always easy to distinguish strikes based on economic and social demands from those whose purpose is fundamentally political. In some cases the strikers' demands were presented first to the government authorities rather than to the employers; for example, in the farm labor strike of 1934, the Socialist farm federation sought legislative decisions against employers rather than utilizing collective bargaining. Then, too, the ideological commitment of the CNT, which tended to transform all strike activity into political protest, must be taken into account. The conflict of the two large-scale labor movements, the UGT and the CNT, both committed to radical social change and both competing for the same constituency or hoping to absorb or fuse with the other, also tended to politicize normal labor conflicts. The rigidity of employers like the small marginal entrepreneurs whose position was so precarious that they could not afford concessions, and the possibility of lockouts in a society suffering from unemployment and underemployment, particularly in the countryside, inevitably drew the government into labor conflicts. As strikes often accompanied violence and tension, they became a matter of public order and therefore a problem for the Ministry of Interior as well as the Ministry of Labor. Socialist domination of the labor arbitration machinery in the first years of the Republic made transactions feasible but at the same time alienated the followers of the CNT.

Unfortunately, the strike statistics for the period are far from complete or accurate.[99] It is therefore difficult to trace the fever curve of labor conflict as distinct from other forms of unrest and tension, such as church burnings, invasions of land by landless farmers, spontaneous clashes, and political crimes and assassinations.[100] There are indications, however, that the causes of these various manifestations of crisis coincided at some times and at others did not, but all combined to create a prerevolutionary atmosphere and growing fear, not only among the privileged but in broad segments of the middle class, including the land-owning peasantry, as well. The society might have tolerated one or another of these manifestations of tension if those responsible had clearly distinguished between legitimate and illegitimate forms of expression, but the rhetoric and symbolic acts, even of the top leadership, tended to make this impossible. Whether this pattern of violence and social tension is beyond the limits of democratic politics would be hard to assert. But certainly the cumulative psychological impact, particularly considering the acceleration of the process of violence, the exaltation of violence by many of the leading political actors, and the ambivalent, if not irresponsible, attitude of governments toward the violence of their partisans, could not but create an unsolvable problem.

It is significant that the late spring of 1936 saw decided efforts at reequilibration of the system and warnings of doom,[101] such as the famous speech by Prieto less than two and one-half months before the outbreak of civil war:

A country can survive a revolution, which is ended one way or another. What a country cannot survive is the constant attrition of public disorder without any immediate revolutionary goal; what a nation cannot survive is the waste of public power and economic strength in a constant state of uneasiness, of anxiety and worry. Naive souls may say that this uneasiness, this anxiety, this worry, is only suffered by the upper classes. In my judgment that is incorrect. The working class itself will soon suffer from the pernicious effects of this uneasiness, this anxiety, this worry, because of the disarray and possible collapse of the economy, because though we aspire to transform the economic structure, so long as it does exist. . . .

Let it not be said, to the discredit of democracy, that sterile disorder is only possible when there is a democratic government in power, because then such disorder would mean that only democracy permits excesses, and that only the lash of dictatorship is capable of restraining them. . . . If disorder and excess are turned into a permanent system, one does not achieve socialism, nor does one consolidate a democratic republic—which I think is our advantage—nor does one achieve communism. You achieve a completely desperate anarchy that is not even advocated by anarchist ideology. You achieve disorder that can ruin the country.[102]

The Army and the Breakdown

A comparative view of the breakdown of Spanish democracy might find that the military pronunciamento in July 1936 was its cause, which would bring the Spanish case closer to a rather simplified Latin American model. However, we feel that, taking into consideration the role of the army, the process of crisis and breakdown in the thirties was more like that of Italy in the twenties. For a long time the army tended to play a role not unlike that of the *Reichswehr* in the crisis of the Weimar Republic rather than that of the "moderating power" of the pre-1964 Brazilian model.[103] Ortega y Gasset, who was anything but sympathetic to the tradition of the Spanish military interventionists, in his only published statement about Spanish politics after 1933 stressed that the army uprising in 1936 was not a classic pronunciamento of the type he had so well defined.[104]

Certainly, military intervention as a moderating power was the model in the minds of many politicians and army officers throughout the years of the Republic. The August 1932 uprising was the last pronunciamento in Spanish history, and it failed dismally as a valid model for the civilians as well as for the majority of the military. In 1934, after the October revolution, in late 1935, and immediately after the 1936 election, the politicians of the extreme Right, like Calvo Sotelo, and Gil Robles himself, explored with trusted high-ranking officers whether the army was ready to play the traditional role of a "moderating power," but they could not effect a favorable response among the officer corps.[105] The army was not ready to act on its own at the urging of the politicians unless the latter assumed responsibility for the action. And to that point the politicians themselves were not ready to go.

The fact was that the army was divided internally as to both its political role and its ideological outlook.[106] Throughout the history of the Republic there were undoubtedly officers, particularly self-retired officers, conspiring against the regime. However, the majority of the senior generals were legalists with no ideological commitments who supported the constitutionally formed legitimate government. Even in July 1936, out of sixteen generals with command of a division and the heads of the two police forces, only four joined the rebellion.[107] Despite professional grievances created by many aspects of the Azaña reforms, and by the style with which they were carried out, the bulk of the officer corps opted for an attentist position. Given the definition of the "Republic for the Republicans," this meant a nonpartisan attitude rather than commitment to the regime, but it did not preclude such officers from having close ties and sympathies with certain more committed officers and political leaders. As long as the institutionalized authorities functioned with some legitimacy and effectiveness, such officers were ready to support them in performance of their duties, as they did during the August 1932 putsch and the 1934 October crisis.

It is symbolic that General Batet, who intelligently defeated the insurrection of the regional government of Catalonia, should have been shot by the rebels in Burgos. It is equally symbolic that López Ochoa, commanding general of the army in Asturias in 1934, opponent of Primo de Rivera, a Mason who attended the funeral of Pablo Iglesias (the founder of the Socialist party), and who had named his daughter Libertad, should be shot in Madrid by the Popular Front. Lerroux was basically right, at least before 1936, when he wrote: ". . . the Spanish army has a frankly liberal spirit; a majority of the officers are indifferent to the form of government and the minority are Republican, or more frequently, Monarchists."[108]

There were other forces at work, of course: the conspiratorial activities of some monarchical generals and officers, both retired and in command; the emergence of the Unión Militar Española as a professional activist organization courted by different political factions; the attraction after October 1934 of Yagüe and a number of younger officers to fascism; and the success on the other side of the spectrum as the Left (especially the Communists) found support among a minority, particularly in the police and the air force and among some noncommissioned officers. The links between military professionals and the paramilitary organizations of all political colors, the public appeals to the army as the backbone of the nation by the extreme Right, particularly Calvo Sotelo, and the aggressive anti-militarism of the Left inevitably contributed to politicization of the officer corps. This link affected decisions concerning command assignments, a highly political matter, arousing the suspicions of the politicians and creating tensions within the officer corps. It seems impossible to imagine in such a highly politicized and polarized society, with political groups advocating violence and preparing to use it, that the armed forces could remain apolitical, committed to supporting the constituted government irrespective of its political color.

Given the double threat of social revolution and regional nationalism perceived as separatism from the Spanish state after 1934, army officers were increasingly open to the notion of an independent political role. In this context, it is important to realize how far the army had moved from the nineteenth-century model of the moderating power. In November 1934, in the middle of the conflict with the president of the Republic about amnesty for officers who had sided with the October rebellion—a dispute which threatened a presidential dissolution of the Chamber and an electoral victory of the Left—the CEDA leader, Gil Robles, explained the situation to the military in the following terms:

For us it was impossible to take the initiative to provoke an exceptional situation even though we do not oppose the army's making known to the president its strong desire to prevent his violating the fundamental norm of the nation, as he was at the point of doing. If I maintain the position of the ministers of the CEDA, there will be no way out of the crisis. Alcalá Zamora will be obliged to give power to a Left government and dissolve the legislature. It will be a true coup d'état, and who shall prevent it?[109]

In spite of the ambiguities of the situation, this message was intended to test the response of the army to an appeal that it use its moderating power. The response was negative. The army did not feel that it had the capacity for the task, and the Center-Right politicians, unlike those of the extreme Right, were not ready to call openly for military support in a coup. On 11 December 1935, when Parliament was on the verge of dissolution by the president, the minister of war, Gil Robles, received a proposal for a coup d'état from his undersecretary, a general. He refused to assume that responsibility and suggested that if the army, united around its natural leadership, felt it had to take power temporarily to save the spirit of the constitution and "prevent a gigantic falsification of revolutionary sign," he would not oppose it. After consultation with fellow officers, the leading generals rejected the suggestion. A letter from Franco to Gil Robles in March 1937 explained the situation in these terms:

. . . Neither the duty of discipline nor the situation of Spain—difficult, but not yet of imminent peril—nor the carefullness with which you proceeded during your whole tenure in the Ministry—which did not authorize me for such a task—permitted me to propose what at that time would have seemed to lack justification or belief in the possibility of success, since the Army, which can rebel when such a sacred cause as that of the Fatherland is in imminent danger, cannot give the appearance of arbiter in political disputes nor define the conduct of parties or the powers of the chief of state. Any action at that time would have been condemned to failure as unjustified had the Army undertaken it; and the latter, which now has rebelled to save Spain, was hoping that, if possible, she would be saved through legal channels that would prevent grave and . . . painful upheavals.[110]

When the results of the election began to be known on 16 February, General Franco contacted the head of the *Guardia Civil* to ask the minister of war of the interim centrist Portela government to declare a state of emergency—a request which he later made directly to the prime minister, who refused after consulting with the president, since the latter approved a state of alarm only. The prime minister, who, hours later, before the final results of the elections were known or the legislature convened, was to give power to Azaña to avoid facing the pressures of the Popular Front masses, explored the possibility of an independent action by the army. Franco, still head of the General Staff, responded that the army did not yet have the moral unity necessary to undertake the task.[111] After the deposition of President Alcalá Zamora on dubious constitutional grounds, and before the election of Azaña, officers under the leadership of López Ochoa proposed that Alcalá Zamora dissolve the legislature and install a military cabinet. This would have been the second dissolution to which he was entitled, according to one interpretation of the constitution. He rejected the idea but apparently hinted that he would not discourage the officers from acting on their own initiative.[112] Again the conspirators could not bring themselves to act without some sort of constitutional mandate.

In all these situations either the politicians or the military considered intervention, but on each occasion the leading officers agreed that action as the moderating power by a relatively united army was possible only if legitimized by civilians holding office constitutionally.

There is no point in recounting here the progress of the various groups of conspirators in the spring of 1936, the slow convergence of the nonpartisan generals with the more political conspirators of the UME, the involvement in May and June of prestigious generals who had heretofore remained aloof from conspiracy, nor the broad support mobilized by the rebels after Franco's commitment and the assassination of Calvo Sotelo on 13 July. What is important for our analysis is to note that the top leadership, particularly General Mola, wanted at all costs to avoid linking what was to be a purely military rebellion to any particular political faction or program and to insure that any civilians joining the uprising were subordinate to the military authority. It is also significant that the leadership deliberately planned the coup to appear Republican, using Republican symbols, an indication of the degree to which monarchical legitimacy no longer served as a rallying symbol. The uprising on 17, 18, and 19 July bore no resemblance to those of the nineteenth century or those taking place in Latin America until quite recently, in which the politicians incite the military to act and then to transfer power to them. In this case the military assumed power themselves, relying on civilian supporters only because of the weakness of the military organization and the need to rally popular support. Faced with what they perceived as a prerevolutionary situation, the military in Spain assumed what Stepan has described as a new professionalism, or at least some elements of it, by abandoning the old role of the moderating power that the semiloyal politicians of the Republic (and many moderates, in the spring of 1936), were ready to assign to them.[113]

Out of the Spanish experience arises the question of whether in a democracy experiencing intense constitutional and social crisis, the intervention of the army as a moderating power, including intervention via an interim military dictatorship, might not sometimes provide greater hopes for the future restoration of democracy than does a total break with the existing institutions by the professional military and the subsequent creation of an authoritarian regime.

Although the army became the ultimate cause of the breakdown, the crisis and loss of legitimacy of the regime and the polarization in the society had progressed to great extremes before the army acted.[114] It would be a mistake to consider this insurrection the main cause. In more than one sense, the regime had already broken down.

BIBLIOGRAPHIC NOTE

The literature on the Republic and the origins of the civil war is large and often highly partisan. Among the major works in English are: Raymond Carr, *Spain, 1808-1939* (Oxford: Oxford University Press, 1966); Gabriel Jackson, *The Spanish Republic and the Civil War, 1931-1939* (Princeton, N.J.: Princeton University Press, 1965); Hugh Thomas, *The Spanish Civil War* (New York: Harper and Row, 1977), a revised and enlarged edition; and Salvador de Madariaga, *Spain: A Modern History* (New York: Praeger, 1958) by a liberal Spanish intellectual who refused to identify in exile with either side (pp. 377-498 on the Republic). The most comprehensive and best-documented work in Spanish is Ricardo de La Cierva, *Historia de la Guerra Civil española, Antecedents: Monarquía y República, 1898-1936* (Madrid: San Martín, 1969). From a different perspective, see Ramón Tamames, *La República: La era de Franco,* 6th rev. ed. (Madrid: Alianza Editorial, 1977), the work of an economist, and Manuel Tuñon de Lara, *La II Republica,* 2 vols. (Madrid: Siglo XXI, 1972), a short work by a well-known social historian. The collection of essays edited by Manuel Ramírez Jiménez, *Estudios sobre la II República Española* (Madrid: Tecnos, 1975), brings together the most recent work of a group of Spanish scholars on aspects often neglected. Ramírez is also the author of *Los grupos de presión en la segunda República Española* (Madrid: Tecnos, 1969), the best monograph on interest groups. In addition to a number of monographic studies on political parties, the following give an overview and rich documentation: Miguel Artola, *Partidos y programas políticos, 1808-1936,* vol. 1, *Los partidos políticos,* and vol. 2, *Manifiestos y programas políticos* (Madrid: Aguilar, 1974–75). On political parties in the Republic, see vol. I, pp. 598–700. See also Juan J. Linz, "The Party System of Spain: Past and Future," in *Party Systems and Voter Alignments: Cross-National Perspectives,* ed. Seymour Martin Lipset and Stein Rokkan (New York: Free Press, 1967), pp. 197–282. On the Left, see Stanley G. Payne, *The Spanish Revolution: A Study of the Social and Political Tensions That Culminated in the Civil War in Spain* (New York: Norton, 1970), and Raymond Carr, ed., *The Republic and the Civil War in Spain* (London: Macmillan and St. Martin's Press, 1971). The latter includes chapters by Edward Malefakis on the Left, R. Robinson on the Right, and Stanley Payne on the army.

Edward E. Malefakis, *Agrarian Reform and Peasant Revolution in Spain: Origins of the Civil War* (New Haven: Yale University Press, 1970), covers much more than the title would indicate. The concluding chapters, "The Destruction of the 'Bourgeois' Republic" and "Could the Disaster Have Been Avoided," should be read in conjunction with this essay since they deal with important questions, particularly in relation to the class conflict in Spain, which we have decided to neglect rather than repeat his work.

A collection of documents that should be consulted and that could serve to support points we are making is found in Ricardo de La Cierva, ed., *Los Documentos de la Primavera Trágica: Análisis documental de los antecedentes inmediatos del 18 de julio de 1936* (Madrid: Ministerio de Información y Turismo, Secretaría General Técnica, Sección de Estudios Sobre la Guerra de España, 1967).

Henry Landsberger and Juan J. Linz, "El caso chileno y la España do los años 30: Contraste y similitud," in *Chile 1970–1973: Lecciones de una experiencia,* ed. Federico G. Gil, Ricardo Lagos E., and Henry A. Landsberger (Madrid: Tecnos, 1977), pp. 399–458, is an attempt to point out some of the similarities and differences in the processes leading to the tragic breakdown of democracy in both countries.

NOTES

1. The low performance of the Spanish Republic, measured operationally, stands out among the countries compared in Ted Robert Gurr and Muriel McClelland, *Political Performance: A Twelve-Nation Study* (Beverly Hills, Ca.: Sage, 1971), which include the Weimar Republic and Yugoslavia. Their summary score for Spain between 1932 and 1936 (p. 72) was −7.80, compared to −6.01 for Germany between 1923 and 1932, −3.95 for Yugoslavia between 1921 and 1929, and −2.57 for France between 1879 and 1940. The depth of the crisis is also reflected in the fact that the linear trends (regression coefficients) of the aggregate returns in seven polarized polities between the two world wars and the present postwar period show Spain to be the most polarized. The sum of the coefficients of extreme Right and extreme Left in Weimar Germany was 6.16, while in Spain it reached 15.9. The weakening of the representation of the Center (respectively, −3.65 and −7.3) is particularly noticeable. For the definition of the coefficients method and data used, see Giovanni Sartori, *Parties and Party Systems: A Framework for Analysis* (Cambridge: Cambridge University Press, 1976), pp. 164–73.

Data on cabinet instability in the period between 14 April 1939 and 17 July 1936 confirm the pattern: average cabinet duration in Spain was 101 days (148 for the Catalan regional governments). The figure for Austria in the early thirties was 149; for Weimar Germany before the Depression (1918–30) it was 210, rising to 258 after 30 March 1930. Average cabinet duration was 260 days in Italy before Mussolini (1918–22), compared to 166 days in Spain during a comparable period (1918–23).

2. Juan J. Linz, "Early State Building and Late Peripheral Nationalisms against the State," in *Building States and Nations: Analysis and Data Across Three Worlds,* ed. S. N. Eisenstadt and Stein Rokkan (Beverly Hills, Ca.: Sage, 1973), vol. 2, pp. 32–116.

3. Pedro Voltes Bou, *Historia de la economía española en los siglos XIX y XX,* 2 vols. (Madrid: Editora Nacional, 1974). The economic history of the period has not yet been thoroughly studied. Leandro Benavides, *Política económica en la II República española* (Madrid: Guadiana, 1972), presents a brief overview with reference to contemporary sources. See also Alberto Balcells, *Crisis económica y agitación social en Cataluña*

(1930-1936) (Esplugues de Llobregat: Ariel, 1971). Balcells, while agreeing on the less dramatic situation in Spain in terms of economic indices and unemployment, rightly notes how that impact was more severe in the absence of unemployment benefits and other social programs.

4. Unfortunately, we have no systematic data to prove this point, since there were no surveys at the time. Indirectly, the small electoral support and membership of monarchist parties, the fact that even the uprising of the army in 1936 was under a Republican flag with manifestoes closing "Live the Republic," the lack of support for monarchical forms of government revealed by surveys in Franco's Spain despite the official reinstauration of a monarchy, the low prestige of the aristocracy, etc., would support our statement.

5. Nothing can better convey a feeling for the vacuum of support for the monarchy after the resignation of Primo de Rivera (January 1930) and particularly in its last hours (April 1931) than the review essay by Jesús Pabón, "Siete relatos de tres días (Estudio preliminar para un libro sobre la crisis de la Monarquía)," in *Días de ayer: Historias e historiadores contemporáneos* (Barcelona: Alpha, 1963), pp. 367-431.

6. On the 1931 municipal elections, see Juan J. Linz, "The Party System of Spain: Past and Future," in *Party Systems and Voter Alignments: Cross National Perspectives,* ed. Seymour M. Lipset and Stein Rokkan (New York: Free Press, 1967), pp. 231-36.

7. On the late founding and weakness of fascism *(strictu sensu)*, see Stanley Payne, *Falange: A History of Spanish Fascism* (Stanford, Ca.: Stanford University Press, 1961); his chapter on Spain in Stein Ugelvik Larsen, Bernt Hagtvet, and Jan Peter Myklebust, *Who Were the Fascists* (forthcoming), with more recent bibliographic references; and Juan J. Linz, "Some Notes Toward a Comparative Study of Fascism in Sociological Historical Perspective, in *Fascism, A Reader's Guide,* ed. Walter Laqueur (Berkeley and Los Angeles: University of California Press, 1976), pp. 3-121. See also the synthesis in Ricardo de la Cierva, *Historia de la Guerra Civil española* (Madrid: San Martín, 1969), chap. 12, pp. 507-75.

8. See reference to Giovanni Sartori's articles and the scholarly discussion provoked by them in our introductory essay.

9. The course of the Republic was punctuated by frequent elections that contributed to the high level of tension, particularly three national elections in less than five years, and the lack of synchronism between the political developments in Catalonia and the rest of Spain. To them we have to add the referenda on the local autonomy statutes. See Javier Tusell, *Las elecciones del Frente Popular,* 2 vols. (Madrid: Edicusa, 1971); idem *La segunda república en Madrid: Elecciones y partidos políticos* (Madrid: Tecnos, 1970); and idem, *Sociología electoral de Madrid (1903-1931)* (Madrid: Edicusa, 1967). See also Miguel M. Cuadrado, *Elecciones y partidos políticos de España (1868-1931)* (Madrid: Taurus, 1969), vol. 2, pp. 853-57, on the 1931 municipal elections, and Jesús de Miguel and Juan J. Linz, "Hacia un análisis regional de las elecciones de 1936 en España," *Revista Española de la Opinión Pública,* 48 (1977): pp. 27-68.

10. See Ferdinand A. Hermens, *Democracy or Anarchy? A Study of Proportional Representation* (Notre Dame, Ind.: Review of Politics, 1941), and his follower Helmut Unkelbach, *Grundlagen der Wahlsystematik: Stabilitätsbedingungen der modernen Demokratie* (Göttingen: Vandenhoeck and Ruprecht, 1956). An early critic who mentioned the Spanish case was Sten S. Nilson, "Wahlsoziologische Probleme des Nationalsozialismus," *Zeitschrift für die gesamte Staatswissenschaft* 110 (1954):279-311, esp. pp. 282-84. For a recent reexamination of the thesis passionately defended by Hermens, see Hans Fenske, *Wahlrecht und Parteiensystem: Ein Beitrag zur deutschen Parteiengeschichte* (Frankfort: Athenaeum, 1972), pp. 30-35. For a balanced analysis, see Giovanni Sartori, *Parties and Party Systems: A Framework for Analysis* (Cambridge: Cambridge University Press, 1976), vol. 1.

11. The Spanish electoral system is similar in this respect to the Argentinian system that created the impossible game in the post-Perón period: coalitions with parties like the Peronists were inevitable and were perceived as a disloyal opposition.

   There is a need for a systematic analysis of the possible alternative outcome of elections with different electoral systems for those years. The failure to enact proportional representation, advocated in principle by the CEDA and strongly favored by the Lliga and other minor parties in 1935, remains unexplained.

12. Juan J. Linz, "Continuidad y discontinuidad en la elite política española, de la Restauración al Régimen actual," in *Estudios de ciencia política y sociología: Homenaje al Profesor Carlos Ollero* (Guadalajara: Gráficas Carlavilla, 1972), pp. 361–423.

13. Fortunately, on the agrarian problem and the failure to tackle the agrarian reform in a politically and technically viable way we have the outstanding monograph by Edward E. Malefakis, *Agrarian Reform and Peasant Revolution in Spain: Origins of the Civil War* (New Haven: Yale University Press, 1970). The low ranking of agrarian reform on the agenda of the leadership of the Republic is reflected in the fact that until May 1932 no serious discussion occurred in the Constituent Cortes and that the obstruction of agrarian reform measures until September by a small minority of the Right would have been defeated if the majority had so desired (Malefakis, *Agrarian Reform*, p. 389).

14. There is no fully adequate history of the church and the Catholic lay movement in the twentieth century, nor is there an adequate treatment of anticlericalism. José Manuel Cuenca, *Estudios sobre la Iglesia española del siglo XIX* (Madrid, 1973), provides some historical antecedents. M. Batllori and V. M. Arbeloa, *Iglesia y Estado durante la Segunda República española: 1931–1936*, is forthcoming. In English, José M. Sánchez, *Reform and Reaction: The Politico-Religious Background of the Spanish Civil War* (Chapel Hill: University of North Carolina Press, 1962), provides an overview. In Spanish, see the chapter in La Cierva, *Historia de la Guerra Civil Española*, pp. 462–81. Even though centered on the civil war period, Antonio Montero Moreno, *Historia de la persecución religiosa en España: 1936–1939* (Madrid: Biblioteca de Autores Cristianos, 1961), provides an overview for the prewar years, including the church burnings, the Asturian Revolution, and the popular anticlericalism in 1936. A good local study based on diocesan documents is Juan Ordóñez Márquez, *La apostasía de las masas y la persecución religiosa en la provincia de Huelva, 1931–1936* (Madrid: Consejo Superior de Investigaciones Científicas, 1968). The sociological study by Severino Aznar, *La revolución española y las vocaciones eclesiásticas* (Madrid: Instituto de Estudios Políticos, 1949), shows the impact of the October revolution on the number of seminarians. For the declarations of the hierarchy, see Jesús Iribarren, ed., *Documentos colectivos del episcopado español, 1870–1974* (Madrid: Biblioteca de Autores Cristianos, 1974). On the other hand, we have the biographies of bishops, including Anastasio Granados, *El Cardenal Gomá: Primado de España* (Madrid: Espasa Calpe, 1969); Ramón Muntanyola, *Vidal i Barraquer, cardenal de la pau* (Barcelona: Estela, 1970); and the book by Juan de Iturralde, *El catolicismo y la cruzada de Franco* (n.p.: Egui-Indarra, n.d.), focused on the links of the church with reactionary elements. Ramón Comas, *Isidro Gomá, Francesc Vidal i Barraquer: Dos visiones antagónicas de la Iglesia española de 1939* (Salamanca: Sígueme, 1977), shows the divergent outlook of two leading churchmen.

To get a feel for the secularizing and anticlerical positions—at their most dignified—see the speeches of Azaña, particularly in the Cortes debate, included in his *Obras completas*, ed. Juan Marichal, 4 vols. (Mexico: Oasis, 1967). See also those of Gordón Ordás in *Mi política en España*, 3 vols. (Mexico D.F.: Imprenta Fígero, 1961–63). There is no sociological-sociopsychological study of popular anticlericalism, nor of the popular manifestations of religiosity in response to it.

On lay Catholicism, the writings of Angel Herrera Oria, director of El Debate, *Obras selectas de Angel Herrera* (Madrid: Biblioteca de Autores Cristianos [BAC], 1943), and Martín Sánchez Juliá, *Ideas claras: Reflexiones de un español actual* (Madrid: BAC, 1959), are revealing. All the works dealing with the CEDA are also relevant to an understanding of the contribution of the religious conflict to the crisis.

15. See Stanley G. Payne, *Politics and the Military in Modern Spain* (Stanford, Ca.: Stanford University Press, 1967), pp. 266–91, on the Azaña reforms (some of them enacted by the provisional government eleven days after the founding of the regime).

16. See Ignacio Hidalgo de Cisneros, *Memorias 2: La república y la guerra de España* (Paris: Editions de la librairie du Globe, 1964), pp. 91–99, on military reactions to Azaña's reforms. The future head of the Republican Air Force in the civil war (a Communist)

documents well the kind of reforms—for instance, retroactively voiding honor court decisions—that even he could not accept.

17. On those unfortunate events and the failure of the government to react effectively, see the memoirs of the minister of the interior at the time, Miguel Maura, *Así cayó Alfonso XIII* (Barcelona: Ariel, 1966), pp. 240–64.

18. Malefakis, *Agrarian Reform*, chap. 8, pp. 205–35, describes in detail how the provisions of the Agrarian Reform Law unnecessarily increased the number of opponents to the regime, yet had no chance, within any reasonable time—given budgetary constraints—to benefit anyone. In addition, they overloaded the bureaucratic machinery with work. Of the 879,371 farms affected by the reform, only 154,716, or 17.6 percent, lay in the eleven latifundio provinces, to which another 11.5 percent were added in the areas of application of the law. The remaining 70.9 percent were affected in their status without, however, any prospect of being actually included in the reform. Had the reform been limited to the eleven principal latifundio provinces, only 20,460 owners would have been affected, even after all the small and medium-sized farms encompassed by the *ruedo* and lease provisions were taken into account. As the law was written, 79,554 owners were forced to register their property.

The enemies of the reform were increased fourfold: more than two thirds of all inventory owners came from northern and central Spain, where land redistribution could not take effect until an enabling law had been passed by the Cortes (pp. 216–17).

19. Carlos Alba Tercedor, "La educación en la II República: Un intento de socialización política," in Ramírez, *Estudios sobre la II República Española*, pp. 49–85.

20. See Linz, "Early State Building," and idem, "Politics in a Multi-lingual Society with a Dominant World Language: The Case of Spain," in *Les États Multilingues: Problèmes et Solutions*, ed. Jean-Guy Savard and Richard Vigneault (Quebec: Université Laval, 1975), pp. 367–444, for an analysis and bibliographic references.

An excellent monograph on the conservative Catalan party is Isidre Molas, *Lliga catalana: Un estudi d'Estasiologia*, 2 vols. (Barcelona: Edicions 62, 1972), that includes an analysis of the party system of Catalonia (2:231–98) and election data for the period (2:267–94), as well as information on Lliga membership, social composition of elites, etc. An overview is provided by Jaume Rossinyol, *Le problème national catalan* (Paris: Mouton, 1969). Jesús Pabón, *Cambó*, 3 vols. (Barcelona: Alpha, 1952–69), is a basic work. For the Catalan Left, see Roger Arnau, *Marxisme català i qüestió nacional catalana, 1930–1936*, 2 vols. (Paris: Edicions Catalanes de Paris, 1974). An earlier overview is contained in Maximiano García Venero, *Historia del nacionalismo Catalán*, 2 vols. (Madrid: Editora Nacional, 1967). Galician regionalism was not a disruptive factor. See Alfonso Bozzo, *Los partidos políticos y la autonomía en Galicia, 1931–1936* (Madrid: Akal, 1976). On the Catalan Estatuto, its origins, enactment, and application, see the excellent study by Manuel Gerpe Landin, *L'estatut d'autonomia de Catalunya í l'estat integral* (Barcelona: Edicions 62, 1977).

21. On Basque nationalism, the most recent comprehensive history is Stanley G. Payne, *Basque Nationalism* (Reno: University of Nevada, 1975). See also Javier Tusel Gómez, *Historia de la Democracia Cristiana en España* (Madrid: Edicusa, 1974), vol. 2, pp. 11–119, particularly on the relations with the CEDA.

22. Quoted in Catalan in La Cierva, *Historia de la Guerra Civil*, p. 378.

23. For an account of the events, see ibid., pp. 369–86, and two contemporary narratives: L. Aymami i Baudina, *El 6 d'Octubre tal com jo l'he vist* (Barcelona: Atenea, 1935), and Jaume Miravitlles, *Crítica del 6 d'octubre* (Barcelona: Libreria Catalonia, 1935).

24. On the case, see Albert Balcells, *El problema agrari a Catalunya 1890–1936: La questió rabassaire* (Barcelona: Nova Terra, 1968); Jesús Pabón, *Cambó, Parte segunda: 1930–1947* (Barcelona: Alpha, 1969), pp. 339–60; and the memoirs of the lawyer who argued the case before the constitutional court: Amadeu Hurtado, *Quaranta anys d'advocat: Historia del meu temps* (Esplugues de Llobregat: Ariel, 1967), chap. 10, pp. 256–98.

25. Manuel Azaña, in a parliamentary debate on 25 June 1934. See his *Obras Completas*, vol. 2, p. 981.

26. Quoted in Pabón, *Cambó, Parte segunda*, pp. 335–36.

27. The basic source is the personal defense by Manuel Azaña himself. See Azaña "Mi rebelión in Barcelona (1934–1935)," first published in 1935, reprinted in *Obras Completas*, vol. 3, pp. 25–179.

28. See Karl Dietrich Bracher, Wolfgang Sauer, and Gerhard Schulz, *Die Nationalsozialistische Machtergreifung* (Cologne: Westdeutscher Verlag, 1960), pp. 136–44, the relevant studies by Karl Schwend, and the memoirs of Frhr. von Aretin.

29. The statements of Izquierda Republicana and Unión Republicana on 5 October 1934 are quoted in La Cierva, *Historia de la Guerra Civil*, p. 429. The Partido Republicano Conservador, Partido Federal Autónomo, and Izquierda Radical Socialista made similar statements. Given the legitimizing of the revolution by the bourgeois parties with those statements, a historical study of their formulation would be important. If we consider the CEDA as a potentially legitimate participant in the political process—which those parties did not—these official notes were at best a semiloyal behavior.

30. On the Sanjurjo uprising, see Payne, *Politics and the Military in Spain*, pp. 277–91, and Alejandro Lerroux, *La pequeña historia: Apuntes para la historia grande vividos y redactados por el autor* (Buenos Aires: Cimera, 1945), pp. 143–46, the latter for his account of a conversation with Sanjurjo and his transmittal of the information to Azaña (without, however, revealing names).

31. In his memoirs (*Obras Completas*, vol. 4, pp. 649–52), Azaña describes in detail a conversation on 2 January 1934 with Fernando de los Ríos, former Socialist minister, on the revolutionary plans of the Socialist party. He later had a similar conversation with Largo Caballero. While he tried forcefully to dissuade them, he does not mention any thought of informing the Lerroux government.

32. Joaquín Chapaprieta, *La paz fue posible: Memorias de un político*, with an introductory essay by Carlos Seco Serrano (Esplugues de Llobregat: Ariel, 1971), pp. 407–13.

33. On the anarcho-syndicalist movement, see José Peirats, *La CNT en la revolución española* (Toulouse: Ediciones de la CNT, 1953). A recent analysis is Antonio Elorza, *La utopía anarquista bajo la Segunda República* (Madrid: Ayuso, 1973). On Anarcho-syndicalism and spontaneous peasant protest, see Malefakis, *Agrarian Reform*, chap. 11, pp. 284–316. For additional references, see Stanley G. Payne, *The Spanish Revolution: Study of the Social and Political Tensions That Culminated in the Civil War in Spain* (New York: Norton, 1970).

34. The official history is Partido Comunista de España, *Historia del PCE*, abbreviated version (Havana: Editora Política, 1964). See also the anti-Communist work by Eduardo Comín Colomer, *Historia del Partido Comunista de España*, 3 vols. (Madrid: Editora Nacional, 1967). On the PCE and dissident Communist parties, see also La Cierva, *Historia de la Guerra Civil*, pp. 352–63, and Guy Hermet, *Les communistes en Espagne: Etude d'un mouvement politique clandestin* (Paris: A. Colin, 1971), pp. 17–34.

35. On the Catalan revolutionary parties and groups, see Arnau, *Marxisme català*, and Isidre Molas, *Lliga catalana*, vol. 2, pp. 277–98. For additional references, see Payne, *Spanish Revolution*. On the POUM—Partido Obrero de Unificación Marxista—see Andrés Nin, *Los problemas de la revolución española*, with a Preface by Juan de Andrade (Paris: Ruedo Ibérico, 1971), and Victor Alba, *El marxisme a Catalunya, 1919–1939*, vol. 1, *Historia del B.O.C.*, vol. 2, *Historia del P.O.U.M.*, vol. 3, *Andreu Nin*, and vol. 4, *Joaquím Maurín* (Barcelona: Portic, 1974–75).

36. A definitive history of the Socialist party, particularly in the years from the death of Pablo Iglesias (1925) to the civil war, remains to be written. Today, we must still rely on the scanty memoirs of participants, collections of speeches by different leaders, polemical tracts, and valuable secondary accounts based on limited evidence. Much monographic research is under way, and the provisional synthesis of developments in the PSOE during the thirties in Malefakis, *Agrarian Reform*, will certainly lead that author to write the work needed. The description of the three main tendencies in the party centered around key personalities like Besteiro, Prieto, and Largo Caballero will be insufficient until we know more about their respective bases of support and are able to place their positions in a comparative ideological analysis of Socialist politics. The terms often used to characterize those three positions—reformism, pragmatism, and maximalism—are in part a misleading

shorthand. Except for Besteiro and Fernando de los Ríos, Spanish Socialist leaders did not articulate their positions intellectually in Marxist terms, as did many of their colleagues abroad. Only a more thorough analysis of their statements and actions over the years, i.e., their intellectual roots, would help us to understand more systematically and comparatively their positions in those fateful years.

Such analysis would also limit excessive emphasis on personality conflicts and enable us to interpret as consistent apparently contradictory positions taken in the course of time, which we suspect—given the personalities of some of the actors—responded to an implicit code. From this perspective, Largo Caballero's collaboration with the dictatorship, his ministerial role in the first bienio, his rejection of further collaboration with the Left-bourgeois parties in 1933, his shift to a clearly revolutionary insurrectionist position which led to the events of October 1934, his rejection of the party's participation in the government in 1936 after the Popular Front victory, and his revolutionary voluntarism might ultimately be as consistent as the "orthodox" Marxism of Besteiro's rejection in principle of party participation in bourgeois political alliances (in 1917, 1923, 1930, and 1931) and the inarticulate but obviously socio-democratic stance of Prieto, which had been maintained since the days of Primo de Rivera. Certainly Besteiro's position was politically non-viable in the 1930s, since the PSOE and the UGT were the two best-organized political forces to the left of center, and there was a divided and far from outstanding bourgeois Left and Center political leadership. Outside support and the personal participation of leaders without the commitment of their parties, could not strengthen a progressive Republic nor satisfy the deprived working-class masses. It would perhaps have made sense if Azaña and Lerroux had worked together against both the Right and the proletarian Left, as the bourgeois forces in the Third French Republic sometimes did. But the non-social democratic position of Largo Caballero, whose roots in the early years of the party need to be traced, would only have made sense if the PSOE had been supported by the whole urban and rural proletariat—divided between Socialists and the syndicalists of the CNT, in addition to minor radical parties—and if the society had for one reason or another found itself in a really prerevolutionary situation after its defeat in the war, in a sudden deep economic crisis rather than a structural crisis aggravated by the depression, and with a much weaker urban and rural middle class ready to defend its interests. It is no accident, as La Cierva has noted (*Historia de la Guerra Civil*, pp. 315–20), that Largo Caballero should have embraced the ideas of the working-class alliances (initially formulated by dissident Communists in Catalonia), since only the united action of all proletarian organizations could aspire to revolutionary action. Under the circumstances the chances for victory in a real revolution, even a well-planned one, were considerably less than even. Only the preemptive counterrevolution of 1936 made possible the unity of revolutionary forces and a civil war.

Besteiro's supporters accused Largo of being a "practical reformist who sometimes can take the appearance of an extreme radicalism" and of a "transition from collaborationist opportunism to bolshevik opportunism."
37. Martin Blinkhorn, *Carlism and Crisis in Spain, 1931–1939* (Cambridge: Cambridge University Press, 1975).
38. Paul Preston, "Alfonsist Monarchism and the Coming of the Spanish Civil War," *Journal of Contemporary History* 7, nos. 3 and 4 (July–October 1972):89–114.
39. For a hagiographic biography, see Felipe Acedo Colunga, *José Calvo Sotelo* (Barcelona: AHR, 1957). For a good example of his disloyal opposition, see the speech of 12 January 1936 appealing for a military insurrection (La Cierva, *Historia de la Guerra Civil*, pp. 628–29).
40. See Payne in his writings on Spanish fascism, particularly *Falange*. In contrast, a fascisticized, monarchical, conservative Right had support among certain elites and intellectuals, and the Carlists retained their local strongholds. See Stanley G. Payne, "Spain," in *The European Right*, ed. Hans Rogger and Eugene Weber (Berkeley and Los Angeles: University of California Press, 1965), pp. 168–207, for additional references. It was this sector of the Right that was most active in stimulating military conspiracies, and that established, in March 1934, contacts with the Italian government to buy arms. It is difficult to estimate the electoral appeal the Carlists and Renovación would have had

running candidates separately, but it certainly would have been below that of the DNVP, except in its worst showing. In 1936 the vote going to the candidates of both parties who appeared on coalition lists was 7.2%.

41. In 1933 the extreme Right had gone into the elections in many (but not all) districts allied with the CEDA; soon, however, it would find the collaboration between that party and Radicals as distasteful as did the Radicals, who followed Martínez Barrio in his split with Lerroux. The attacks became increasingly bitter in late 1934 and continued well into the election campaign of 1936, which the extreme Right led under the slogan "Let us vote so that some day we can stop voting." The CEDA, on the other hand, was optimistic about the potential electoral success, overestimating the effect of its organizational and financial resources. From a pro-Bloque Nacional point of view, see Santiago Galindo Herrero, *Los partidos monárquicos bajo la Segunda República* (Madrid: Rialp, 1956), pp. 259–65, which contains correspondence between Gil Robles and Calvo Sotelo. Gil Robles, *No fue posible la paz* (Esplugues de Llobregat: Ariel, 1968), pp. 406–23, describes in detail the tension in the course of the campaign. See also La Cierva, *Historia de la Guerra Civil,* pp. 497–501 and 619.

42. Unfortunately, there is no monographic study on the Esquerra and no scholarly biography of Companys comparable to that of Cambó. See, however, Angel Ossorio Gallardo, *Vida y sacrificio de Companys* (Buenos Aires: Losada, 1943); Josep M. Poblet, *Vida i mort de Lluís Companys* (Barcelona: Pórtic, 1976); Joan B. Culla i Clarà, *El catalanisme d'esquerra (1928–1936): Del grup de "L'Opinió" al Partit Nacionalista Republicà d' Esquerra (1928–1936)* (Barcelona: Curial, 1977); and J. M. Poblet, *Història de l'Esquerra Republicana de Catalunya* (Barcelona: Dopesa, 1976). On the Catalan elite, see Ismael E. Pitarch, *Sociologia dels Polítics de la Generalitat (1931–1939)* (Barcelona: Curial, 1977). The sources of Catalan politics quoted above all deal extensively with the role of the Esquerra.

43. In English, see Frank Sedwick, *The Tragedy of Manuel Azaña and the Fate of the Spanish Republic* (Columbus: Ohio State University Press, 1963). However, the best biographical interpretative sketch is Juan Marichal, *La vocación de Manuel Azaña* (Madrid: Edicusa, 1968). Marichal also edited the monumental four-volume collection, *Obras completas* (see n. 14).

44. There is no scholarly biography of the Radical leader. The following volumes were written without access to archives but are informative and personal: Lerroux, *La pequeña historia;* idem, *Mis memorias* (Madrid: Afrodisio Aguado, 1963). On the Radical party, see Octavio Ruiz Manjón, *El Partido Republicano Radical, 1908–1936* (Madrid: Tebas, 1976).

45. There is no monograph on the Radical-Socialist party, one of the largest in the Constituent Cortes. However, the collection of writings of one of its leaders—Gordón Ordás, *Mi política en España*—gives much information and conveys its style and ideology. The party split into three tendencies in 1933. In later years some of its members would end in the "Center-Right of the Left"—the Unión Republicana. See Manuel Ramírez Jiménez, *Las reformas de la II República* (Madrid: Tucar, 1977), pp. 91–169.

46. Richard A. H. Robinson, *The Origins of Franco's Spain: The Right, the Republic and Revolution, 1931–1936* (Pittsburgh, Pa.: University of Pittsburgh Press, 1970) has been the object of severe criticism by Paul Preston. See Paul Preston, "The 'Moderate' Right and the Undermining of the Second Republic in Spain, 1931–1933," *European Studies Review* 3, no. 4 (1973):369–94. On the polemic, see R. M. Blinkhorn, "Anglo-American Historians and the Second Spanish Republic: The Emergence of a New Orthodoxy," *European Studies Review* 3, no. 1 (January 1973):81–87.

47. There are no published memoirs of Indalecio Prieto, but many interesting and insightful autobiographical articles are included in his *Convulsiones de España,* 2 vols. (Mexico: Oasis, 1967), which include his civil war memoirs.

A prime example of the elimination of real leaders from positions of responsibility and the substitution of second-rate men as stand-ins occurred with the pushing of Azaña into the presidency. The Left Socialists vetoed Prieto as a prime minister, and Casares Quiroga (whose lack of qualifications is almost as much a matter of agreement as his dependency on Azaña) was appointed instead. See the account by Juan Marichal, based on an interview with Araquistain, in Azaña, *Obras,* vol. 3, pp. XXXI–XXXII. Prieto, for his part, later expressed doubt that Azaña was really displeased with his inability to assume the premiership. See La Cierva, *Historia de la Guerra Civil*, p. 667.

48. Emilio Lamo de Espinosa, *Política y filosofía en Julián Besteiro* (Madrid: Edicusa, 1972); Andrés Saborit, *Julián Besteiro* (Buenos Aires: Losada, 1967). On 5 August 1933 Besteiro cautioned the young Socialists who said, "Democracy does not serve us for anything; let us stop (talking) and go toward dictatorship." Besteiro responded, "Many times one is more revolutionary resisting one of those collective madnesses than letting oneself be carried away by the drift of the masses to harvest immediate success and assured applause, at the risk that later the masses will be the ones harvesting the disappointments and suffering" (quoted in Saborit, *Julián Besteiro*, p. 240; see also p. 232).

49. The maximalist position is articulated in Largo Caballero, *Discursos a los trabajadores: Una crítica de la República, Una doctrina socialista, Un programa de acción*, with Foreword by Luis Araquistain, 2d ed. (Madrid: Gráfica Socialista, 1934). Araquistain was also the editor of *Leviatán: Revista Mensual de Hechos e Ideas*, the intellectual organ of that position. The critique by Gabriel Mario de Coca, *Anti-Caballero: Crítica marxista de la bolchevización del partido socialista (1930-1936)* (Madrid: Editorial Engels, Foreword dated March 1936). Indalecio Prieto, R. González Peña, Toribio Echevarría, Amador Fernández, Alejandro Jaume, Antonio Llaneza, etc., *Documentos Socialistas: Colección inquietudes de nuestro tiempo* (n.p.: Gráficas Sánchez, n.d. [probably 1935]), represent the other side in the split of the party.

On the radicalization of the Socialists, the best account is still Malefakis, *Agrarian Reform*, pp. 317-42. The more moderate wing of Spanish socialism perceived the dilemma posed by maximalism when it stated, in the spring of 1936: "The revolutionary verbalism is not, by far, the revolution, but it can be the counterrevolution if it precipitates events of uncorrectible imprudence, the worst of which is the division of the party." See Miguel Artola, *Partidos y programas políticos 1808-1936*, 2 vols. (Madrid: Aguilar, 1974-75), vol. 1, pp. 668-69.

50. See the sources quoted in note 14, particularly Angel Herrera.

51. For an excellent analysis of some of the "constraints" in the 1930s and the "defensive" character of the CEDA that distinguished it both from other European Christian-Democratic movements born more slowly and in more auspicious times and from the Partido Social Popular (founded just before the dictatorship), see Oscar Alzaga, *La primera democracia cristiana en España* (Esplugues de Llobregat: Ariel, 1973), pp. 305-21. The failure of the social policies of the Center Right is treated, with emphasis on the agrarian policies, in Malefakis, *Agrarian Reform*, pp. 342-63. It is handled with restraint in the memoirs of Chapaprieta and viewed critically by Paul Preston in *The Spanish Right under the Second Republic: An Analysis* (Reading: Occasional Publication no. 3 of the University of Reading, Graduate School of Contemporary European Studies, 1971), and in José R. Montero Gilbert, "La CEDA: El partido contrarrevolucionario hegemónico de la II República" in *Estudios sobre la II República Española*, ed. Manuel Ramírez (Madrid: Tecnos, 1973), pp. 89-128. It is a brief summary of his excellent two volume work, *La CEDA: El catolicismo social y político en la II República* (Madrid: Ediciones de la Revista de Trabajo, 1977).

The complex problem of loyalty, semiloyalty, or disloyalty is answered very differently by authors of different ideological persuasions. In our view no answer is possible for the role of the party over the whole period, since changing situations and pressures affected its stance. Obviously in the late spring of 1936 its position could not be that of 1935. On its semiloyalty/disloyalty after 1936, see La Cierva, *Historia de la Guerra Civil*, pp. 740-44. The basic sources are the two volumes by the leader of the party, Jose María Gil Robles, *No fue posible la paz*, and *Discursos Parlamentarios* (Madrid: Taurus, 1971). The latter contains an introductory essay by Carlos Seco Serrano (pp. vii-1).

52. William J. K. Irwin, "The CEDA in the 1933 Cortes Elections" (Ph.D. diss., Columbia University, 1975), and Javier Tusell, *Las elecciones del Frente Popular* (for the 1936 election). La Cierva, *Historia de la Guerra Civil*, pp. 615-19, and the memoirs of Gil Robles and Chapaprieta all convey a sense of the ambiguities, contradictions, and compromises in the coalitions made across the electoral map by this major party.

53. The origins, formation, and meaning of the Popular Front are complex issues, partly obscured for partisan purposes. One detailed account is contained in La Cierva, *Historia de la Guerra Civil*, pp. 579-610. The basic sources are the memoirs and speeches of Azaña

and Gordón Ordás, the small book by Diego Martínez Barrio, *Páginas para la historia del Frente Popular* (Buenos Aires: Publicaciones del Patronato Hispano Argentino de Cultura, 1943), Prieto, *Posiciones socialistas,* pp. 13ff., and José Díaz for the Communists. The initial idea was a Frente Republicano, but a variety of circumstances led to the heterogeneous final coalition, whose program, proclaimed on 15 January 1936 included references to some points of disagreement between Republicans and the Marxist parties. For the program, see Artola, *Partidos y programas,* vol. 2, pp. 454–55.

54. On the negotiations to form electoral tickets in the Catalan provinces, see Isidre Molas, *Lliga catalana,* vol. 1, passim; for the electoral results, see pp. 267–94.

55. Strangely enough, many party leaders were aware of the dangerous implications of the electoral system. For example, Ventosa of the Lliga declared: "For the reform of the electoral system is essential; without proportional representation and with the bonus that is now given to the majority, political stability will never be achieved. It will provoke the alternative crushing of one block of parties by another and nothing else" (ibid., vol. 2, pp. 197–202).

56. A problem faced by Gil Robles, and one which he recognized, was the antidemocratic position of the Juventud de Acción Popular (JAP). (See *No fue posible la paz,* pp. 189–203.) This created many difficulties for him. However, it could be argued that the pseudo-fascist rhetoric of the JAP deflected the youthful potential for fascism into channels which in practice proved to be nonviolent.

57. Juan J. Linz, "Continuidad y discontinuidad en la élite política española," tables on pp. 395, 397, and 398.

58. The image of public immorality associated with the Radical party, which ultimately destroyed this Center force (in the straperlo and Nombela affairs, though these were *pecata minuta* compared to the Stavisky affair), must be seen in the context of a relatively high level of personal honesty in the politicians of the monarchy and Republic. Without taking those affairs into account, the crisis of late 1935, after a limited reequilibration of the political system after October 1934, cannot be understood. On the affairs and the dubious role of Alcalá Zamora in their political exploitation, see La Cierva, *Historia de la Guerra Civil,* pp. 502–5; Chapaprieta, *La paz fue posible,* pp. 243–91; Gil Robles, *No fue posible la paz,* pp. 295–313; and Lerroux, *La pequeña historia,* chaps. 13–19, passim. Pabón, *Cambó,* vol. 2, pp. 433–58, also contains an excellent account. Philip Williams, "The Politics of Scandal," in *Wars, Plots, and Scandals in Postwar France* (Cambridge: Cambridge University Press, 1970), pp. 3–16, analyzes the political dynamics of scandals in a way that could be applied to this case.

59. There is general agreement that in 1935 not only the extreme Right and the Agrarios, but a considerable number of CEDA deputies, opposed the more progressive social and tax policies of the CEDA ministers and Chapaprieta, even though Gil Robles gave them his support. The specific pressure-group politics involved and their links with the parties deserve further study. See Gil Robles, *No fue posible la paz,* pp. 279–80, 349–51, 355–58, and Chapaprieta, *La paz fue posible,* pp. 292–305. On interest-group politics in the Republic, see Manuel Ramírez Jiménez, *Los grupos de presión en la Segunda República Española* (Madrid: Tecnos, 1969).

60. Balcells, *El problema agrari a Catalunya.*

61. There is no scholarly biography of Niceto Alcalá Zamora, the first president of the Republic, and our views of his role are inevitably colored by the accounts of his opponents, particularly Lerroux and Gil Robles. For his defense, see *Los defectos de la Constitución de 1931* (Madrid: Imprenta de R. Espinosa, 1936), and Niceto Alcalá Zamora, *Memorias (Segundo texto de mis memorias)* (Barcelona: Planeta, 1977) Appendix 5, "Los Ataques de Lerroux," pp. 478–535. Before the formation of the presidential governments at the end of 1935, he had established the custom of receiving cabinet members without the knowledge of the prime minister and of forcing on prime ministers his personal friends in the formation of cabinets. See Largo Caballero, *Mis recuerdos: Cartas a un amigo* (Mexico: Ediciones Unidas, 1954). In his memoirs, Azaña, in addition to Lerroux and Gil Robles, comments on these tendencies and their impact on the political process.

62. La Cierva, *Historia de la Guerra Civil,* pp. 609, 659, and 702–3; Chapaprieta, *La paz fue posible,* pp. 378–81. From the complaints of both the Right and Left about the behavior of the courts, one could think that they were less biased than in Weimar Germany.

63. José Ortega y Gasset exemplifies in a paradigmatic way the dilemmas of a detached, passionately patriotic, politically sophisticated, but vocationally intellectual man witnessing the breakdown of a regime he had helped found and continued to support as the only alternative. His brilliant critical analysis of the fatal errors of all participants contributed inevitably to an alienation from the regime but could not become—in spite of his own faint hopes—a rallying point for a constructive alternative. No one optimistic about the viability of the regime can ignore his analysis, which can be found in *Obras Completas*, vol. 11, *Escritos políticos II (1922–1933)* (Madrid: Revista de Occidente, 1969). Symbolic of that tragedy was that after 3 December 1933, except for an epilogue to his *Rebellion of the Masses* for English readers, published in 1937, he would remain silent on Spanish politics.

64. For the text of the constitution, and Article 81, see Nicolás Pérez Serrano, *La Constitución Española (9 Diciembre 1931), Antecedentes, Texto, Comentarios* (Madrid: Revista de Derecho Privado, 1932) with commentary on each article. Let us not forget that the normal six-year term of office of Alcalá Zamora would have lasted until 10 December 1937. Similarly, the legislature elected on 14 July 1931 could have lasted legally until the same date in 1935, had it not been dissolved by the president in a call for new elections. The legislature constituted after these elections, on 8 December 1933, if it had exhausted its term, would have lasted until the same date in 1937, rather than until 7 January 1936. In view of the Spanish experience, one might ask if premature dissolution in a polarized and tense society, even when it allows the expression of changes in public opinion, does not do a disservice to the stability of democratic institutions and allow parties to escape their responsibilities.

65. There is no systematic analysis of the role of the intellectuals in politics and society in this period that covers the whole ideological spectrum and the role of magazines and of the press. Two important contributions are Carlos M. Rama, *La crisis española del siglo XX* (Mexico: Fondo de Cultura Económica, 1960), and Manuel Tuñón de Lara, *Medio siglo de cultura española (1885–1936)* (1971). Particularly useful on Marxist thought is J. C. Mainer, *Literatura y pequeña burguesía en España (Notas 1890–1940)* (Madrid: Edicusa, 1972). On Miguel de Unamuno, see Elías Díaz, *Revisión de Unamuno: Análisis crítico de su pensamiento político* (Madrid: Tecnos, 1968). On José Ortega y Gasset, see Gonzalo Redondo, *Las empresas políticas de Ortega y Gasset, "El Sol," "Crisol," "Luz" (1917–1934)*, 2 vols. (Madrid: Rialp, 1970). In addition, see Juan Marichal, *La vocación de Manuel Azaña*, and José L. García de la Serrana, "Los intelectuales en la II República," in *Estudios sobre la II República Española* ed. Manuel Ramírez, pp. 131–40. Very revealing on the political climate among the intellectuals and the impact of events is Julio Caro Baroja, *Los Baroja (Memorias Familiares)* (Madrid: Taurus, 1972), pp. 255–340. It is important to note that at the end of the dictatorship the intellectual community, despite its ideological differentiation, seems to have had some common ground, but with the civil war it was forced to take sides and in part disperse into exile.

On the presence of university professors in the legislatures of the Republic, and their party affiliation, see Juan J. Linz, "Continuidad y discontinuidad en la élite política española," pp. 402–5. In 1931 there were thirty-nine professors among the 464 deputies, in 1933, twenty, and in 1936, twenty-nine, but only eight served in all three Cortes and only fifteen in the first and third legislatures. In view of these data it appears that while the new regime might initially have deserved the name "the Republic of professors," it did not deserve it by 1936. Of the fifty-two professors who were deputies, eight were Socialists, fourteen were followers of Azaña, and four were followers of the Agrupación al Servicio de la República, but there were also seven of the CEDA and at least six more who were members of the parties supporting the governments of 1933–35.

66. For the thinking of the extreme Right, see Ramiro de Maeztu, *Obra* (Madrid: Editora Nacional, 1974). The intellectual organ of the extreme Right, *Acción Española*, was not founded until December 1931 and apparently had a limited circulation.

67. The Sanjurjada was the last of the pronunciamentos in Spain, if we define them as Ortega y Gasset did in his *Invertebrate Spain* (New York: Norton, 1937), chap. 9. It was also a total failure of planning; it rallied neither broad military nor civilian support, and its rapid defeat showed that at that point the regime could consolidate itself. It also convinced the leadership of the Center Right and the more moderate rightist masses that their efforts had to be directed at an electoral victory. It unfortunately created in the bourgeois Left a certain

disdain for the threats that might come from the army; this might have contributed to the false sense of security that characterized Casares Quiroga in 1936, which in turn led him to disregard the complaints of the Right. It also left as a heritage to the second bienio of Lerroux-Gil Robles after 1933 the issue of amnesty of the participants, which in turn undermined the legitimacy of their response to the October revolution. For an account of events see Payne, *Politics and the Military in Modern Spain*, chap. 15, and the bibliographical references there.

68. See Malefakis, *Agrarian Reform*, pp. 203–4, on the renewed spirit of Republican unity that facilitated the passage of the agrarian reform.

69. The bibliography on the October revolution in Asturias and the attempts to support it elsewhere is extensive. Recent works published in Spain include Bernardo Díaz-Nosty, *La comuna asturiana: Revolución de octubre de 1934* (Madrid: ZYX, 1974); J. A. Sánchez G. Saúco, *La revolución de 1934 en Asturias* (Madrid: Editora Nacional, 1974), with a Foreword by Vicente Palacio Atard, also published in his book, *Cinco historias de las república y de la guerra* (Madrid: Editora Nacional, 1973); and Francisco Aguado Sánchez, *La revolución de Octubre de 1934* (Madrid: San Martín, 1972). However, contemporary writings are more useful in understanding the impact of those events on the participants and the society. See Manuel D. Benavides, *La revolución fue así: Octubre rojo y negro* (Barcelona, 1937); and Manuel Grossi, *La insurrección de Asturias (Quince días de revolución socialista)* (Barcelona: Gráficas Alfa, n.d. [1935]). (There is a French translation of the latter, published in Paris by Etudes et Documentation Internationales in 1972.) See also Antonio Ramos Oliveira, *La revolución española de octubre: Ensayo político* (Madrid: Yunque, 1935); Reporteros Reunidos, *Octubre Rojo (Ocho días que commovieron a España),* Manual de Historia Política de España (Madrid: Rubiños, 1935); Aurelio de Llano Roza de Ampudia, *Pequeños anales de quince días (La revolución en Asturias) Octubre de 1934* (Oviedo: Talleres Tipográficos, 1935); and Ignacio Núñez, *La revolución de octubre de 1934,* 2 vols. (Barcelona: José Vilamala, 1935). The account by General Eduardo López de Ochoa, *Campaña militar de Asturias en octubre de 1934* (Madrid: Yunque, 1936), is very revealing.

70. A motion on 25 May 1936 by Sánchez Román's National Republican Party (PNR), which had initially supported the formation of a Left Republican coalition but finally refused to join it when the Popular Front included the Communists, called for emergency measures to prevent further deterioration of the situation. Miguel Maura's articles in *El Sol* between 18 and 27 June were also calling for a "national republican dictatorship." The PNR proposals were an excellent example of the kind of measures that might defuse a situation which would otherwise lead inevitably to one or another type of dictatorship or civil war, and initiate a process of reequilibration. For the texts, see Payne, *Spanish Revolution*, pp. 202–4.

71. That policy was the natural alternative when Azaña maintained his commitment to the Socialists, and the relations between the two leaders became more difficult. The composition of the legislature elected in 1933 made it inevitable, but it should not be forgotten that the Radicals and the CEDA had already cooperated in the elections in many provinces. See Irwin, "The CEDA in the 1933 Cortes Elections," passim.

72. On Azaña's fear of victory, see Juan Marichal's Introduction in Azaña, *Obras Completas,* vol. 3, pp. xxvii–xxix, which quotes the relevant texts from a conversation with A. Ossorio and Azaña's diary (entry of 19 February 1936).

73. The mismanagement of the aftermath of the October crisis is well summarized in La Cierva, *Historia de la Guerra Civil*, pp. 435–56.

74. See Calvo Sotelo's speech on 6 November, quoted in ibid., p. 422. Julián Soriano Flores de Lemus, *Calvo Sotelo ante la II República: La reacción conservadora* (Madrid: Editora Nacional, 1975), covers only part of the period and is not the monographic study we need of Renovación Española and its leader.

75. On the problem of the repression of those responsible for the revolution, and the political implications of that repression, see the lengthy discussions in the memoirs of all the participants. For a summary, see La Cierva, *Historia de la Guerra Civil*, pp. 441–42, 443–44.

76. On the last two cabinet crises of 1935—so central to our analysis of the creation of a power vacuum by the intervention of Alcalá Zamora, which could only be filled by a new election of plesbiscitarian character that would polarize the society (not unlike those after weak

presidential cabinets under Hindenburg)—see the memoirs of two participants: Chapaprieta, *La paz fue posible*, pp. 328–83, and Gil Robles, *La paz no fue posible*, pp. 358–403. See also the account by Pabón, *Cambó*, pp. 459–67, which sees the problem through the eyes of the great Catalan leader who had warned Gil Robles of the dangers of a conflict with the president "that would oblige him to sacrifice his party or enter into a campaign that could lead the country into anarchy" (p. 460).

77. It might be noted that between January and April of 1935 the bourgeois Left, under the leadership of Azaña, started to articulate a position that included the moderate Socialists and might have offered another platform for reequilibration, but the inevitable constraints of electoral arithmetic demanded formation of a much broader alignment, i.e., the Popular Front, for the 1936 election. See La Cierva, *Historia de la Guerra Civil*, pp. 587–88.

78. In this context the dating of the change in the Socialist movement—PSOE, UGT, and the agrarian trade union (FNTT)—is of more than historical interest. Was it a response to the disintegration of the Socialist-Republican Coalition, Hitler's ascent to power, the electoral success of the anti-Azaña coalition, the perception of the CEDA in the light of the events of 1934 in Austria, or the articulation of latent ideological tendencies whose expression had been submerged under the dictatorship and the instauration of the Republic?

On the change in orientation of the Socialist party, see Paul Preston, "Los orígenes del cisma socialista: 1917–1931," *Cuadernos de Ruedo Ibérico* 49–50 (January–April 1976):12–40, which traces the divisions of the thirties back to positions taken earlier, particularly the Primo de Rivera dictatorship. See also Marta Bizcarrondo, "La crisis del partido socialista en la II República," *Revista del Instituto de Ciencias Sociales de la Diputación de Barcelona* 21 (1973), and David Ruiz, "Aproximación a Octubre de 1934," *III Coloquio de Pau* (1972).

For an analysis of the evolution of the maximalist Socialist leader, see Blas Guerrero, "La radicalización de Francisco Largo Caballero: 1933–1934," *Sistema* 8 (January 1975):73–83. See also Marta Bizcarrondo, *Araquistain y la crisis socialista en la II República Leviatán (1934–1936)* (Madrid: Siglo XXI, 1975). Paul Preston has edited a selection of texts with an introductory essay: *Leviatán (Antología)* (Madrid: Turner, 1976). See Santiago Carillo, *Demain l'Espagne: Entretiens avec Régis Debray et Max Gallo* (Paris: Seuil, 1974), pp. 31–35 and 42–48, on the radicalization of the Socialist youth organization and the cooperation and later fusion with the Communist youth.

For a collection of contemporary texts, manifestoes, analyses, and a long introductory essay demonstrating the ideological convergence and contacts between minor revolutionary groups like the BOC (Bloc Obrero y Camperol) with the PSOE even before and immediately after the 1933 election, see Marta Bizcarrondo, *Octubre del 34: Reflexiones sobre una revolución* (Madrid: Ayuso, 1977). These contacts encountered the hostility of the USC (Unió Socialista de Catalunya), which supported the regional Esquerra government. Bizcarrondo also discusses Largo Caballero's subsequent trip to Barcelona in February 1934.

The maximalist view is well reflected in a statement made by Luis Araquistain in *Claridad*, 13 February 1936: "The historical dilemma is fascism or socialism, and only violence will decide the issue." The statement concluded that since what passed for "fascism" in Spain was weak, socialism would win.

79. On the failure to be generous with Catalonia as region and to distinguish the people and institutions from the error of its government, see Pabón, *Cambó*, pp. 415–21. Such a policy would also have reinforced the ties with the Lliga, a participant in late 1935 governments, and its position in Catalan politics. Such a policy was advocated by Hurtado, *Quaranta anys d'advocat*, vol. 3, pp. 322–25.

80. For the violence from 31 January to 17 July, reported in *El Sol* of Madrid and in *La Nación* and *La Prensa* of Buenos Aires, see tables. The two Argentine papers were used to cover periods in which censorship prevented publication of news. The data probably underestimated the violence; certainly, use of more sensationalist papers on both sides of the political spectrum would raise the figures. The type of violence reported changes over time as the gravity increased. The data were collected by Margaret Scobie for Edward Malefakis; they were coded by Rocío de Terán, and the calculations were made by Ramiro Cibrián.

81. This point is brilliantly stated by Manuel Azaña in the politico-literary dialogue "La Velada de Benicarló" (written in 1937), included in *Obras Completas*, vol. 3, pp. 379–460. The theme had already appeared in a speech on 3 April 1936; see *Obras Completas*, vol. 3, p. 304.

82. While it is possible roughly to quantify the political and social violence, particularly the number of deaths, and to emphasize the psychological and political impact of some assassinations or attempts on the life of political leaders, we cannot fully assess the impact of the rhetoric of violence from Parliament to the daily newspaper and or the politicization and violence in daily social interaction. A good description of the kind of day-by-day occurrences that led to fear and hatred can be found in an article by the great writer Miguel de Unamuno in *Ahora*, 8 June 1936, quoted in La Cierva, *Historia de la Guerra Civil*, pp. 691–92.

83. This atmosphere of violence extended to the Cortes, from the opening session after the election to the last dramatic meeting of the Diputación Permanente after the assassination of Calvo Sotelo. See the text of the dramatic June–July parliamentary debates in which a Communist deputy said that Gil Robles would die with "his shoes on." For the text, see Fernando Díaz-Plaja, ed., *La historia de España en sus documentos: El siglo XX—La guerra (1936–1939)* (Madrid: Faro, 1963), pp. 13–148.

84. See Maura, *Así cayó Alfonso XIII*, pp. 240–64, esp. pp. 251–53.

85. On the Casas Viejas massacre, see Malefakis, *Agrarian Reform*, pp. 258–61. The parliamentary debate on that tragedy and the notes in Azaña's diary at the time are extremely illuminating. They illustrate how isolated revolutionary acts (so characteristic of the Anarchists), the brutality of the forces of order, insufficient information on such events, slowness in perceiving the political danger, and cynical manipulation by disloyal and semiloyal oppositions contribute to the erosion of the legitimacy of a regime and personal authority of its leaders. (For Azaña's interventions in the debate, see *Obras Completas*, vol. 2, pp. 531–45, 574–665; for his diary, see idem, vol. 3, pp. 447–74.) Undoubtedly the dangerous distance between Lerroux and Azaña—two founders of the regime—was increased by those developments. On this last phase of the first bienio, see La Cierva, *Historia de la Guerra Civil*, pp. 239–42.

86. The problem of the repression of the revolution, especially the illegal actions in Asturias, its serious political implications, and the political incapacity to face the problem honestly are well treated by La Cierva, *Historia de la Guerra Civil*, pp. 447–56; the author is a historian who cannot be suspected of leftist bias. The parliamentary and public campaign of Gordón Ordás in particular deserved more serious attention from the government. That lack of response and the censorship prevailing at the time allowed the Left to build an enormous emotional response that lasted until the outbreak of the civil war and even manifested itself in the debate in the Diputación Permanente of the Cortes over the assassination of Calvo Sotelo.

87. The anarcho-syndicalist revolutionary rhetoric and sporadic, more-or-less ill-coordinated uprisings in Catalonia, Zaragoza, and isolated villages were politically important in the first two years of the Republic, because they contributed to a crisis of authority and tensions in the government coalition. See Peirats, *La CNT. en la revolución española;* Elorza, *La utopía anarquista;* Malefakis, *Agrarian Reform;* and John Brademas, *Anarcosindicalismo y revolución en España (1930–1937)* (Barcelona: Ariel, 1974). However, since it was the expected behavior of this principled opposition, which was absent from Parliament and any public office, given its spontaneous and romantic or primitive character, the political significance was different from the actions of the Socialist party in 1934 and 1936. The PSOE and the UGT were seen as responsible and disciplined organizations, which had not been outlawed even under the dictatorship; their leaders sat in Parliament and had just been cabinet members, PSOE members controlled local governments, etc. In addition, our ecological analysis suggests that the violence in 1936 was mainly in traditionally Socialist regions of the country (even though some conflicts were probably caused by the CNT-FAI and took place between their members and the Socialists and other Marxist groups), while some Syndicalist areas—like Catalonia—were relatively quiescent.

88. The Radical minister of interior from 31 March to 4 October 1936, Rafael Salazar Alonso gives an interesting, even when perhaps exaggerated, account of the social tension

in 1934; see *Bajo el signo de la revolución* (Madrid: San Martín, 1936). On that semirevolutionary strike, see Malefakis, *Agrarian Reform,* pp. 335–40. The strike was defeated by a mixture of concessions, lack of support by many workers, and by the security measures of the government. The dead numbered only thirteen, mostly victims of conflicts between strikers and those refusing to join. There were 7,000 arrests, but except for the leaders, most were detained only for short periods of time. Four Cortes deputies were briefly arrested, but only one for more than a night. The strike had catastrophic consequences for the morale of the farm workers' federation.

In any discussion of the rural revolutionary or semirevolutionary outbreaks of Anarchists and Socialists, it should not be forgotten that a large part of the peasantry was made up of small property holders and stable tenants who were either moderate Republicans, CEDA supporters, or even Carlists. See Edward Malefakis, "Peasants, Politics, and Civil War in Spain, 1931–39," in *Modern European Social History,* ed. Robert Bezucha (Lexington, Mass.: D. C. Heath, 1972), pp. 194–227.

89. Mass rallies and demonstrations organized by the parties as shows of strength contributed much to the crisis atmosphere. A good example was the rally organized on 22 April 1934 by the CEDA youth organization—Juventud de Acción Popular—on which La Cierva comments, "It was morally impossible that the Spanish left would not mistake the demonstration of El Escorial for a Fascist rally. The general strike called in Madrid was not able to prevent the ceremony, but clearly marked an expression of resentment and protest" (*Historia de la Guerra Civil,* p. 260). The same would be true for the massive gathering on 6 September 1934 in the Asturian religious sanctuary of Covadonga and for the march of 100,000(?) persons during six hours through Barcelona on 29 April in support of the Generalitat in its conflict with the central government and the Constitutional Court. On the JAP—its organization, relation to the CEDA, ideology, and style—see Montero, *La CEDA,* vol. 1, pp. 582–656.

90. See La Cierva, *Historia de la Guerra Civil,* for the 2 April 1936 appeal in *Claridad* to create people's militias.

91. Cambó, one of the real moderates of the Right, wrote: "The excitement of the masses is the indispensable preparation for a fascist coup or a proletarian revolution . . . these mass rallies can never be used by a party that wants to maintain a center position" (quoted in Pabón, *Cambó,* p. 433).

92. The data on the casualties of dead and wounded in the Asturias Revolution are given in La Cierva, *Historia de la Guerra Civil,* pp. 425–26, who quotes the research in Llano y Roza de Ampudia. *Pequeños anales de quince días,* p. 206ff.

93. On the violence and persecution of the Falange, see the account in La Cierva, *Historia de la Guerra Civil,* pp. 692–96. An ecological analysis of the provinces with higher violence rates, particularly those where socioeconomic structural conflicts do not seem to have been important, suggests that the presence of the Falange contributed to the violence. The same is probably true for the PCE presence (using candidacies in the February elections as an indicator of presence).

94. Ivan Maisky, in his *Spanish Notebook* (London: Hutchinson, 1966), reports that when Alvarez del Vayo visited him (as Soviet ambassador in London) on 11 July he told him that "The Socialist youth league has created its own militia" and concluded that the Republic was "not in serious danger. There are forces in the country sufficient to avert or in any event crush any attempt at a military coup." Asked about the size of the Socialist militia, he said: "In Madrid it numbers up to 15,000 or so. . . . Not at all badly trained . . . as to arms, things are not too good. . . . But the people are with us." This is a good example of the excessive self-confidence that paramilitary forces can inspire. A week later the civil war started. We do not know if the existence of such militias and the plans for a purge of the army was one of the factors precipitating and strengthening the military resolve against the regime.

95. Let us not forget that the Falange, while not formally outlawed, was persecuted not only by the Socialist militia but by the government, which closed its headquarters (27 February 1936). Its leader, José Antonio Primo de Rivera, was under arrest after March 1936 and had been condemned to prison from April onward. We should also not forget that none of its leaders had parliamentary immunity. On this period, see Payne, *Falange,* pp. 101–15; La Cierva, *Historia de la Guerra Civil,* pp. 692–96.

96. It should not be forgotten that Largo Caballero went free in November 1935 for lack of proof of his leadership of the October revolution, and that Azaña, despite the eagerness of the government to implicate him, also went free in April 1935.
97. See table. From a sociological-political point of view, the absolute level is perhaps less important that the universally shared perception, the geographic spread, and the intensity and dramatic nature of cases which occurred in the national capital.

   Another indicator of the political breakdown—also found in Italy—is the substitution of elected municipal authorities by the Ministry of Interior. For data, see Rafael Salazar Alonso, *Bajo el signo de la Revolución*. Casares Quiroga made 270 substitutions between 1931 and 1933 (pp. 116–21), and Salazar Alonso 193 during his own tenure as minister (pp. 122–29); there were a total of 1,116 substitutions out of the 8,346 elected municipal authorities in the country after the October revolution (p. 129).

   Another sign of the impending crisis and the prevailing climate of fear and violence is the fact that 270,000 new gun licenses were taken out in the thirty-six months between mid-1933 and 1936, according to official figures. See Payne, *Spanish Revolution*, p. 195.
98. The figures are given in Renzo de Felice, *Mussolini il fascista: La conquista del potere* (Turin: Einaudi, 1966), p. 87. See also his data on violence, pp. 35–39.
99. Manuel Ramírez, "Las huelgas durante la II República," *Anales de Sociología* 1 (1966):76–88. The number of strikes was: 734 (1931), 681 (1932), 1127 (1933), 594 (1934), 181 (1935), and 1108 between January and July 1936. The monthly figures of the *Boletín del Ministerio de Trabajo* for 1936 are: 26, 19, 47, 105, 242, 444, and 225 until July 17.
100. On farm invasions and accelerated agrarian reform in 1936, see Malefakis, *Agrarian Reform*, pp. 364–87. The settlement from March to July involved 110,921 peasants and the occupation of 572,055 hectares.
101. An example of such strange eleventh-hour efforts to establish bridges between impossible allies are the contacts in May 1936 between Prieto and José Larraz (a man close to the CEDA), perhaps in search of support for a centrist alternative after a possible split of the PSOE and the thought of a split of the CEDA to support such a solution (La Cierva, *Historia de la Guerra Civil*, p. 669–70; Gil Robles, *No fue posible la paz*, pp. 615–627; Tusell, *Historia de la Democracia Cristiana*, vol. 1, pp. 357–59). The last such effort to formulate a program that could lead to a compromise with the military, which had already begun its rebellion, led to the formation on the night of 18 July of the Martínez Barrio cabinet. See the account in Maximiano García Venero, *Madrid, Julio 1936* (Madrid: Tebas, 1973), pp. 334–41 and 345–47, based on the recollections of a leading participant, and the memoirs of Azaña, *Obras completas*, vol. 4, p. 714.
102. Prieto, in a speech in Cuenca on 1 May 1936. Quoted in Payne, *Spanish Revolution*, p. 197. The complete text is in Indalecio Prieto, *Discursos Fundamentales* (Madrid: Turner, 1975), pp. 255–73, with an introductory essay by Edward Malefakis.
103. Alfred Stepan, *The Military in Politics: Changing Patterns in Brazil* (Princeton, N.J.: Princeton University Press, 1971). See part 2, "The 'Moderating Pattern' of Civil-Military Relations: Brazil, 1945–1964," pp. 57–66.
104. José Ortega y Gasset, *Invertebrate Spain*, trans. M. Adams (London: Allen and Unwin, 1937).
105. See Gil Robles, *No fue posible la paz*, pages quoted below.
106. Ramón Salas Larrazábal, *Historia del Ejército Popular de la República*, 4 vols. (Madrid: Editora Nacional, 1973), is an excellent analysis of the structure of the armed forces, including the police, under the Republic and of the political orientations of the officers. Larrazábal provides very detailed information on the response of different services and units to the uprising in July, and calculates the number of officers and enlisted men on both sides. On the basis of those data, he concludes that some 20 percent of the officers sided with the government, and others who were in principle undecided made their choice depending on the winner in the area in which they were located. Many who would have rallied to the government or served it probably changed their minds once the proletarian revolution had started. He also notes that the cleavage lines were largely ideological rather than social, since members of military families frequently fought on opposite sides.
107. Ibid., pp. 186–90. The following table, which gives the alignment of eighty-two generals on 18 July 1936 by location at the beginning of the conflict, is based on his data.

	Government Area	Rebel Area	Total
Serving	22	17	39
Expelled or sent to the reserves	7	10	17
Exiled	1	—	1
Gone over to the enemy	2	2	4
Executed	15	6	21
	47	35	82

108. Lerroux, *La pequeña historia*, p. 346. This view is confirmed in Hidalgo de Cisneros, *Mis memorias*, p. 98, when he writes: "At the advent of the republic there was a minority of republicans in the army and another minority of bitter reactionaries; the remainder, that is, the great majority, were neutral or indifferent, felt no hate nor love for the new regime, but accepted it and obeyed it." But he also notes the change in the course of the years for the reasons he points out; causes that "seen in isolation might appear of little weight, but which were intelligently used by the enemies in a predisposed milieu." Let us note the very different initial climate of opinion in Spain from that in the Weimar Republic. An excellent analysis of the social structure of the armed forces is found in Julio Busquets, *El militar de carrera en España: Estudio de sociología militar* (Barcelona: Ariel, 1967).

109. On the consultations between Gil Robles and the army leadership in November 1934, see Gil Robles, *No fue posible la paz*, p. 147, and La Cierva, *Historia de la Guerra Civil*, pp. 445-46.

110. The feelers put out by Gil Robles toward the army leadership after the president vetoed any possibility that he might form a government, and decided to dissolve the legislature instead on 11 December 1935, are described by him in *No fue posible la paz*, pp. 364-67 and 376-78. For Franco's letter on those events, see Payne, *Politics and the Military in Modern Spain*, pp. 308-9 and 505. For a description of similar explorations after the election returns came in in 1936, see Gil Robles, *No fue posible la paz*, pp. 492-502.

111. See La Cierva, *Historia de la Guerra Civil*, pp. 639-40.

112. Chapaprieta, *La paz fue posible*, pp. 407-13.

113. Alfred Stepan, "The New Professionalism of Internal Warfare and Military Role Expansion," in *Authoritarian Brazil*, ed. Alfred Stepan (New Haven: Yale University Press, 1973), pp. 47-65; see particularly table 2.1, p. 52. Accounts of the conspiracy, the negotiations of military leaders, like Mola, with the leaders of the extreme Right and the refusal to commit themselves to any particular politico-ideological program, the tone of the manifestoes of the rebels, the declaration of the Burgos military junta against all partisan activity (in theory including that of those actively supporting the uprising), the late creation (1938) of the first civilian government, etc., all support our interpretation. This was not the role of the military as a moderating power considered by many politicians in the spring of 1936 (see Chapaprieta, *La paz fue posible*, note 112) or even the type of intervention considered by Gil Robles.

114. Another "explanation" of the breakdown of the democratic Republic has been foreign intervention. The Left and many liberals blame Hitler and Mussolini, and Franco propagandists blame international communism. Both quote false documents, make wrong inferences from circumstantial evidence, give excessive significance to the activities of foreign agents, and have in their favor facts of minor significance in the total picture. Undoubtedly, the international climate and the foreign intervention in the civil war, once initiated, made those interpretations plausible. For our argument here—the breakdown of democracy—it is irrelevant who would have won the civil war if military aid had not been forthcoming to one or the other side at key junctures. Once a civil war had started, after the failure of the military uprising in many parts of Spain and given the inability of the government to defeat it without the support of the revolutionary proletariat, the outcome could not have been continuity with the democracy established in 1931. A Republican victory could perhaps have led to the reestablishment of democracy in the shorter run as it might have brought Spain into World War II; and it might have encouraged, after liberation

by the Allies, a postwar political development similar to that of other European nations. But too many "ifs" are involved to be even mentioned here.

For our analysis, the relevant fact is that the potential foreign support, the contacts established with foreign states and movements, were not sufficiently important to determine the course of action followed either by the counterrevolutionary forces (particularly the army) or for those hoping or talking of revolution.

On this problem, see the outstanding scholarly monograph by Angel Viñas, *La Alemania Nazi y el 18 de julio* (Madrid: Alianza Editorial, 1974), which contains new documentation and extensive critical references to the literature. The efforts by the extreme Right to buy arms from the Italian government in 1934 had not led very far; the Falange received some funds from the Italians, but neither of those developments was of central importance in leading to the final crisis. See John F. Coverdale, *Italian Intervention in the Spanish Civil War* (Princeton, N.J.: Princeton University Press, 1975), pp. 37–65.

Biographical Notes

RISTO ALAPURO received his doctorate from the University of Helsinki in 1973. He pursued postdoctoral studies at the University of Michigan during 1973 and 1974 and has been a lecturer in sociology at the University of Helsinki since then. Dr. Alapuro has published books and articles on the student movement and peasant mobilization in Finland.

ERIK ALLARDT is a Research Professor at the Academy of Finland and Chairman of the Finnish Political Science Association. He received his doctorate from the University of Helsinki in 1952 and has been a Visiting Professor at the University of California at Berkeley, the University of Illinois, and the University of Wisconsin. From 1968 to 1971 he was editor of *Acta Sociologica*. With Stein Rokkan he edited *Mass Politics: Studies in Political Sociology* and with Yrjö Littunen, he edited *Cleavages, Ideologies, and Party Systems*. His book, *Sociologi,* is currently in its sixth edition in Finnish.

PAOLO FARNETI received his Laurea in Jurisprudence from the University of Turin in 1960 and his doctorate in sociology from Columbia University in 1968. He is currently a Professor of Political Science at Turin and Director of the Centro Studi Scienza Politica, Turin. Formerly he was the Lauro de Bosis Lecturer at Harvard University. His publications include *Theodor Geiger e la coscienza del la società industriale, Sistema politico e società civile,* and *L'Italia contemporanea.*

M. RAINER LEPSIUS is Professor of Sociology at the University of Mannheim and has been President of the German Sociological Association since 1971. He received his Ph.D. degree in the social sciences from the University of Munich in 1955. He has published over twenty monographs and essays on such themes as the sociology of intellectuals, industrial sociology, radical nationalism, inequality, regime change, and democracy in Germany as a historical and sociological problem.

JUAN J. LINZ is Pelatiah Perit Professor of Political and Social Science at Yale University. He received his doctorate from Columbia University in 1959 and has taught at Columbia University, Stanford University, the University of Madrid, and the Universidad Autónoma of Madrid. He is Chairman of the Committee on Political Sociology of the International Sociological and Political Science Associations. His publications include "Totalitarian and Authoritarian Regimes," in *Handbook of Political Science*, ed. F. Greenstein and N. Polsby; "Some Notes toward a Comparative Study of Fascism in Comparative Sociological Perspective," in *Fascism,* ed. W. Laquer; and numerous monographs and essays on Spanish elites and entrepreneurs, quantitative history, and parties and elections in Spain and Germany.

WALTER B. SIMON received his M.S. degree in social psychology from the University of Washington in Seattle and his doctorate in sociology from Columbia University. He has taught sociology at several North American universities and is presently teaching at the University of Vienna. His published work deals with the concept of the authoritarian personality, the phenomenon of social movements, aspects of socialization and pedagogy, language politics, and the political implications of cultural pluralism.

ALFRED STEPAN is Professor of Political Science at Yale University and frequently serves as Chairman of Yale's Council on Latin American Studies. He received his doctorate from Columbia University in 1969 and has taught at Yale since then. He has been a Guggenheim Fellow and, from 1978 to 1979, will be a Visiting Fellow at St. Antony's College, Oxford University. He has published *The Military in Politics: Changing Patterns in Brazil* and *The State and Society: Peru in Comparative Perspective*. He is the editor of *Authoritarian Brazil: Origins, Policies, and Future* and co-editor, with Bruce Russett, of *Military Force and American Society*.

Index

Academic Karelia Society, 125
Acción Republicana, 165
Acquisition classes. *See* Classes, acquisition
Adenauer, Konrad, 120 n. 28
Agrarian crisis (Germany/1927–28), 53–54
Agrarian Reform Law (Spain), 153, 202 n. 18
Agrarian Union (Finland), 122, 128, 130, 134, 135
Agricultural workers, 7, 13, 15. *See also* Peasants
Agriculture: in Finland, 128, 135, 141 n. 39; in Germany, 53–54; occupations in Italian, 15; reform in Spanish, 153, 154, 180; strikers in Italian, 14
Aguirre y Lecube, José Antonio de, 185
Alba Bonifaz, Santiago, 150
Alcalá Zamora, Niceto, 150, 159, 165, 171, 174, 185, 187, 197, 207 n. 61, 208 n. 64, 209 n. 76; personality of, 173
Alianza Obrera, 162
Alphons XIII, King, 143, 173
Anarcho-syndicalist labor movement (Spain), 143–44, 145, 151, 155, 164, 166, 176, 183, 185, 186, 190, 211 n. 87
Anticlericalism: in Austria, 88, 89, 95; in Spain, 153, 154, 156, 167–68, 175, 190. *See also* Clericalism
Antimarxism (Austria), 88–89, 95
Anti-Semitism, 53, 64, 73, 81, 89
"Arditi," 17
Army: Austrian volunteer, 110, 117; Finnish, 124–25, 127, 128, 133; German, 56, 68, 74, 118; Italian, 7, 11, 13, 16, 19, 21, 29, 118; rightist upheavals and, 18; SA as, 68; Socialist (Austria), 88; Spanish, 142, 143, 144, 152, 153, 155, 159, 161, 166, 176, 178, 182, 190, 191, 192, 194–98, 213 n. 106, 214 n. 108
Army officers: demobilization of Italian army and, 16; Spanish, 143, 144, 178, 195–96, 197, 213 n. 107
Article 48 (Weimar constitution), 47

Asturian revolution (Spain), 176, 184, 189, 190, 191, 195
Austria, 146, 150, 169; anti-Marxists in, 88–89; economic crisis in, 98–100; fascism in, 93–98; German nationalists in, 91–93; Germany and, 83, 91–92, 100, 104, 107, 111, 115, 118; history of First Republic of, 80–84; National Socialist party growth in, 107–12; National Socialist triumph in, 112–19; party coalition in, 81–101 passim, 103–7; proclerical conservatives in, 89–91; socialists in, 84–88
Austrian Parliament: composition of (1930s), 102–3, 107–12; dissolution of, 113–14, 115
Austromarxists, 85–86, 88, 106, 107; theory of, and coalition, 105. *See also* Marxists, Austria
Authority, 139; Austrian government and, 114; charisma and, 61–63; in Weimar Republic, 36–38, 44, 50
Autonomy, loss of: defined, 6; in Italy (1919–21), 8–12, 13, 16, 17, 19; political society and, 4–5, 7
Azaña Díaz, Manuel, 153, 155, 156, 158, 159, 161, 162, 165, 171, 174, 177, 178, 179, 182, 185, 186, 189, 197, 203 nn. 31, 36, 205 n. 47

Banks (German), 55, 59
Barcelona, October rebellion and, 156–60, 162, 176, 181, 183, 187
Barracks. *See* "Politics of the barracks"
Basque Nationalist party. *See* Partido Nacionalista Vasco
Basque problem in Spain, 153, 155, 156, 160, 164, 185
Batet Mestres, General Domingo, 195
Bauer, Otto, 86, 106, 111
Besteiro Fernández, Julián, 166, 167, 203 n. 36, 206 n. 48
Bismarck, Otto von, 120 n. 28

219

Library of Congress Cataloging in Publication Data
Main entry under title:

The Breakdown of democratic regimes, Europe.

    Includes index.
    1. Europe—Politics and government—20th century—
Addresses, essays, lectures. I. Linz Storch de Gracia,
Juan José, 1926–   II. Stepan, Alfred C.
JN94.A2B73   320.9'4'05   77–28750
ISBN 0–8018–2022–7